A Lasting Prophetic Legacy

A Lasting Prophetic Legacy

Martin Luther King Jr., the World Council of Churches, and the Global Crusade Against Racism and War

THOMAS A. MULHALL

WIPF & STOCK · Eugene, Oregon

A LASTING PROPHETIC LEGACY
Martin Luther King Jr., the World Council of Churches, and the Global Crusade
Against Racism and War

Wipf & Stock
An Imprint of Wipf and Stock Publishers
199 W. 8th Ave., Suite 3
Eugene, OR 97401

www.wipfandstock.com

ISBN 13: 978–1-62032–753-1

Manufactured in the U.S.A.

To Mary, Aoife, and Thomas Jr.

Contents

Foreword

THE ADJECTIVE "GLOBAL" IS increasingly associated with the name, life, and activities of Martin Luther King Jr. The world in which King lived was, due to scientific and technological revolutions, becoming increasingly smaller, and his familiarity with that world was such that he variously labeled it "a global village," "the world house," and "the worldwide neighborhood." In view of this rapidly shrinking global scene, King hoped that people in America and abroad would develop a more explicit and enlightened world perspective, and that the Christian church, in particular, would become a force in strengthening the spectrum of social justice and the advancement of human rights and democratic freedoms across the globe. This explains in part the significance of this rich, provocative, and groundbreaking book by Thomas Mulhall, which highlights King's call for a more enlightened vision of the church's universality in an interrelated and interdependent world.

With the appearance of this book, Mulhall joins the ranks of a select group of scholars who are rediscovering and reclaiming the global Martin Luther King Jr. Mulhall is most interested in the vision and sense of mission that King shared with South African anti-apartheid activists like Albert J. Luthuli and representatives of the World Council of Churches (WCC) such as Eugene Carson Blake, particularly in terms of the struggle against racism and war. By reorienting its focus to King's global concerns, this book goes beyond the King who is commonly associated with churches and social activism in the United States and, more precisely, the American South. Thus, "the global King" and his ideas, activities, and contributions, while treated primarily in his own historical context, are also exposed for serious study, inspiration, and appropriation in this contemporary world.

Mulhall highlights King's sense that the civil rights movement in America was crucially linked to global events. This is important for understanding the shared vision and sometimes collaborative efforts of the civil rights leader, South African activists, and voices of advocacy and activists in the WCC. King must have found in this kind of an alliance of conscience a microcosm of what he envisioned as a global beloved community. Indeed, it testified to the power of his belief in the social nature of human existence, or, as he also put it, "the interrelated structure of all reality."[1]

Mulhall concludes that the struggle against racism and war constitutes a vital part of the prophetic legacy of both King and the WCC. At the same time, Mulhall shows that the prophetic was inextricably intertwined with not only the spiritual, but also the social, political, and economic in both cases. Even so, his stress on the *prophetic* is noteworthy because it evokes the image of an ecclesial-based anti-racism and anti-war crusade, or a movement grounded in spiritual, moral, and ethical forces. Interestingly enough, this is exactly how King, South African activists like Albert Luthuli, and WCC representatives such as Eugene Carson Blake viewed their struggle for a world free of hatred, bigotry, intolerance, and violence. The idea was that global justice, peace, and community necessitated, first and foremost, changes in the hearts of human beings before these could be translated and incorporated into the social, political, and economic order of societies. In other words, genuine spiritual transformation was seen as a necessary precondition for not only prophetic advocacy, but for much-needed enduring social, political, and economic transformation.

A book like this appears at a time when a new surge of both King's and the WCC's influence needs to be felt across the world. We need to study and learn from King and the prophetic voices in the WCC, and also the great freedom and justice crusaders of South Africa, because they still have something to say about the many issues impacting our global future, such as the need for durable peace in nations torn by ethno-national conflict, religious strife, political turmoil and divisions, and terrorism. They challenge us to address the need for a heightened consciousness of the interconnectedness, interrelatedness, and interdependence of human beings. Nothing could be more important in our increasing and often frustrating encounters with globalization and its discontents. Mulhall's book reminds us of the importance of developing a richer vision of the church universal in an increasingly globalized world.

Lewis V. Baldwin
Vanderbilt University
July 2013

---

1. King, *Testament to Hope*, 254.

Acknowledgments

THIS BOOK WOULD NEVER have been completed but for the encouragement and advice given to me by Professor Lewis V. Baldwin. Prior to that, my research over the last decade or so on Martin Luther King Jr. and the World Council of Churches had turned into many cul de sacs. I will be forever grateful to Ms. Cynthia Lewis of the Martin Luther King Jr. Center for Non-violent Social Change, who inspired me along my present path. Ms. Lewis and Ms. Elaine Hall were always helpful to me in locating documents from the King Library and Archives in Atlanta, Georgia. The staff at the World Council of Churches Library and Archives in Geneva also deserves special thanks for facilitating my access to documents relevant to this study. I cannot forget the kindness shown to me at the many libraries I visited, particularly the British Library in London, the Trinity College Library Dublin and the Irish School of Ecumenics, the Kimmage Development Studies Centre Library in Dublin, and the University of Ulster Jordanstown Library. Many thanks are due to Christian Amondson of Wipf and Stock for giving me the opportunity to bring my work to publication, and my appreciation also goes to Alex Fus for copyediting my manuscript. Professor Rufus Burrow took the time to read my early drafts and offer useful advice for which I am eternally grateful. My appreciation also goes to Professor Noel Erskine, who provided a complimentary endorsement of my work. Professor Hak Joon Lee gave me every encouragement when it was needed. Finally, I would like to thank Dr. Vicki Crawford, Director of the Morehouse College Martin Luther King Jr. Collection, for giving me a fascinating insight into Dr. King's alma mater.

Introduction

MARTIN LUTHER KING JR. is best known for his role as a civil rights leader in the tumultuous days of 1960s America. While it is widely accepted that he exerted one of the greatest influences on social consciousness in the United States, his importance beyond these shores has been very much underrated. King was a true Christian socialist, but this leaning has been understated because in Cold War America, socialism was mistakenly associated with communism. King's worldwide perspective was evidenced by his visits to Africa and Asia in the late 1950s. He recognized before many of his contemporaries that the demise of colonialism would have far-reaching repercussions for African Americans and others who were subjected to widespread discrimination. Indeed, the birth of emerging democracies in Africa and Asia would reverberate throughout the Western world, where at times lip service was paid to equality for all. King worked hard to bring his influence to bear on these historical changes. King also saw the potential of the church to gain greater credibility on the world stage through the World Council of Churches (WCC). A confluence of events helped King to encourage the WCC to be active in this regard. Reverend Eugene Carson Blake became General Secretary of the WCC in 1966, a crucial time in King's career. Having followed King's struggle closely, and being a civil rights activist in his own right, Blake was well-positioned to support King as needed in his new role within the WCC. The Vietnam War, which both opposed, began to escalate sharply from 1965 onwards, and each of these clergymen took it upon themselves to actively oppose American foreign policy in Southeast Asia. Furthermore, their speeches and activities in regard to segregation, apartheid, and the Vietnam War show sufficient similarities to point to their mutual influence in domestic and foreign affairs. King demonstrated his confidence in the WCC when he replied to a series of questions in an interview with *Redbook Magazine* in November 1964, one of which related to peace initiatives. King responded, "The World Council of Churches has made very clear through recent proclamations and resolutions that war is immoral and that some alternative to it must be found."[1]

This book has been written to highlight how Martin Luther King Jr. worked though the WCC to bring an end to racism and war worldwide. Evidence shows that the WCC wanted to replicate King's nonviolent methodology elsewhere in the world, where war and strife prevailed. The admiration with which the WCC regarded King would be shown during the terms of General Secretaries Dr. Willem Visser 't Hooft,[2] and Dr. Eugene Carson Blake. King's posthumous influence was also apparent when the WCC's Fourth Assembly in Uppsala, Sweden, which he was to have opened, agreed to call a Consultation on Racism at Notting Hill, London in May of 1969. This consultation led to the adoption of a designated Programme to Combat Racism that was particularly targeted at South Africa's apartheid system, which King had campaigned against.

This book details how King's US efforts to bring an end to the evils of apartheid in South Africa brought him into contact with some of the great activists for change, including Chief Albert Luthuli,[3] the Methodist lay preacher whose nonviolent work paralleled King's activities with organizations such as the American Committee on Africa (ACOA)[4] and the American Negro Leadership Conference on Africa (ANLCA).[5] King made it clear in pronouncements that he supported African leaders like Nelson Mandela[6]

1. Peters, "Our Weapon is Love," *Redbook*, August 1956, 42–43, 71–73.

2. Willem Adolph Visser 't Hooft (September 20, 1900–July 4, 1985) was a Dutch theologian who became the first General Secretary of the World Council of Churches (WCC) in 1948, a position he held until 1966.

3. Chief Albert John Luthuli (1891–July 21, 1967), also spelled Lutuli, was elected President of the African National Congress (ANC) in 1952. He was awarded the 1960 Nobel Prize for his role in the nonviolent struggle against apartheid, making him the first African to be recognized with the honor.

4. The American Committee on Africa (ACOA) was founded in New York in 1953 by George Houser with a group of civil rights activists who had organized support for the historic Defiance Campaign in South Africa the previous year. The Africa Fund, founded in 1966, worked with ACOA to provide key support for independence movements throughout Africa. During the anti-apartheid movement, the African Fund became the principle contact point for progressive trade unionists and politicians by encouraging US firms and stockholders to divest in South Africa and publishing up-to-date lists of US companies involved there.

5. The American Negro Leadership Conference on Africa (ANLCA) was formed in 1962, with Philip Randolph and Martin Luther King Jr. as co-chairmen and Theodore E. Brum as director.

6. Nelson Mandela (July 18, 1918–December 5, 2013)) was born in Transkei, South Africa, and joined the ANC in 1944 as a political activist against the National Party's apartheid policies. Mandela was tried for treason for his role in ANC's military wing, known as Umkhonto we Sizwe (spear of the nation), but eventually guided the nation's

and Robert Sobukwe.[7] However, King recognized that he needed a bigger stage to promulgate his vision of peace and brotherhood in an increasingly militarized world. Although highly successful in accessing publicity prior to 1964, King received a tremendous boost when he was honored with the Nobel Peace Prize that year. Besides giving him added confidence in imparting his much-needed message for world peace, the recognition also provided enhanced opportunities to gain the ears of world leaders.

Martin Luther King Jr.'s civil rights activism in the US has been studied in great depth, but his influence on international affairs has been by and large neglected. King scholars such as Lewis V. Baldwin have been pushing the boundaries with books like Baldwin's *Toward the Beloved Community: Martin Luther King Jr. and South Africa* (1995) and *The Voice of Conscience: The Church in the Mind of Martin Luther King, Jr.* (2010). Baldwin's *"In a Single Garment of Destiny": A Global Vision of Justice,* published in 2013, illustrates King's stance on global liberation struggles through his own words and deeds. Baldwin presents new archival material that shows King advocating for human rights globally and working alongside Eleanor Roosevelt,[8] Chief Albert Luthuli, and Thich Nhat Hanh[9] on issues from racism to war, poverty, and religious intolerance. The problems King highlighted are still relevant today, but Baldwin is one of the few scholars who has written extensively on the international importance of King's work. This study continues Baldwin's line of research by focusing on King's international influence as one of the great leaders of the twentieth century.

This book consists of nine chapters. Chapter 1 focuses on Martin Luther King Jr.'s understanding of the purpose and role of the Christian church. The black church had a formative influence on King, and he had the distinction of being the son and grandson of Baptist preachers. Before 1944, when he entered Morehouse College in Atlanta at the age of fifteen, he had been thoroughly immersed in the fundamentalist tradition of black Baptist Protestantism in the South. Having performed well academically at Crozer Theological Seminary near Chester, Pennsylvania, King moved on

---

peaceful transition to democracy as South African's first black president.

7. Robert Sobukwe (December 5, 1924–February 27, 1978) was a South African political dissident who founded the Pan Africanist Congress (PAC) in opposition to the apartheid government. Sobukwe served as president of PAC from 1959 to1963.

8. Eleanor Roosevelt (October 11, 1864–November 7, 1962) was the First Lady of the US from 1933 to 1945. She supported the New Deal policies of her husband, President Franklin Delano Roosevelt, and became an advocate for civil rights. She remained influential in politics and civil rights activism throughout her life.

9. Thich Nhat Hanh (October 11, 1926) is a Vietnamese Buddhist monk and peace activist who travels internationally to host retreats and talks. He met with Martin Luther King Jr. during the Vietnam War to discuss the conflict.

to complete his PhD at Boston University. He was eager to study under Dr. Edgar Brightman, whose ideas on "personalism" had stimulated King's interest. Personalism insisted that human personality, which is intrinsic in all individuals, was the ultimate value in the world. King's belief in the essential worth of all human beings was thus reaffirmed.[10] King's belief in the goodness of the human personality was tested in the long and bitter Montgomery Bus Boycott in late 1955, which brought King national and international acclaim. He was thrust into a leadership position that he did not seek and for which he was largely unprepared. As one of the most prominent black leaders in the emergent civil rights movement, King was certain that the church had a role to play in the vital issues of the day—not only civil rights, but also war and peace. Chapter 1 explores how this remarkable Baptist minister became politicized.

Chapter 2 traces Eugene Carson Blake's leadership of the National Council of Churches (NCC) and the WCC. Blake, like King, was an activist for civil rights, and they may have influenced each other in their spiritual and pastoral roles. Blake worked during a period when the WCC was undergoing great changes, including increased membership from newly independent countries in Africa and Asia. A new period of ecumenism was being born. King was aware that the WCC could be highly influential in matters of mutual concern, and there is evidence of great respect between the two leaders. Their role, King confirmed, was "to hound every Christian layman everywhere with a nagging conscience."[11] Blake followed a similar path, and he consistently condemned racism and the Vietnam War throughout his time within the WCC.

Chapter 3 examines how Martin Luther King Jr. and the WCC worked in tandem to eliminate racism worldwide. The WCC had condemned racism since its formation in 1948, but despite its abhorrence of this practice, little was done to initiate practical solutions until the successful civil rights campaigns in the US precipitated action within the WCC. This change was facilitated by the good working relationship between King and General Secretaries Willem Visser 't Hooft and Eugene Carson Blake. King's influence is evident in his invitation to preach at the World Conference on Church and Society in Geneva in July of 1966, and then later at Uppsala, Sweden in 1968, which led to the WCC's Programme to Combat Racism in 1969.

Chapter 4 shows that from his earliest days as a spiritual leader and church pastor, King spoke of a broader vision for the resolution of worldwide strife. This chapter details King's early interest in the quest for freedom

10. Kirk, *Martin Luther King, Jr.*, 17–18.

11. Baldwin, *Voice of Conscience*, 196.

throughout Africa and Asia. He followed decolonization with great interest, and saw that US civil rights activists had much to learn from their African and Asian brothers. King despised the practice of apartheid, and he built up a strong rapport with Chief Albert Luthuli in South Africa. With King's help, the ACOA campaigned tirelessly to raise funds for the alleviation of distress, especially in South Africa. King and Luthuli never met, as the latter was under severe travel restrictions for most of his active life, and King was considered persona non grata to the South African government, and hence no entry visa was granted to him.

Chapter 5 explores Martin Luther King Jr.'s early opposition to the Vietnam War in 1965 and 1966. In those years, there were very few prominent clergymen who were prepared to condemn this conflict in Southeast Asia. But Eugene Carson Blake, as King's contemporary, was not afraid to speak out on the moral issues of the day. Both clergymen spoke out robustly against the war from 1967 onwards, and there is certainly a lot of common ground in their speeches in this regard. It is important to put King's courage into context, as the 1950s and 60s were times of great fear for the West, with the Cold War raging between East and West. Communism was seen as the great evil, and anyone percieved to be a Communist supporter or quasi-supporter in the US was subjected to ongoing harassment. J. Edgar Hoover, as Director of the FBI, listed King as a threat to the state, largely because of his association with former Communists, his civil rights activities, and his allegedly casual attitude toward extramarital relationships. King needed tremendous strength of character to overcome the ongoing campaign of vilification Hoover perpetuated against him. That he was successful despite this persecution is further testament to his great ability. Chapter 5 will show that King's growing opposition to the Vietnam War moved in tandem to that of the WCC.

Chapter 6 explains that although King had been invited to open the Fourth Assembly of the WCC at Uppsala, Sweden in July of 1968, he was assassinated in April of that year. Nevertheless, his legacy was brought to bear on the deliberations of the Assembly, which came to several very important decisions as a result of King's success in the civil rights campaign in the US. In recognition of the potential of King's methodology to bring about change through peaceful means, the WCC adopted the Martin Luther King Resolution, which proposed "A Martin Luther King Study for Non-Violent Social Change."[12] This was a great tribute to King, who gave his life to build a brotherhood of man through non-violent means. This chapter goes on to

---

12. Eugene Carson Blake to William A. Cooper, October 28, 1968, WCC General Secretaries, Correspondence: Frequent 1938–(1966–1970), WCC Archives, Geneva, Switzerland.

explore how the WCC proposed to implement this resolution, and possible obstacles to that end. King would also have been happy that the intractable problem of apartheid, in which he had taken a great interest, was high on the agenda at the Uppsala Assembly. The WCC had called on Christians to encourage and support all efforts to bring about change through non-violent means, to construct a society permeated by justice and reconciliation.[13] Momentum had been building up for years within the WCC for action on racism, not just well-intentioned rhetoric against it. I contend that King's successes on the civil rights front, along with his obvious support from the top echelons of the WCC, resulted in that organization adopting a proactive stance against racism.

Chapter 7 analyzes how the elimination of racism became a priority for the WCC. This coincided with Blake's tenure in the organization's leadership. The Uppsala Assembly decision in July of 1968 led to the Consultation on Racism at Notting Hill, London in May of 1969. Consultants from around the world convened over several days under the chairmanship of George McGovern,[14] a US Senator from South Dakota. Intense negotiations took place while policy papers were mulled over and dissected by a diverse range of participants, from Rev. Francis House[15] to O. R. Tambo,[16] Rev. Michael Scott,[17] and Rev. Channing Phillips[18], to name a few. Because apartheid was seen to be so reprehensible, there was a heavy concentration on South Africa. Notting Hill was followed by the Canterbury Consultation, and the end result was the World Council of Churches' Programme to Combat Racism. This outcome, I contend, owed a lot to the consistent campaigning by

13. "WCC's Statements and Actions on Racism, 1948–1979," Programme to Combat Racism, 4223.16.3/2, WCC Archives, Geneva, Switzerland.

14. George Stanley McGovern (July 19, 1922–October 21, 2012) was a member of the US House of Representatives from South Dakota who openly opposed the Vietnam War and later served as the US Ambassador to the United Nations.

15. Reverend Francis House (August 9, 1908– September 1, 2004) was Archdeacon of Macclesfield and became the first secretary of the WCC Youth Department. In 1955, he became the WCC's Associate General Secretary for Ecumenical Action.

16. Oliver Reginald Tambo (October 1917–April 1993) was a South African anti-apartheid activist and a leading figure in the African National Congress (ANC). In 1955, Tambo became Secretary General of the ANC.

17. Reverend Guthrie Michael Scott (June 30, 1907–September 14, 1982) was an Anglican clergyman who opposed apartheid. He was the first petitioner to appear before the United Nations to bring the troubles of South-West Africa (now Namibia) to international attention.

18. Channing Emery Phillips (March 23, 1928– November 11, 1987) was a minister, civil rights leader, and social activist who led Robert F. Kennedy's 1968 presidential campaign in the District of Columbia.

Martin Luther King Jr. to end racism worldwide through nonviolent means. The relationship between King, Blake, and the WCC played a crucial role.

Chapter 8 discusses the early years of the Programme to Combat Racism. As Blake observed, the UN had called apartheid "a crime against humanity." This program had concluded that racism was "not confined to certain countries or continents, but that it is a world problem."[19] The focus turned to Southern Africa, and in particular, South Africa. It was not long before the WCC became embroiled in great controversy over the Special Fund Grants that were made to various organizations working toward the elimination of racism. The monies were intended for humanitarian purposes only. When it became known that funds were transferred to the Patriotic Front, which was alleged to be involved in terrorism, an almighty argument arose. Although the sums involved were not overly large, the symbolism of the WCC's gesture was enormous. It was hard to escape the politicization of the WCC's agenda.

Chapter 9 reflects on the significance of Martin Luther King Jr.'s ongoing influence on world events over the four decades following his untimely death. Undoubtedly, progress has been made in some areas, but it is difficult to ignore the fact that the lessons that should have been learned from the Vietnam War have been somewhat forgotten. The slaughter of innocents continued with the invasions of Iraq and Afghanistan. The Middle East also remains a highly volatile region, with conflicts in Libya, Syria, Egypt, and Lebanon, to name but a few. Europe also suffered under the breakup of the former Yugoslavia, with the ensuing crimes of genocide and ethnic cleaning. Furthermore, the problem of racism is still pervasive in Africa and Asia, and indeed throughout the world, and so King's international exhortations for peaceful coexistence needs to be revisited and acted upon to ensure the continuance of earthly peace.

19. Blake, Eugene Carson, "Laymen Have a Ministry to Fulfil," *UNIAPAC International*, 995.1.02/4 Works (1971), WCC Archive, Geneva, Switzerland.

Abbreviations

ACOA	American Committee on Africa
AMRO	Amsterdam-Rotterdam Bank
ANC	African National Congress
ANCLA	American Negro Leadership Conference on Africa
BCC	British Council of Churches
CCIA	Churches Commission on International Affairs
CALCAV	Clergy and Laymen Concerned About Vietnam
CORE	Congress of Racial Equality
DRC	Dutch Reformed Church
EABC	European American Banking Corporation
EEC	European Economic Community
EKD	Evangelical Church in Germany
ELTSA	End Loans to South Africa
FOR	Fellowship of Reconciliation
FBI	Federal Bureau of Investigation
IIP	International Institute for Peace
JPIC	Justice, Peace, and Integrity of Creation
MIA	Montgomery Improvement Association
MK	Umkhonto we Sizwe
NAACP	National Association for the Advancement of Colored People
NATO	North Atlantic Treaty Organization
NCC	National Council of Churches

NLF	National Liberation Front
NUL	National Urban League
PAC	Pan Africanist Congress
PPC	Poor People's Campaign
PCR	Programme to Combat Racism
POQO	The Azanian People's Liberation Army, later APLA
SACC	South African Council of Churches
SACP	South African Communist Party
SCLC	Southern Christian Leadership Conference
SNCC	Student Non-Violent Coordinating Committee
SODEPAX	The Joint Committee on Society, Development and Peace
UNESCO	United Nations Educational, Scientific, and Cultural Organization
UNIAPAC	International Christian Union of Business Executives
WASP	White Anglo-Saxon Protestants
WCC	World Council of Churches
ZANU	Zimbabwe African National Union
ZAPU	Zimbabwe African People's Union

1

The Call to Service

Martin Luther King Jr. on the Purpose and Role of the Christian Church

MARTIN LUTHER KING JR. was first and foremost a Christian and a church-man who only later became politicized. His civil rights activism, his opposition to racism, and to the Vietnam War was guided by his religious convictions. His commitment to these convictions was clear from the start, when as the newly elected president of the Montgomery Improvement Association (MIA), he emphasized the Christian doctrine of love: "Our nation must be guided by the deepest principles of our Christian faith."[1] Although King gained national and international recognition as a civil rights leader, he was quite clear in how he saw himself: "I am many things to many people, but in the quiet recesses of my heart, I am fundamentally a clergyman, a Baptist preacher."[2]

King was originally an advocate for the African American community, but when he saw the parallel effects of poverty on the white poor, he embraced their plight as well. King's view of racism in the US developed

---

1. King, *Stride Toward Freedom*, 62.

2. Quoted in Carson, "African-American Social Gospel," 173. See also King, Martin Luther King Jr., "Doubts and Certainties Link: An Interview With Martin Luther King Jr.," transcript, BBC, London, April 4, 1968, King Papers, Box 14, King Center Library and Archives, Atlanta, GA.

to consider the interaction of economic interests and military power as he moved outside the confines of the black civil rights movement towards Christian Socialism. Then, as a Christian activist with a global platform, he felt obliged to speak out against the Vietnam War, the threat of nuclear proliferation, and the evils of racism in a global context.

King's understanding of the Christian church was formed by the prophetic heritage of the Bible, his black church origins, his exposure to liberal and progressive-minded black ministers and academics at Morehouse College, Crozer Theological Seminary, and Boston University. Above all, King saw himself as a Christian minister with deep roots in the southern black Baptist Church.[3] Lest there be any doubt about King's influences, scholar James H. Cone answers the rhetorical question, "What traditions did he turn to in moments of crisis during his ministry?" without hesitation: "In moments of crisis when despair was about to destroy the possibility of making a new future for the poor, King turned to the faith contained in the tradition of the black church."[4]

The success of the Montgomery Bus Boycott propelled King to national and international fame. The problem for him then was to capitalize on that success and on his status as a Baptist minister. As King said, "The church too must face its historic obligation in this crisis," for in the final analysis, "the problem of race is not a political but a moral issue."[5] Lack of cooperation from the white church led King to remark, with some dismay, "One of the disappointing experiences of the Montgomery struggle was the fact that we could not get the white ministerial association to sit down with us and discuss the problem. With individual exceptions, the white ministers from whom I had naively expected so much, gave little."[6] Nevertheless, King envisioned the church playing a far greater role than it had yet entertained, saying, "I see the church as the conscience of the community, the conscience of the nation, and the conscience of the state, and consequently, the church must be involved in all of the vital issues of the day, whether it's in the area of civil rights, whether it's dealing with the whole question of war and peace."[7]

"The Churches' Influence on Secular Society," an essay published by *Time* in 1967, cast the modern civil rights movement in an important light: "Beginning with the 1954 Supreme Court decision against school

3. See Baldwin, "Preacher, Pastor, and Prophet," 41.

4. Cone, "Black Theology—Black Church," 207.

5. King, "Church and the Race Crisis," 1140–41.

6. Ibid.

7. "Sunday with Martin Luther King, Jr.," transcript of radio statement, WAAF-AM, Chicago, IL, April 10, 1966, 2–4, King Center Library and Archives, Atlanta, GA, quoted in Baldwin, *Voice of Conscience*, vii, 77.

segregation, the civil rights movement was a major cause of the churches' new activity. Most denominations already paid lip service at least to integration, but the growing national concern and the direct challenge to the Christian conscience brought a flurry of new resolutions and exhortations. In the 1960s the civil rights struggle moved the churches further along from talk to action."[8]

King, however, saw the church as a staunch upholder of the status quo, for he observed, "Nowhere is the tragic tendency to conform more evident than in the church, an institution which has often served to crystallize, conserve, and even bless the patterns of majority opinion. The erstwhile sanction by the church of slavery, racial segregation, war, and economic exploitation is testimony to the fact that the church has hearkened more to the authority of the world than to the authority of God."[9] On April 19, 1961, King spoke about the introduction of slavery and the reasons why the white man deemed it necessary to justify the institution. To disguise an obvious wrong, slavery had to be rationalized and draped "in the beautiful garments of righteousness," said King. Religion and the Bible, he argued, were used to perpetuate this deceit:

> And so many argued that the Negro was inferior by nature because of Noah's curse upon the children of Ham. The Apostle Paul's dictum became a watchword, "Servants, be obedient to your master." And then one of the brethren had probably read the logic of Aristotle and he could put his arguments in the framework of an Aristotelian syllogism. He could say that all men were made in the image of God, this was a major premise. Then came the minor premise, God, as everyone knows, is not a Negro. Then came the conclusion, therefore the Negro is not a man. He could put his argument in that logical framework.[10]

The conditions of slavery, and later, segregation, had a deleterious effect on the lives of black people, who only began to make substantial progress when the upheaval of two world wars, migration from rural plantations to the cities, and increasing education all combined to lead the "Negro masses" to "re-evaluate themselves."[11] To make matters worse, the white churches

8. "Churches' Influence," 20–21.

9. King, *Strength to Love*, 21.

10. King, Martin Luther, Jr., "The Church on the Frontier of Racial Tension," address at Southern Baptist Theological Seminary, Louisville, KY, April 19, 1961, King Papers, Box 2, January 1, 1961–December 22, 1961, King Center Library and Archives, Atlanta, GA.

11. Joyce, Frank H., "People Against Racism," Programme to Combat Racism, Notting Hill Consultation 1969, 4223.1.03, WCC Archives, Geneva, Switzerland.

had a deliberate policy of excluding blacks from positions of power within their infrastructure. As King declared, "It is to their everlasting shame, that white Christians developed a system of racial segregation within the church, and inflicted so many indignities upon its Negro worshippers that they had to organize their own churches."[12] King explained that whenever a crisis emerged in society, the church had a significant role to play in the area of human relations: "First, the church must urge its worshippers to develop a world perspective. Whenever men develop a world outlook, they rise above the shackles of racial prejudice and racial hatred." King, aware of the interrelatedness of all men, advised, "when we find individuals caught in the shackles of racial prejudice, they are the victims of narrow provincialism and sectarianism. So the church must urge its worshippers to rise above the narrow confines of their individualistic concerns to the broader concerns of all humanity."[13] King, with notable prescience, further declared, "So you see, the world in which we live today is a world that is geographically one. And in order to solve the problems in the days ahead, we must make it spiritually one."[14]

The interrelated structure of reality had a profound effect on King. Having traveled to India in 1959, he found the poverty there appalling, and went on to say that the destiny of the United States was tied up with India and with all other nations. King often quoted John Donne, the seventeenth-century British poet, who had described this interconnectedness in graphic terms: "No man is an island, entire of itself; every man is a piece of the continent, a part of the main . . . Any man's death diminishes me, because I am involved in mankind, and therefore never send to know for whom the bell tolls; it tolls for thee." The message from King was quite clear: "The church must get this over in every community, in every section of this nation, in every country of this world."[15]

Scholar Paul R. Garber argues that King saw the modern black freedom movement as a continuation of an ancient freedom movement, in which, according to Exodus, God spoke through Moses, saying, "Let my people go." King recalled the courageous events of the exodus: the inhumane slavery inflicted on the Hebrews, their dramatic escape from the cruel Egyptians, the miraculous passage of the Israelites through the Red Sea, and

---

12. Quoted in Baldwin, *Voice of Conscience*, 103. See also Joyce, "People Against Racism," Notting Hill Consultation 1969, 4223.1.03, WCC Archives, Geneva, Switzerland.

13. King, "Frontier of Racial Tension," April 19, 1961, King Center Library and Archives, Atlanta, GA.

14. Quoted in ibid.

15. Ibid.

the drowning of the pursuing Egyptian army.[16] King asserted that this event illustrated the underlying goodness of the universe, which he emphasized through the words of James Russell Lowell, a nineteenth-century American poet and diplomat:

> Truth forever on the scaffold, wrong forever on the throne
> Yet that scaffold sways the future, and behind the dim unknown
> Standeth God within the shadow keeping watch above His own[17]

It was significant that the slaves wisely noted, and King believed, "that the exodus of the Israelites from Egyptian bondage contradicted the claims, made frequently by slaveholders and other pro-slavery advocates, that God intended Africans and their descendants to be slaves."[18] Baldwin observed that King believed in the use of parallelism in his sermons, noting that "He skillfully and effectively emphasized slavery in Egypt, the Exodus, the experience of the Israelites in the wilderness, Jesus' identification with outsiders, God's ultimate triumph over evil, and other great Biblical themes as historical realities to which he and his people could relate on a very personal level."[19] According to Baldwin, as with slaves in early generations, the tradition of the exodus, grounded in the Old Testament, was reconstructed when blacks confronted the forces of oppression on the streets, at lunch counters, and in jails throughout the South. King, inspired by the exodus model, "cast the Negro church in the roles of chosen people and suffering servant."[20] In doing so, King showed his certainty that his people had been chosen by God for a special destiny, and that by practicing nonviolence and accepting unmerited suffering for a greater good, they were taking on "a kind of messianic role in history."[21] King had concluded from reading British historian Arnold Toynbee[22] that "Negroes" had rediscovered "in Christianity certain original meanings and values" that made them capable of injecting a "new spiritual dynamic" into Western civilization.[23]

For King to complete this messianic vocation, he felt that it was absolutely necessary for black people to remain true to the tenets of the

16. See Garber, "Black Theologian," 404. See also Exodus 7:16 (NAB).

17. Miller, *Voice of Deliverance*, 14.

18. Baldwin, *Voice of Conscience*, 105.

19. Baldwin, "Preacher, Pastor, and Prophet," 82.

20. Baldwin, *Voice of Conscience*, 112.

21. Ibid.

22. Arnold Toynbee (April 14, 1889–October 22, 1975) was a British historian educated at Oxford and an acknowledged expert on international affairs.

23. Baldwin, *Voice of Conscience*, 112.

Christian faith, which was not the way the vast majority of white Christians in America behaved. Coretta Scott King, King's widow, described it like this: "Martin believed that white Christianity had failed to act in accordance with its teachings. However, my husband felt that it was not the Christian ethic which must be rejected, but that those who failed Christianity must be brought—through love—to brotherhood, for their own redemption as well as ours. He believed that there was a great opportunity for black people to redeem Christianity in America."[24]

For inspiration, King turned to the Hebrew prophets of the eighth century, who had stood against authorities in the interests of the poor and dispossessed: "King discovered in the prophets Amos, Hosea, Micah and others, the echoes of the same concerns that he had when he spoke out against America's racism, her militarism, her idolatry, and her use of every strategy to mistreat the poor and the oppressed."[25] King found similarities between religion practice in modern America and in eighth-century Hebrew society, when religion appeared externally healthy, but on the inside was rotten to the core. Frequently, this insight led King to quote Amos 5:24: "But let justice run down as waters, and righteousness as a mighty stream."[26] The portrait of the church as Good Samaritan was very alluring for King, for it reflected the behavior of "a certain man" who, in Jesus' parable, went to the assistance of a "wounded man" on the Jericho Road (Luke 10:29–37), ignoring "the external accidents of race, religion and nationality." For King, dipping into the New Testament for parables "emphasized the importance of embracing a universal altruism that transcends race or skin color."[27] The story of the Good Samaritan was for King "meaningful and instructive" not only for Judaism, but for its ramifications with other religions worldwide.[28]

The Southern Christian Leadership Conference (SCLC), which King organized with other church leaders in 1957, chose as their motto, "To Redeem the Soul of America." As a result, "the powerful impulse to redeem the moral, social, and political character of the nation tinged the civil rights movement with the crusading righteousness of the church, and freedom marches became 'redemptive experiences.'"[29] The concept of the "beloved community" and its realization was King's primary goal. "We Are Still Walking" was one of King's first published articles; in it he reflected, "we are striv-

24. Quoted in Baldwin, "Messianic Vision," 13.

25. Quoted in Baldwin, "Preacher, Pastor and Prophet," 47.

26. Quoted in Baldwin "Preacher, Pastor, and Prophet," 47.

27. Baldwin, *Voice of Conscience*, 89.

28. Ibid.

29. Ibid., 120–21.

ing for the removal of all barriers that divide and alienate mankind, whether racial, economic, or psychological."[30] Shortly before the SCLC was formed, King described its objectives: "The ultimate aim of SCLC is to foster and create the 'beloved community' in America where brotherhood is a reality . . . SCLC works for integration. Our ultimate goal is genuine intergroup and interpersonal living—integration."[31]

That SCLC was a success cannot be denied, for after a faltering start, Adam Fairclough notes that "It became a dynamic force within the civil rights movement and one of the most effective political pressure groups in American history."[32]

King acknowledged that the spiritual songs of the slaves, which expressed a particular fascination with Moses and the chosen people, along with the folk music of the freedom riders, was a powerful force in the motivational repertoire of the civil rights movement. Spirituals such as "Joshua Fit the Battle of Jericho," "Go Down, Moses," "There is a Balm in the Gilead," and "Woke up This Morning with My Mind Stayed on Freedom," had given powerful expression to the tragedies, betrayals, and hopes of their ancestors in the challenge to survive.[33] King explained the significance of the songs to the movement, saying, "We sing the freedom songs today for the same reasons the slaves sang them, because we too are in bondage, and the songs add hope to our determination that 'we shall overcome, black and white together, we shall overcome someday.'"[34]

King delivered a version of his sermon, "A Knock at Midnight," at Mount Zion Baptist Church in Cincinnati in early 1967. His sermon referred to how the slaves, in their spirituals, spoke of their faith that the "midnight" of oppression and despair would one day give way to the bright "morning" of freedom and hope. King noted that slaves included both heartache and hope in their songs, and he declared, "our slave foreparents taught us so much in their beautiful sorrow songs, one of which you sang so beautifully this morning. They looked at the midnight surrounding their days. They knew that there was sorrow and agony and hurt all around. When they thought about midnight they would sing, 'nobody knows the trouble I see, nobody knows but Jesus.' And fairly soon they were reminded that morning would come, and they started singing, 'I'm so glad, trouble don't

30. King, Martin Luther, Jr., "We Are Still Walking," *Liberation*, December 1956, 6–9, quoted in Zepp, *Social Vision*, 207.

31. Ibid., 211.

32. Fairclough, *To Redeem the Soul*, 13.

33. Baldwin, *Voice of Conscience*, 103.

34. Ibid., 127.

always last."[35] King's reading of the Old Testament, along with the history of slavery, produced images for King that were illustrated by the alienation African Americans felt from the Statue of Liberty's symbolism: "On the Statue of Liberty we read that America is the mother of exiles, but it does not take us long to realize that America has been the mother of its white exiles from Europe. She has not evinced the same maternal care and concern for her black exiles who were brought to this country in chains from Africa."[36]

In 1962, James Meredith[37] attempted to attend classes at the University of Mississippi against blatant racist opposition. The incident was widely reported, and nearly a decade after the historic Brown v. Board of Education decree outlawing segregation in public schools, King, with some puzzlement, asked the pertinent question, "Who is their God?" As King explained in his essay of the same name in the *Nation*, "I have traveled much of the length and breadth of Mississippi. On lazy summer afternoons and cold mornings, I've seen tall church spires and sprawling brick monuments dedicated to the glory of God. Often did I wonder, 'What kind of people worship there? Who is their God?' When I review the painful memory of the last week at Oxford and cannot recall a single voice 'crying in the wilderness,' the questions are still the same: 'What kind of people worship there? Who is their God?'"[38]

King saw that the role of the church was to make it perfectly clear that segregation was a moral evil that no Christian could accept: "The church must make it clear," he wrote, "that if we are to be a true witness of Jesus Christ, we can no longer give our allegiance to a system of segregation." Segregation was wrong, "because it substituted an I-it relationship for the I-thou relationship." The problem was that the perpetrator of segregation had a false sense of superiority, and the victim was left feeling inferior. As King said, "the underlying philosophy of segregation is diametrically opposed to the underlying philosophy of Christianity."[39] King saw the church having a responsibility in getting to "the ideational roots of racial prejudice," usually based on irrational fears and misunderstandings. The false ideas disseminated by politicians to further their political careers was something

35. Quoted in Baldwin, "Messianic Vision," 9–10.

36. King, Martin Luther, Jr. "Speech at SCLC Staff Retreat," Frogmore, SC, November 14, 1966, Box 11, June–December 1966, King Center Library and Archives, Atlanta, GA.

37. James Howard Meredith (June 25, 1933) is a civil rights activist and writer. During President John F. Kennedy's administration, he became the first African American student to seek entry to the segregated University of Mississippi in 1962.

38. King, "Who Is Their God?" 210.

39. King, "Role of the Church," *New York Amsterdam News*, September 15, 1962

King believed could be rebutted by the church: "The church can say to men everywhere that the idea of an inferior or a superior race is a false idea that has been refuted by the best evidence of the anthropological scientists."[40]

In July of 1963, King wrote in the *New York Amsterdam News* that the church was "the guardian of the morale of the community." Religion, he said, "must always be concerned about man's social condition." He saw religion operating on the vertical plane along with the horizontal insofar as it should seek "not only to integrate men with God, but to integrate men with men and each man with himself." The end result, he thus concluded, was that true religion was a "two-way road, on the one hand it seeks to change the souls of men, and thereby unite them with God; on the other hand it seeks to change the environmental conditions of men so that the soul will have a chance after it is changed."[41] For example, King challenged the church and churchmen to take on the responsibility of creating the proper moral climate to enable fair employment practices to prevail.[42] King represented a younger generation of black clergy who were involved in the civil rights movement. By engaging in direct action tactics and preaching authoritatively to the white churches on their shortcomings, King became a force to be reckoned with. James F. Findlay asserts, "by 1963 he was without question the leading black interpreter of the civil rights struggle, in all its moral urgency, to white church people throughout the country."[43]

In King's opinion, the white church in general exemplified the hypocrisy, bigotry, and intolerance prevalent in society. He had encountered this attitude during the Birmingham campaign, when he "heard numerous Southern religious leaders admonish their worshipers to comply with a desegregation decision because it is the law," but King longed to hear white ministers declare, "follow this decree because integration is morally right and because the Negro is your brother."[44] When King witnessed gross injustices inflicted "upon the Negro," he "watched white churchmen stand on the sidelines and mouth pious irrelevancies and sanctimonious trivialities." King stood firmly in the midst of a momentous crusade for racial and economic equality, only to hear many ministers sidle out of the struggle by saying, "these are social issues with which the gospel has no real concern." King criticized many churches for committing themselves to an "otherworldly

40. Ibid.

41. King, "Profound Moral Issue," *New York Amsterdam News*, July 20, 1963.

42. Ibid.

43. Findlay, "Religion and Politics," 69.

44. These and the quotations that follow are taken from King, "Letter from Birmingham Jail," 773.

religion," which made a "strange, unbiblical distinction between body and soul, between the sacred and the secular." One can imagine King's frustration as he sat in Birmingham Jail contemplating the future: "We are moving toward the close of the twentieth century with a religious community largely adjusted to the status quo—a tail-light behind other community agencies rather than a headlight leading men to higher levels of justice." In Birmingham, King replied to those who called him an "outsider" by stating that he felt obliged to speak God's truth to people, whenever it was necessary. Thus, he continued: "I am in Birmingham because injustice is here. Just as the prophets of the eighth century B.C. left their villages and carried their 'thus saith the Lord' far beyond the boundaries of their home towns, and just as the Apostle Paul left his village of Tarsus and carried the gospel of Jesus Christ to the far corners of the Greco-Roman world, so am I compelled to carry the gospel of freedom beyond my home town. Like Paul, I must constantly respond to the Macedonian call for aid."[45]

The Civil Rights Act of 1964 was one of the truly landmark pieces of legislation in US history. The law was only passed under the pressure of a number of King-led civil rights campaigns and intense church lobbying by liberal Protestant churches with the assistance of Jews and Catholics.[46] James F. Finlay confirms that politicians on Capitol Hill recognized that the American churches were playing an unusual and important role in efforts to get the legislation passed. Senator Hubert Humphrey, in shepherding the bill through the Senate, ultimately felt that the churches were "the most important force at work."[47] Senator Richard Russell, his colleague from Georgia, agreed even as he sharply commented that in supporting civil rights, "men of the cloth" had applied a "philosophy of coercion" comparable to the "doctrine that dictated the acts of Torquemada in the infamous days of the inquisition."[48] Andrew Young[49] confirmed that lobbying by Eugene Carson Blake, Methodist Bishops Lord and Mathews, Bob Spike, and the WCC Commission on Religion, among others, succeeded in pressuring Senator Hickenlooper of Iowa, who was opposed to the bill.[50] Thus, the bill was finally passed, having overcome a Southern filibuster.

45. King, *Why We Can't Wait*, 77.

46. McGraw, "Andrew J. Young," 324–330.

47. Findlay, "Religion and Politics," 66.

48. Ibid.

49. Andrew Young (March 12, 1932), an American politician, civil rights leader, and clergyman, joined King in leading the SCLC. Following King's assassination, he worked with King's successor, Ralph Abernathy, until Young's resignation in 1970.

50. McGraw, "Andrew J. Young," 324–330.

In a 1965 interview, King was asked if he could recall any mistakes he had made in leading the movement. He replied, "Well, the most pervasive mistake I have made was in believing that because our cause was just, we could be sure that the white ministers of the South, once their Christian consciences were challenged, would rise to our aid."[51] As with the Montgomery Bus Boycott, this failed to happen, and King was "chastened and disillusioned." As the campaigns progressed and direct appeals were made to white ministers, the majority declined to help, and some even "took stands against us," claiming "it was not the proper role of the church to intervene in secular affairs." When asked if he disagreed with this view, "most emphatically," King answered, "the essence of the Epistles of Paul is that Christians should rejoice at being deemed worthy to suffer for what they believe. The projection of a social gospel, in my opinion is the true witness of a Christian life. This is the meaning of the true *ekklesia*—the inner, spiritual church." King felt that the church was stagnant and had lost direction: "The church once changed society. But today, I feel that too much of the church is merely a thermometer, which measures rather than molds public opinion." King qualified his answer to say that it was the leadership of the white church, with some exceptions, that he was disappointed with.

Scholar Ira G. Zepp notes that "it is significant that one of the greatest debts King acknowledges to anyone is the tribute he pays to Raushenbusch."[52] King was deeply influenced by Walter Rauschenbusch, and in "My Pilgrimage to Nonviolence," having commended the theologian for doing "a great service for the Christian church," he wrote in praise of him: "It has been my conviction ever since reading Rauschenbusch that any religion which professes to be concerned about the souls of men, and is not concerned about the social and economic conditions that scar the soul is a spiritually moribund religion only waiting for the day to be buried." King added, "a religion that ends with the individual, ends."[53]

King gave credit when it was due, and the voting rights campaign in Selma, AL, was a triumph of support from white religious communities. Four hundred white clergymen from various denominations and faith traditions arrived in Selma, and contributed to what King described as "the greatest and warmest expression of religious unity of Catholic, Protestant, and Jew in our nation's history."[54] The preaching and pastoral aspects of

---

51. This and the quotations that follow are taken from Haley, "Playboy Interview," 65–68, 70–74, 76–78.

52. Zepp, *Social Vision*, 31.

53. Quoted in ibid.

54. Quoted in Baldwin, *Voice of Conscience*, 176.

King's ministry were closely related to the prophetic aspects. This relationship was illustrated by his appearance on *Face the Nation* in August of 1965, when Martin Agronsky of CBS News questioned King on his speaking out against the US involvement in Vietnam, and he explained:

> I happen to be a Minister of the Gospel and I take that ministry very seriously, and in that capacity I have not merely a priestly function but a prophetic function, and I must ever seek to bring the great principles and insights of our Judeo-Christian heritage to bear on the social evils of our day. And I happen to feel that war is obsolete and that it must be cast into unending limbo, and that if we continue to escalate this war, we move nearer to the point of plunging the whole of mankind into the abyss of annihilation.[55]

Indeed, the issue of war and peace has always been a difficult one for the church, for it often requires agonizing decisions. It places the church in a precarious position somewhere between two extremes: "at one end, the belief that all war is wrong, on the other, the notion that God is on the side of one's own country," which is perhaps one area where the churches are "notably at a loss."[56] The enthusiastic backing that both Protestant and Catholic churches gave to the US in World War I still resonated in King's time, and the unrealized great expectations for a peaceful society that followed were still painful. The subsequent disillusionment gave a renewed impetus to pacifist organizations, one that was to be rebuffed once again by US involvement in World War II in 1941. The churches accepted the war, bowing to what the *Christian Century* called an "unnecessary necessity."[57]

On December 6, 1965, King addressed the Synagogue Council of America on the issue of peace and war, and he returned again to his role as a Baptist minister when he claimed that it was worthless to seek integration at a lunch counter if the world was in imminent danger of disintegration:

> Beyond this I am a minister of the gospel. I am mandated by this calling above every other duty to seek peace among men and to do it even in the face of hysteria and scorn. Moreover, as a minister and civil rights leader I have scathingly denounced the silence of good white people in the South. I have described their fear to speak out on discrimination as ultimately more

55. Martin Luther King Jr., interview by Martin Agronsky, *Face the Nation*, CBS, August 29, 1965, King Papers, Box 9, August 1–December 31, 1965, King Center Library and Archive, Atlanta, GA.

56. "Churches' Influence," 20–21.

57. Ibid.

damaging and immoral than the open deeds of the segregation-
ists. If I could exonerate their silence in the presence of evil I
cannot maintain my own silence when a more terrible scourge
afflicts the world.[58]

The mid-sixties had arrived, and it was a pivotal time marked by the
politics of civil and voting rights enforcement, the war against poverty, and
the Vietnam War, all of which had become "inextricably intertwined."[59]
There was a significant shift in King's thinking in the years between 1965
and 1968 as he was faced with fundamental flaws in the American way of
life: "We have moved into an era where we are called upon to raise certain
basic questions about the whole society. We are still called upon to give aid
to the beggar who finds himself in misery and agony on life's highway. But
one day, we must ask the question of whether an edifice which produced
beggars must not be restructured and refurbished. This is where we are
not."[60] In one of King's most important speeches, given on November 14,
1966, in Frogmore, SC, he censured his country for its mismanagement of
both national and foreign policy in his call for a "restructuring of the whole
of American society." King could not comprehend why there were forty million poor people in the richest country in the world:

> I am simply saying that God has left enough and to spare in
> this world for all of his children to have the basic necessities
> of life, and God never intended for some of his children to live
> in inordinate superfluous wealth while others live in abject,
> deadening poverty. And somehow I believe that God made it
> all. I believe that God made the coal. I believe that the gasoline
> that goes in my automobile is there because God made it, and I
> believe firmly that the earth is the Lord's and the fullness thereof
> … I think the earth is the Lord's, and since we didn't make these
> things by ourselves, we must share them with each other.[61]

September of 1966 brought King to Dallas, TX, where he addressed
the International Convention of Christian Churches. In talking about the
spectacular strides in science and technology in the US and the unlimited
horizons that seemed to stretch ahead, King spoke of "a poverty of the

58. King, Martin Luther, Jr., "Speech to the Synagogue Council of America," New
York, December 5, 1965, King Papers, Box 9, August 1–December 31, 1965, King Center Library and Archive, Atlanta, GA.

59. Jackson, *Civil Rights to Human Rights*, 218.

60. King, *Autobiography of Martin Luther King*, 346.

61. King, "Speech at SCLC Staff Retreat," King Center Library and Archives, Atlanta, GA.

spirit" which stood in glaring contrast to the "technological abundance."[62] King warned that progress required increased material powers that "spell enlarged peril." This deficit of morality required appropriate action, for "this tragic problem presents the church with a great challenge. As the chief moral guardians of the community the church must work with passionate determination to solve the problem of racial injustice. It has always been the responsibility of the church to broaden horizons, challenge the status quo, and break the mores when necessary."[63]

In 1967, King was actively involved in preparation for the SCLC's Poor People's Campaign, and he saw that the crisis had international ramifications: "Can a nonviolent, direct-action movement find application on the international level, to confront economic and political problems? I believe it can. It is clear to me that the next stage of the movement is to become international."[64] On April 4, 1967, exactly a year before his death, King delivered an outstanding speech, "Beyond Vietnam,"[65] at Riverside Church in New York City. He spoke movingly about his receipt of the Nobel Prize and his commitment to the "brotherhood of man," but King had a far bigger burden to shoulder:

> I would yet have to live with the meaning of my commitment to the ministry of Jesus Christ. To me, the relationship of this ministry to the making of peace is so obvious that I sometimes marvel at those who ask me why I am speaking against the war. Could it be that they do not know that the good news was meant for all men—for communist and capitalist, for their children and ours, for black and for white, for revolutionary and conservative? Have they forgotten that my ministry is in obedience to the one who loved his enemies so fully that he died for them?[66]

62. Martin Luther King, Jr., "Beyond Discovery Love," address at the International Convention of Christian Churches, Dallas, TX, September 25, 1966, King Papers, Box 11, King Center Library and Archive, Atlanta, GA.

63. King, "Beyond Discovery Love," September 25, 1966, King Center Library and Archive, Atlanta, GA.

64. King, Trumpet of Conscience, 62.

65. "Beyond Vietnam," or as it is also called, "A Time to Break Silence," was delivered before a meeting of Clergy and Laymen Concerned About Vietnam (CALCAV). This was a no-holds-barred speech in which King attacked the Johnson administration for prolonging a wholly unnecessary and catastrophic war in Southeast Asia. King also linked the war and the civil rights movement for the first time. A barrage of negative responses from the media followed, but King felt that his conscience compelled him to speak out against the horrendous casualties being suffered by both the Vietnamese and American servicemen. King, "Time to Break Silence," 231–44.

66. Ibid.

King, in addition to his arduous speaking schedule at home, engaged earnestly with the World Council of Churches (WCC), the World Convention of Churches of Christ, and other Christian communities worldwide, daring them to "first discern what God is calling . . . [them] to do in the presence of international conflict" and to make their "witness known, not merely through pronouncement but by the submission of their bodies as a living witness to the truth of Christ."[67] Eric Lincoln described King's contribution to the black church and to Christianity in glowing terms when he wrote, "The late Dr. Martin Luther King, Jr., did more than anyone in modern times to exemplify the spirit of Christianity and this tremendous benefit was to all of Christendom, not just the Black church. Christianity itself was against the wall and King's high moral leadership and eventual martyrdom did more to re-establish credibility and interest in the faith than all of the councils and pronouncements of the last hundred years."[68]

67. Quoted in Baldwin, *Voice of Conscience*, 209.
68. Lincoln, "Decade of Change," 7.

2

To Set the Captives Free

Martin Luther King Jr., Eugene Carson Blake, and the Social Mission of the WCC

THE WCC's EUGENE CARSON Blake admitted that the civil rights movement in the 1950s and the 1960s failed to achieve all its goals, but this did not deter one activist from recounting this memory of him: "There was both a heroism about Dr. Blake without which Protestantism would have been even more cowardly than it was in those hectic days, and an arrogance about him so necessary to do what was needed to be done."[1] One of the aims of this book is to show the extent to which Martin Luther King Jr. served as an international spokesman for peace. Working in tandem with the WCC, he was able to promulgate his message with the help of his association with this formidable organization. King was fortunate that Blake was General Secretary of the WCC beginning in 1966, when his timely support for King's work was of great importance. Both clergymen lived through the turbulent days of the civil rights movement and the tragedy of the Vietnam War, momentous events that showcased both leaders' conscientious condemnation of US domestic and foreign policy. For example, in August of 1967, King and Blake appeared alongside Tram Van Bo, South Vietnam's foreign minister, to discuss the morality of the Vietnam War on the CBS religious program,

---

1. Brackenridge, *Eugene Carson Blake*, 105.

16

Lamp Unto My Feet. The episode, "Vietnam, the Battle Behind the War," was taped at the WCC "Pacem in Terris" conference held in Geneva on May 29, 1967. The conference was called "Pacem in Terris" after the encyclical on peace of Pope John XXIII. This was certainly an opportunity for King and Blake to compare notes on their respective stances.[2] King may have had a "Dream," but Blake certainly did all in his power to help bring that "Dream" to fulfillment.

Following King's death, Blake presided over the adoption of the Martin Luther King Resolution to study nonviolent means to resolve international disputes. Later, Blake was instrumental in pushing the WCC's Programme to Combat Racism with special regard to South Africa, which was one of King's great concerns. Blake's speeches over the years clearly show King's ongoing influence on his deliberations. That is, even after King's death, he still had a champion fighting his cause. This was especially significant in terms of the WCC's opposition to racism, which King had campaigned relentlessly against in the previous twelve years. Some critics might argue that because Blake and King were both Christian ministers, why should they not support similar causes for their brethren? But my analysis will show that there was more to their relationship than a casual respect for each other.

The 1960s saw significant changes in the ecumenical movement when many Eastern and Oriental Orthodox Churches became full members of the WCC, bringing with them new perspectives and new concerns. As former colonies in Africa and Asia gained independence, the WCC expanded to include many churches from the Third World, adding to the organization's global vitality. In the 1950s and 1960s, Blake became known as an enthusiastic supporter of both King's work and of the civil rights movement in the US, an affinity that would have global ramifications.

Blake grew up in Missouri, where racial segregation was so routine "that he was scarcely aware that racism existed."[3] According to Brackenridge, "Theoretically," Blake said, "I knew about the wrongness of social prejudice. But as a small boy it never occurred to me that I was in a segregated school." As he matured, Blake became more sensitive to the conditions endured by minority groups. Blake realized that total or absolute justice was unlikely, saying, "I am Niebuhrian enough not to be romantic," and he once said that "proximate justice is what we should seek." Blake's

---

2. *Bridgeport Post* (Bridgeport, CT), August 6, 1967. See also Wadlow, "Martin Luther King, Jr."

3. Quoted in Brackenridge, *Eugene Carson Blake*, 77–78.

early experiences caused him to seek the objective of "proximate justice" as a pastor, administrator, and citizen.[4]

It was not long before he had an opportunity to put his principles to the test. In moving from Albany, NY, to Pasadena, CA, Blake refused to sign a neighborhood covenant restricting the resale of property to "undesirables," meaning blacks or other minorities.[5] One of Blake's most conspicuous public stands on racial issues during his time in Pasadena was his leadership in the Interracial Commission of the Pasadena Council of Social Agencies in 1948. Blake had two objectives that seem to resonate with King's, both of which seem reasonable in today's Western world: first, "to secure for minorities the full rights and privileges of citizens of the community," and second, "to get members of minority groups to assume responsibility of citizenship within the community."[6] Blake was chosen as head of the commission because he had a reputation for aggressive leadership allied with humanitarian concerns. He soon discovered that he was walking a tightrope between those who felt the commission was too radical and other critics who thought it was too conservative. The municipal swimming pool, which had a segregated policy, was where the battle lines were drawn. The National Association for the Advancement of Colored People (NAACP) successfully contested the legality of Pasadena's policy. The pool was subsequently closed for a number of years, allegedly due to malfunctioning equipment. Blake's commission persuaded the local authorities to reopen the pool, adhering to court guidelines forbidding color limitations. Numerous other problems surfaced in housing, employment, and education, and there would be few successes in unraveling Pasadena's deeply ingrained discrimination. But for Blake, these challenges offered a fast learning curve. "During this period," he said, "I learned more about minorities and interracial problems that I had ever learned before."[7]

In 1951, Blake was elected stated clerk of the Presbyterian Church in the US. He succeeded in transforming this role from being just the "keeper of minutes and committees" to being a dominant leader in the Oikoumene.[8] Through bulletins and conferences with US presidents and congressional leaders in attendance, he and other religious leaders sought to bring a moral Christian conscience to the problems of the day: racism, a

---

4. Ibid.

5. Ibid., 80.

6. Ibid., 82.

7. Ibid., 81–83.

8. The word "ecumenical" derives from the Greek *oikoumenē*, which means the "whole universe."

belligerent religious right, zealous anti-communists like McCarthy,[9] anti-Catholic rhetoric, and the Vietnam War.[10] Practicing what he preached, he championed minority rights, and in 1951, he declared that whites could not solve problems for blacks. Like King, Blake insisted that any real solution could only come about through joint action: "The problem is not that Americans do not know what must be done under the law, but they are not quite ready to face all the implications of a small world in which the majority of people are of the darker races. The problem can be solved only by each community doing its very best to promote discussion amongst the leaders of the various racial groups."[11]

The historic Brown v. Board of Education US Supreme Court decision on desegregation in 1954 was a watershed moment. The court announced that segregation of black children in public schools was unconstitutional, rejecting the previous Plessey v. Ferguson 1896 ruling on the doctrine of "separate but equal." This decision caused consternation in communities through the US, and Blake, in ways that resembled King's activities, worked hard to bring about reconciliation. As stated clerk of the General Assembly and President of the National Council of the Churches of Christ in America (NCC) from 1954 to 1957, he released several statements in support of desegregation and asked for cool heads to prevail. In 1956, Blake and Moderator Paul S. Wright issued a letter to Presbyterian pastors and sessions, calling on them to "not form hasty judgments, nor condemn others, nor assume partisan positions which will in no way work for peace, lest what we condemn in others we may discover within ourselves."[12] Blake became closely identified with efforts to implement the Supreme Court decision, and this provoked a nasty response from some quarters. An anonymous critic had this to say: "Your reckless statement proposing the use of troops to enforce racial integration in the South marks you a fanatic and trouble maker of the first order. Your warped racial views have no visible support in the ranks of the general membership of your(?) [sic] church. Most of the members would stand aghast at the sight of a Negro entering their church."[13]

Blake continued to receive hostile letters, not unlike those received by King. Nevertheless, criticism did not lessen his efforts in support of the aims

9. The McCarthy era (1950–1957), named after Senator Joseph McCarthy, was marked by accusations against thousands of Americans of being Communists or Communist sympathizers. The investigations were mainly directed at government employees, actors, teachers, and trade unionists.

10. Crow, "Eugene Carson Blake," 228–36.

11. Quoted in Brackenridge, *Eugene Carson Blake*, 84–85.

12. Ibid., 85.

13. Ibid., 89.

of the civil rights movement.[14] In Blake's capacity as stated clerk, he worked hard to remove all vestiges of separation and segregation from the church body. When the General Assembly met in Indianapolis in 1959, the local committee had the responsibility for acquiring accommodations for visitors. When one local hotel refused to register a black United Presbyterian clergyman, Blake demanded that we "pull everybody out of that hotel and pull them out right away."[15] Although accommodation was at a premium, those involved thought that Blake's behavior was exemplary. In the future, he ensured that all bookings were made through his office to prevent a reoccurrence of this overt prejudice. Blake's personal commitment to racial equality was as robust as the official commitment of his denomination. The General Assembly had affirmed its support for a non-segregated church and a non-segregated society from as far back as 1946, a decade before King rose to prominence in Montgomery, AL.[16]

Blake had visited South Africa in 1959, where he found that the Nationalist Party in power was committed to a strict policy of apartheid, which provided for the separate development of each of the four racial groupings of the population. This comprised of European, African (Bantu), colored, and Asiatic peoples inhabiting an area twice the size of France. As Blake skeptically remarked, Americans were doubtful, in view of their own experience, that "separate but equal" could work better in South Africa than it had in the US. Blake cynically concluded, "nothing I saw in South Africa made me any less skeptical of this than I was before I made my trip."[17] Blake, in analyzing his fact-finding mission to South Africa, made a few suggestions, especially in relation to the Dutch Reformed Church, which supported apartheid. He addressed his remarks not only to white Americans, but also to African American Christians "who will undoubtedly have more influence on the African continent in the next decades than any of us whose skins are white."[18] Therefore:

1. Let us recognize and emphasize every good and Christian motivation that exists among the leaders and members of the Dutch Reformed Church in South Africa. They are troubled and they are sincerely disturbed at what they feel is a world misunderstanding of them and their position.

2. While giving full credit for the Anglican and other English speaking churches' minority witness against apartheid by deed and word, let us not

14. Ibid.
15. Ibid., 90.
16. Ibid., 90–91.
17. Blake, *Next Decade*, 64–65.
18. Ibid. 66–67.

suppose that the differences between these churches are due entirely to an ethical or theological superiority. I found as much desire for free Christian understanding and witness among the Dutch reformed, as I did among the other churches in South Africa.

Blake called for South African Christians of all races to be involved in the ecumenical movement and its councils, which he felt would benefit all. It was necessary, he said, that "our own Christianity," conditioned by theological, social, and political history, would not spoil, through arrogance, "such witness as we make."[19] Blake concluded on a salutary note when he reflected, "for even then the Christian church is apt to be as much embarrassed as it is today when it contemplates the gulf between its members' Christian professions and their political and economic actions."[20]

In an address titled "The Moral Responsibility of the Church in a Secular Society," Blake stated that church officials in South Africa were afraid "that their congregations will be divided and weakened if any stand is taken against the policy of government."[21] Indeed, many feared that "for the church to meddle in politics will lead it away from its true vocation and duty." Blake, concluded in some despair, "with these reasons to keep them silent, the white churches in South Africa are revealed as weak and ineffective, as irrelevant and peripheral in a great crisis in their nation."[22] As King saw it, the church had a pivotal role to play, but it first had to recapture its prophetic zeal. Otherwise, the church "will become little more than an irrelevant social club with a thin veneer of religiosity. If the church does not participate actively in the struggle for economic and social justice, it will forfeit the loyalty of millions and cause men everywhere to say that it has atrophied its will."[23]

The pictures of blacks being attacked by dogs in Birmingham, AL, incensed Blake and provoked this response: "I decided that I just couldn't stand for such behavior any longer . . . I was angry and I went to the Des Moines General Assembly in that mood."[24] The general board of the NCC met in June of 1963 in New York, where they did some soul-searching on the role members should take on in the civil rights struggle. The board's questions called to mind those raised in King's "Letter from Birmingham

19. Ibid.

20. Ibid.

21. Blake, "Moral Responsibility," 1–4.

22. Ibid.

23. King, "Beyond Discovery Love," September 25, 1966, King Center Library and Archive, Atlanta, GA.

24. Brackenbridge, *Eugene Carson Blake*, 92.

Jail," for they asked, "were pulpit pronouncements enough? Could the Christian conscience be satisfied by mere pious expressions of sympathy for the Negro?"[25] Blake, as executive head of the United Presbyterian Church in the USA's General Assembly, former president of the National Council, and one of the America's most respected clergyman featured on the May 26, 1961, cover of *Time*, did not think so. Blake turned to a fellow board member and said quietly, "Some time or other we are all going to have to stand and be on the receiving end of a fire hose."[26]

The following month, Blake was one of 283 whites and African Americans, including twenty-six Protestant, Catholic, and Jewish clergymen, who were arrested following an integration march to the Gwynn Oak Amusement Park in Baltimore, MD. The sixty-four-acre park had a long history of excluding African Americans. Arrested alongside Blake were Bishop Daniel Corrigan, Director of the National Council of the Protestant Episcopal Church, the Rev. Dr. William Sloan Coffin Jr., Chaplain of Yale University, Rabbi Morris Lieberman of the Baltimore Hebrew Congregation, and Monsignor Austin J. Healy of the Roman Catholic Archdiocese of Baltimore. The march was sponsored by the Congress of Racial Equality and despite careful planning, soon turned ugly. A crowd of about one thousand whites inside the park shouted, "Dump 'em in the bay," "Black nigger, white nigger," "Castrate them," and "Send 'em to the zoo!" Despite the agitated crowd, the police managed to prevent any actual violence. Although Blake and nine fellow clergymen were arrested, the demonstration succeeded in pressuring the owners to stop discrimination, and all charges were later dropped.[27]

But Blake had a bigger agenda when he asked, "when, if ever, is it right to break the law?" a question King often raised. He went on to explain that breaking the law was not something to be done lightly, that anarchy was a terrible thing, and that disorder makes civilization impossible. Blake noted that Presbyterians had a tradition of honoring the law, both civil and ecclesiastic. He advised that anyone who had lived through a riot or revolution ought to appreciate civil order and the police who enforce it. But he warned that he did not believe that it was never right to break the law, asking, "what about Christians or Jews under Hitler, what about the Boston Tea Party?" He then pointed to the whole series of arrests in the New Testament, when Christians regularly refused to obey some laws, even though the Apostle Paul taught that "the powers that be are ordained by God" (Paul Rom 13:1). Blake then turned to the racial crisis: "But has the present effort by American

25. "March on Gwynn Oak Park," 19.

26. Ibid.

27. Ibid.

Negroes to win equality now in voting, in education, in job opportunity and advancement, in housing and in public facilities—even amusement parks—anything to do with witnessing to Jesus Christ, as in the first century?"[28]

Blake confirmed, as did King, that it was perfectly clear that "all of the highest authorities in the Church of Jesus Christ do so believe." He referred to his own general assembly, which had repeatedly made it clear "that the white man's treatment of the Negro even in the church itself is morally wrong and a betrayal of Christ." Blake observed, as did King, that the Pope had made it clear that the Roman Catholic understanding was similar. Blake made reference to the WCC and its willingness to lose several South African churches (particularly the Dutch Reformed Church) "rather than weaken its witness to the Christian importance of racial equality and justice." Blake pleaded with his listeners for the courage "to consider what may be your Christian duty in this battle for justice and equality in 1963 in the USA."[29] Blake noted inequalities for African Americans in some states, such as the lack of voting rights, access to public accommodations, and so on. The people who were preventing a Christian solution, he said, were not the Governor Wallaces in Alabama or the Governor Faubuses in Arksanas. Blake was quite direct when he proclaimed that those responsible for the stalemate in August of 1963, "are we white Christians who have isolated . . . our minds from the realities of the injustice our laws and social patterns impose upon Negroes by forgetting all about them whenever they become quiet and patient."[30] Blake was outspoken for a white clergyman at this time, and was cognizant of the fact that a large proportion of his own brethren did not share his views. Just as Martin Luther King Jr. had done, Blake turned his attention overseas to Africa, where "less qualified people of their own race" had attained their freedom. Blake warned that the patience of African Americans had run out, and that "if there is increasing violence in the US it will not be the fault of Negroes, striving for fairness and justice, it will be the fault of all of us who, in apathy and ignorance, let injustice continue." Blake rebuked the Christian church for its lack of empathy regarding race relations when he described the church as being "like a religious holy embroidery on a secular culture which is essentially more and more selfish and fearful the wealthier and more comfortable we become."[31]

R. Douglas Brackenridge, in writing *Eugene Carson Blake: Prophet with Portfolio,* explained that Blake, because of his radical views, had to cope

28. Quoted in Houck and Dixon, *Rhetoric, Religion,* 566–74.

29. Ibid.

30. Ibid.

31. Ibid.

with ambivalent feelings from even his closest friends. He was still admired as a man of integrity, but many questioned whether he had "gone off the deep end" on racial issues.[32] Blake was prepared to travel the same road as King despite the hazards ahead, and in spite of warnings that treading such a path "may lead you to arrest, ridicule, or poverty, or even physical danger." Blake asked his flock to follow, stating that the much-publicized July 4, 1963, demonstration in Maryland was not of importance unless "it symbolizes and encourages the members of our church to act in a new pattern of witness to Jesus Christ with regard to racial equality and justice."[33] Blake also helped to organize the historic march to the Washington Mall for jobs and freedom in August of 1963. Standing side by side with King on the podium, he spoke persuasively on behalf of his church and for himself, highlighting some past failures but expressing optimism for the future: "We come in hope that those who have marched today are but a token of the new and massive, high determination of all men of religion and patriotism to win in this nation under God, liberty and justice for all. And we come—late we come—we come in that love revealed in Jesus Christ which reconciles into true community all men of every color, race, and nation who respond in faith and obedience to him."[34]

Blake was active in the interfaith coalition for John F. Kennedy's proposed civil rights legislation, which in 1964 was passed into law under President Lyndon B. Johnson's administration. In lobbying before a House Judiciary Subcommittee on July 24, 1963, with Father F. Cronin, S.S., and Rabbi Irwin M. Blank, Blake had warned that unless the legislators took immediate action, the present social revolution could easily degenerate into civil chaos. A Blake explained, the demand for justice regardless of color, race, or national origin had been underestimated and the time had passed for "tokenism or demands for endless patience."[35] Recognition for Blake's important role in civil rights activism came from several sources, including a personal letter from King, who wrote, "1963 was a significant year for the civil rights movement. We were able to make greater strides in that year than ever before. It goes without saying that your creative witness and magnificent support went a long, long way toward making 1963 the momentous year that it proved to be in civil rights."[36] Blake's acceptance speech in assuming the role of General Secretary to the WCC in 1966 gave an indication

32. Brackenridge, *Eugene Carson Blake*, 98.

33. Quoted in Houck and Dixon, *Rhetoric, Religion*, 566–74.

34. Brackenridge, *Eugene Carson Blake*, 103.

35. Ibid.

36. Ibid., 104–105.

as to his vision as a leader for social justice: "I need hardly remind you that this mission includes a ministry of reconciliation not only of God and man and of confessional and church divisions, but also of reconciliation across all the divisions of our world—divisions caused by geography, culture, race poverty, affluence, ideology, sin and fear, which, unless reconciled by the gospel, will prevent world peace and even threaten world disaster."[37]

Blake's predecessor, General Secretary Willem Visser 't Hooft, was described as aloof and sensitive to criticism, primarily a scholar and diplomat. Blake, as he readily admitted, was no theologian, but President Arthur McKay of Chicago's McCormick Theological Seminary attributed to him "an instinctive theological savvy about the issues that are facing the church."[38] Furthermore, "Blake has done more than merely preach about Negro rights; in 1963 he was arrested for attempting to integrate an amusement park in Maryland."[39] Upon his appointment in 1966, Blake received many congratulations, including this one from King: "Men of all colors and from various positions of servitude and affluence throughout the world take a firmer grip on hope for overcoming the evils of racism and poverty as you assume the role of General Secretary. We regard you are our gift to the world and with you we shall overcome."[40] As General Secretary, Blake was determined to make the WCC a truly representative world body in which Orthodox and Third World churches would have a full say in all matters. Like King, he had a vision for a world community, but he also recognized the limitations of man, saying, "the majority of our people (and I dare say of any people) tend both to be short-sighted and selfish. To make any impression upon selfishness, you must realize you are dealing with the ultimate values in human life."[41]

Blake emphasized the importance for the church hierarchy in their calling to help change society: "I simply say that those who have any responsibility for leadership in any Christian church must continue to hope that those who still profess Christianity will not continue acting like selfish, godless materialists."[42]

In July of 1966, Blake made reference to the World Conference on Church and Society in Geneva when King delivered a very well received

37. Crow, "Eugene Carson Blake," 228–36.

38. Quoted in "American in Geneva," 1–2.

39. Ibid.

40. Quoted in Brackenridge, *Eugene Carson Blake*, 150.

41. Blake, Eugene Carson, "The Ecumenical Movement and Its Relation to a World Community," *Westdeutscher Rundfunk*, October 1966, 995.1.01/1, Works (1966), WCC Archives, Geneva, Switzerland.

42. Ibid.

sermon known as "A Knock at Midnight" at Saint Pierre Cathedral that was broadcast throughout Europe. At the 1966 Conference, their concerns surrounding racism, war, and poverty were well-voiced. Blake wrote to King on July 18, 1966, thanking him for his participation: "You should have received by this time the official letter of appreciation of the officers of the Church and Society Conference for your sermon and your willingness to give a little of your precious time to recording it for our use here in Geneva. I am happy to report that the reception both on television and in the Cathedral was excellent and effective."[43] The Conference is discussed in greater detail in Chapter 3.

The conference was composed of representatives of Protestant and Orthodox churches from all over the world, and for the first time, representatives of the churches of the Third World were able to attend in sufficient numbers to be heard. The majority of the church conference was composed of lay members, and most of these were specialists in anthropology, sociology, economics, political science, and technology. As Blake remarked, over the conference's two short weeks the specialists, theologians, and other church leaders became something of a representative world community despite all their differences.[44]

Blake gave an insightful speech titled "The Ecumenical Movement and Its Relation to a World Community," in December of 1966. He explained that many people thought that the ecumenical movement was only of interest to pastors, priests, and perhaps lay church members. However, he insisted that "everyone in the whole world ought to be interested in any movement which gives some promise of gathering the people of our shrinking planet into one community."[45] Such aspirations were shared in King's pursuit of his "beloved community." As King highlighted, "If we are to have peace on earth, our loyalties must become ecumenical rather than sectional, our loyalties must transcend our race, our tribe, our class, and our nation; and this means we must develop a world community."[46]

Blake saw the two most difficult domestic problems in the US as racial equality, justice, and integration, as well as the problem of poverty in the

---

43. Eugene Carson Blake to Martin Luther King Jr., July 18, 1966, WCC General Secretaries, Correspondence: Frequent (1937–1977), 42.11.08, WCC Archives, Geneva, Switzerland.

44. Blake, "Ecumenical Movement," October 1966, 995.1.01/1, WCC Archives, Geneva, Switzerland.

45. Ibid.

46. King "A Christmas Sermon on Peace," Ebenezer Baptist Church, Atlanta, GA, December 24, 1967, King Papers, Box 13, King Center Library and Archives, Atlanta, GA.

midst of greater wealth than any nation had ever known. He saw the two problems as being related, since one of the results of racial prejudice against blacks was the poverty that followed. Certainly this was another aspect of racial inequality that King had regularly brought attention to. Blake's insight was that part of the problem for whites was a lack of imagination about issues of race and poverty. As he put it, "most white Americans cannot imagine what it would be like to have a black skin in our country," and he added the "Christian life requires such imagination."[47] The golden rule should be applied, "Do unto others as you would that they should do unto you." According to Blake, many black leaders were turning away from white liberals because they felt that the white man "often does not understand well enough to know how to love his Negro neighbor."[48] Indeed, as King related, "Racism is still the coloured man's burden and the white man's shame. And the world will never rise to its full moral, political, or even social maturity until racism is totally eradicated."[49]

Blake appeared on *Face the Nation* on December 15, 1966, for an interview with news correspondents Martin Agronsky and Joseph Benti of CBS News and with Edward B. Fiske of the *New York Times*. Fiske noted that the Vatican was setting up a new Commission on Peace and Justice, and he asked Blake what possibilities he saw for cooperative efforts in this area between the WCC and the Vatican. Blake answered that both bodies were optimistic about "the fact that they were deciding to carry out the intention that was expressed by Vatican Council II."[50] This cooperative effort represented a move towards fostering justice as a long-range basis of peace, with particular regard to Asia, Africa, and Latin America. Blake added that there was not going to be any peace unless there was "a better sharing of the wealth of the world in one community." He saw this as an issue around which the WCC and the Roman Catholic Church needed to develop a Christian conviction that changed the question from "how generous ought we rich people to be, to how do we really form a world community, and use the resources of the one world which technology has now made?"[51]

47. Blake, "Ecumenical Movement," October 1966, 995.1.01/1, WCC Archives, Geneva, Switzerland.

48. Ibid.

49. King, Martin Luther, Jr., "Honorary Degree Congregation Speech," University of Newcastle, Newcastle-Upon-Tyne, UK, November 13, 1967, http://www.ncl.ac.uk/congregations/assets/documents/MLKspeech.pdf.

50. Eugene Carson Blake, interview by Martin Agronsky, *Face the Nation*, CBS, December 25, 1966, WCC General Secretaries, 995.1.03/1 Speeches (1966), WCC Archives, Geneva, Switzerland.

51. Ibid.

It is important to examine Blake's views on government policy as applied to Third World countries. Although Vietnam is the subject here, there is no reason to doubt that Africa would be treated in a different manner. Martin Agronsky questioned Blake on the use of the Vietnam's national resources, how they might be used either for making war or for the alleviation of poverty, and what function the church might have in order to remain relevant to this disbursement. Blake responded that they were doing everything they knew "to avoid the churches becoming merely embroidery on a materialistic culture."[52] The leadership in the NCC and WCC was "not to represent the convictions of the rank and file but to try to represent to them what we understand the gospel of Jesus coming into the world means." Blake saw a difficulty here "when it is against your fear or against your prejudice, or even against your hatreds, which are in all of us in part."[53]

It has been my contention that Blake was influenced by the success of Martin Luther King Jr. and the civil rights movement. Later, his position within the WCC from 1966 onwards gave him substantial influence within that organization and ample opportunity to air his views. In reflecting on how the church can change society, Blake argued that charity was not enough, saying, "the cup of milk for the undernourished child is necessary, yes. But the people in developing countries must be helped to help themselves."[54] Suggestions included providing better seeds to triple the crop yield, a call for less discriminatory tariff policies, by which the nations of the North Atlantic Community strangle the economies of nations in the southern half of the world, and a pledge of 1 percent of the US gross national product to help developing countries.[55] Blake offered an example of successful mobilization against adversity when he invoked Christians' support of Martin Luther King's SCLC and the Delta Ministry to build grassroots organizations for poor blacks in the South. As Blake explained, classes in citizenship and political skills began long before black militants popularized the term "participating democracy." These were the forerunners of the Freedom Democratic Party, which in 1964 established the principle that blacks were to be part of all Southern delegations to National Democratic Conventions.[56]

---

52. Blake, interview by Agronsky, *Face the Nation*, December 25, 1966, 995.1.03/1 Speeches (1966), WCC Archives, Geneva, Switzerland.

53. Ibid.

54. Blake, Eugene Carson, "Ways the Church Can Transform Society," *Face to Face*, December 1968, 995.1.01/6 Works (1968), WCC Archives, Geneva, Switzerland.

55. Ibid.

56. Ibid.

Blake delivered a major address in April of 1967 in which he criticized President Johnson's escalation of the Vietnam War. He warned that US action was tragically "unable to distinguish friend from foe," and the end result was that, "the United States seems to be stumbling on toward final disaster."[57] Johnson, who already considered King persona non grata, now added Blake's name to his list of "unacceptable" religious representatives in the White House.[58] Blake followed the same path as King, forever defending the church and religious organizations against charges of antipatriotic behavior and constantly defending the civil rights movement. Blake spoke out again in June of 1967, at a time when King was under fierce pressure for his condemnation of the Vietnam War in his much-heralded speech, "Beyond Vietnam." Blake argued that "the ecumenical movement is first of all a Christian movement based upon the Christian faith in Jesus Christ, the Bible, and upon the living traditions of the churches, Catholic and Evangelical."[59] And to correct any misrepresentation, he continued: "The greatest misunderstanding about this movement, promoted assiduously by some of its critics, is that it is essentially a socialist, communist, anti-American political and social movement with no real dependence upon a theological understanding of the gospel or any traditional morality or faith."[60] Blake urged caution when dealing with international affairs, sensitive that others might have varying views: "We need of course to remember that Christians altogether are but a minority of the world's population. We must be careful not to slip into a new triumphalism which attempts to dictate to mankind."[61] Further clarifying his stance, he continued by offering to collaborate: "We must find the way to organize our Christian activity so that men of other faiths and of no faith are encouraged to join in these efforts and are not repelled by our arrogance as we seek to serve the whole of humanity in its critical need of development, justice and peace."[62]

Blake and King, if not explicitly influenced by one another, certainly spoke along a similar vein. For example, in answer to a question posed by Vorwarts, the central body of the Social Democratic Party of Germany, in

57. Brackenridge, *Eugene Carson Blake*, 173–74.

58. Ibid.

59. Blake, Eugene Carson, "Report of General Secretary to Uppsala Assembly," Uppsala, Sweden, July 9, 1968, 995.1.03/6 Speeches, 1968, WCC Archives, Geneva, Switzerland.

60. Blake, Eugene Carson, "The Ecumenical Movement," Washington, DC, June 29, 1967, 995.1.03/3 Speeches (1967), WCC Archives, Geneva, Switzerland.

61. Blake, "Report of General Secretary," July 9, 1968, 995.1.03/6 Speeches, WCC Archives, Geneva, Switzerland.

62 Ibid.

January of 1969 inquiring about Blake's attitude toward "Church and Politics," Blake replied, "the church influences the political life of the community by its emphasis on justice, love (even for the enemies), hope and peace; in other words, the church enters the political realm through Christian ethics."[63] King explored this political reality for the church before the National Convention on Religion and Race, arguing, "religion at its best deals not only with the relations of man to his fellow men but with the relations of man to the universe and to ultimate reality. But a religion true to its nature must also be concerned about man's social conditions. Religion deals not only with the hereafter but also with the here."[64]

Blake also made a speech in Munich on December 1, 1970, in which he gave a brief historical outline of the WCC's longstanding commitment to the struggle for racial justice. The WCC, with Blake as General Secretary, hoped to use King's methodology to resolve other conflicts. Hence, Blake observed, "In 1963 at the time of the March on Washington led by Martin Luther King, the Central Committee at Rochester addressed itself especially to the situation in the USA and South Africa."[65] Blake acknowledged with shame that many Christians hesitated to actively support the struggle for racial justice, or worse, "were on the wrong side of it."[66] The Central Committee decided that the churches should start with the removal of all racial barriers in their own fellowship. Only then could they be free to pray for both parties in the rising conflict. The Central Committee protested against the situation in South Africa, where millions of Africans were condemned to live in areas of "separate development" despite the majority of the population being black .[67] Blake then alluded to King's televised sermon at the 1966 Conference on Church and Society in Geneva. As Blake explained, this conference laid the foundation for the WCC's Programme to Combat Racism (PCR) in 1969, which demanded concrete action. Regretfully, he concluded that "it is not enough for churches and groups to condemn the sin of racial arrogance and oppression. The struggle for radical change in

63. Blake, Eugene Carson, "The Uppsala Conference: Six Months After," *Kristeligt Dagblad*, March 1969, 995.1.01/8 Works (1969), WCC Archives, Geneva, Switzerland.

64. King, Martin Luther, Jr., "A Challenge to the Churches and Synagogues," address at the Conference on Religion and Race, Edgewater Beach Hotel, Chicago, IL, January 17, 1963, King Papers, Box 3, January 1, 1963–May 25, 1963, King Center Library and Archive, Atlanta, GA.

65. Blake, Eugene Carson, "Address to Meeting with Dietzfelbinger: Proposed Introductory Remarks," 995.1.05/13 Speeches (1970), WCC Archives, Geneva, Switzerland.

66. Ibid.

67. Ibid

structures will inevitably bring suffering and will demand costly and bitter engagement."[68]

King likewise saw the US being distracted from resolving the realities at home by needless adventures abroad, asking, "Why has our nation placed itself in the position of being God's military agent on earth, and intervened recklessly in Vietnam and the Dominican Republic? Why have we substituted the arrogant undertaking of policing the whole world for the high task of putting our own house in order?"[69] Perhaps King also thought that if racism were seriously tackled at home, this enlightened domestic approach would be reflected in America's racially charged foreign policy. Blake had invited King to be a key participant at Fourth Assembly of the WCC at Uppsala, Sweden, in July of 1968, but unfortunately, he was assassinated shortly before it began.

Blake preached that the most obvious results of the nineteenth century's industrial revolution and the twentieth century's technology revolution was the vast increase in population and subsequent widespread poverty on a scale never before seen. Blake saw the connection between the rapidly increasing world population and the unwillingness of powerful nations to use their technological resources in support of the poverty-stricken: "We of the West neglect the findings of any way to deliver goods to the poor . . . The result of increasingly affluent societies with ugly pockets of poverty . . . It is no wonder that hatred and bitterness rise among the poor people."[70] Blake observed that a combination of greed and fear in the US had so far prevented the richest nation in the world from diverting its private and public financial priorities to produce and deliver even a minimum standard of food, housing, clothing, education and healthcare to all citizens. Instead, as Blake alleged, the US continued to spend its immense wealth "for war, for space adventures, and the multiplication of luxuries for those at the top of the competitive struggle, whether of management or labor unions."[71] The problem was further exacerbated by the self-interest of individuals, families, and class groups combined with a fear of the poor, and the threatened revolution was preventing political parties from offering the American electorate

---

68. Ibid.

69. King, Martin Luther, Jr., "The State of the Movement," address at SLC Staff Retreat, Penn Community Center, Frogmore, SC, November 28, 1967, King Papers, Box 13, King Center Library and Archive, Atlanta, GA.

70. Blake, Eugene Carson, "The Moral Aspects of Poverty," *Presbyterian Life*, April 1, 1971, 995.1.02/3 Works (1971), WCC Archives, Geneva, Switzerland.

71. Blake, Eugene Carson, "Mandeville Lecture: Towards a World Community of Man," San Diego, CA, March 28, 1972, 995.1.05/16 Speeches (1972), WCC Archives, Geneva, Switzerland.

an opportunity to vote for a better way of life. The US could not be viewed in isolation, for in the increasingly interdependent world that technology had produced, the problems of population, production, and distribution of goods was becoming even more severe.[72] King echoed Blake's concerns when he preached, "I am convinced that if we are to get on the right side of the world revolution, we as a nation must undergo a radical revolution of values. We must rapidly begin in the shift from a thing-oriented society to a person-oriented society. When machines and computers, profit motives and property rights, are considered more important than people, the giant triplets of racism, extreme materialism, and militarism are incapable of being conquered."[73]

Poverty was a constant theme for Blake. In his article "The Moral Aspects of Poverty," Blake asserted that poverty is not a question of simple economics, but one of morality and spirituality. He quoted from the Old Testament to argue for generosity towards the poor: "You shall not harden your heart or shut your hand against your poor brother" (Deut 15:7–11).[74] Blake also castigated the shortcomings of contemporary Christianity, saying, "The truly tragic aspect of Christian morality just now is that many of us pay lip service to individual charity in order to avoid the challenge of restructuring of our whole society."[75] King had previously confronted poverty in his Frogmore speech in November of 1966, when he announced, "there are more slums in our country today then there were twenty-five years ago."[76] As King found out in his war on poverty, and as Blake argued, "an American politician runs risks if he tries to seek votes with a program of higher taxes to eliminate poverty at home or for foreign aid."[77] Sadly, Blake concluded that "there is as yet no American Christian conscience geared to the realities of the world in which we now live," though he sought an answer in a broader alliance that included the "Roman Catholic Church, through the Pontifical Commission on Justice and Peace, and the World Council of Churches."[78]

72. Ibid.

73. King, "Time to Break Silence," 231–44.

74. Blake, "Moral Aspects of Poverty," April 1, 1971, 995.1.02/3 Works (1971), WCC Archives, Geneva, Switzerland.

75. Ibid.

76. King, "Speech at SCLC Staff Retreat," November 14, 1966, King Center Library and Archives, Atlanta, GA.

77. Blake, "Moral Aspects of Poverty," April 1, 1971, 995.1.02/3 Works (1971), WCC Archives, Geneva, Switzerland.

78. Ibid.

Blake's particular concern for South Africa's apartheid system was revealed when he disclosed that the United Methodist Church had started examining how its funds were used at national level. He explained that the Board of Missions in 1968 had withdrawn its investment portfolio from a bank that continued to make loans to South Africa, enabling that government's policy of racial segregation.[79] As Blake explained, "because of the coincidence of whiteness with military, economic, social, and cultural power in the world," white racism was identified by the WCC's PCR as the necessary focus of its efforts.[80] He observed that even with the breakup of political colonialism, the economic and cultural domination of the white man continued in South Africa. The white minority regimes increasingly used violence and terror against colored people, mostly black men, who sought their freedom. Blake asserted that economic injustice towards blacks in South Africa was a major part of apartheid, but it was also important to remember "that the attempt in that unhappy country is to see to it that black Africans, the coloreds, and dark skinned Asians are and remain the exploited proletariat. Poor white men can rise in the social and economic scale."[81]

The ecumenical movement's position on race was entirely clear, grounded as it was in the New Testament, for it held that discrimination, whether legal or illegal, against any person or groups because of race was morally wrong.[82] Blake felt that it was significant to state that all world gatherings under the sponsorship of the WCC would be multiracial. Despite much smaller memberships in Asia and Africa, eight of the twenty-six-member Executive Committee of the WCC were men and women of color. Under the general authority of the Central Committee, this Executive Committee has been responsible for the WCC's Programme to Combat Racism since 1969.[83] Blake explained that the Programme had been rooted in Christian concerns for the previous fifty years. Steps were taken along the way, and at the Second Assembly in 1954, the WCC adopted the

79. Blake, interview by Agronsky, *Face the Nation*, December 25, 1966, 995.1.03/1 Speeches (1966), WCC Archives, Geneva, Switzerland.

80. Blake, "Mandeville Lecture," March 28, 1972, 995.1.05/16 Speeches (1972), WCC Archives, Geneva, Switzerland.

81. Ibid.

82. Blake, Eugene Carson, "The Progress, Promise and Problems of the Ecumenical Movement," address at the Inauguration of the Irish School of Ecumenics, Dublin, Ireland, November 9, 1970–Spring 1971, 995.1.02/3 Works (1971), WCC Archives, Geneva, Switzerland.

83. Blake, "Mandeville Lecture," March 28, 1972, 995.1.05/16 Speeches (1972), WCC Archives, Geneva, Switzerland.

anti-racism stance it still holds. However, it was not until 1968 that, despite all the WCC's good resolutions and intentions, any real dent was made to racism in member churches or society at large.[84] Blake explained that the ecumenical movement sought to bring the moral insights of the gospel to bear upon the real decisions of men, societies, and nations. However, he did add a caveat: "Fortunately, the churches are not in a position to impose their conclusions upon the world."[85]

Because the American press was as uninterested in Southern Africa as the British press was in Vietnam, it was not until a year had lapsed that vigorous attacks on the WCC's Programme to Combat Racism began in the US. The WCC and its supporting churches were widely charged with promoting violence in Southern Africa, thereby relinquishing the correct Christian position of nonviolence and reconciliation.[86] In response to these accusations, the WCC argued that the more extreme and primary violence was being committed by the white minority governments of Southern Africa, which had become police states. Although the Programme to Combat Racism made grants to liberation movements identified by the WCC, these funds were for the purpose of promoting justice, equality and freedom. The money was dispensed to improve health and education services and to help the dependents of political prisoners (strictly as they requested).[87] Blake thought that it was interesting that pacifist Christians, authentic pacifist organizations, and peace churches generally understood and approved of these race grants. By contrast, many churches and people who relied on military might and atomic terror to establish peace in the world attacked the programs as a support of violence.[88] In such changing times, Blake argued that it was clear that the old norms for a "just war" were no longer useful to help churches or individuals to decide whether any war or revolution was justified, and that to maintain their own moral credibility, churches had to refrain from uncritically supporting any nation's warfare, including US involvement in Vietnam. But it was equally clear that the revolution for freedom in Mozambique[89] had to be judged by the same standards as those

84. Ibid.

85. Blake, "Progress, Promise and Problems," November 9, 1970, 995.1.02/3 Works (1971), WCC Archives, Geneva, Switzerland.

86. Blake, "Mandeville Lecture," March 28, 1972, 995.1.05/16 Speeches (1972), WCC Archives, Geneva, Switzerland.

87. Ibid.

88. Ibid.

89. Mozambique is a former Portuguese colony. In 1962, the Mozambique Liberation Front (Frelimo) commenced a guerrilla campaign for independence. This was achieved eleven years later in 1975.

by which the Dutch, Norwegian, and French resistance movements against the Nazi occupation had been judged.[90] Blake concluded that the end result of all this controversy was that for the first time, the WCC had been able to trigger a widespread discussion of European and North American churches' involvement in white racist structures. Blake felt that such a debate could only do good.[91]

Another line of attack used against the WCC's PCR was the old charge that it was inspired by Communists. This was typical of the same reactionaries who charged that King was being manipulated by Communists to instigate revolution. But as King explained in terms that Blake would have understood clearly, "One day somebody should remind us that, even though there may be political and ideological differences between us, the Vietnamese are our brothers, the Russians are our brothers, the Chinese are our brothers; and one day we've got to sit down together at the table of brotherhood. But in Christ there is neither Jew nor Gentile . . . In Christ there is neither Communist nor Capitalist."[92]

Blake delivered a speech in June of 1970 titled "The Ambiguous Role of Religion in Relation to World Peace," in which he questioned whether the world's religious communities could bring their high aims and aspirations into a positive parallel influence on problems connected with peace, rather than acquiesce to ambiguous role of religion. Again, he invoked King's name to illustrate his point: "Saints and leaders such as Jeremiah and Isaiah, King Ashoka and St. Francis, Al Garali and Shah Waliullah, Mahatma Gandhi and Martin Luther King have in the name of religion contributed to peace at different times and in different ways."[93] In further reference to the ambiguity surrounding the church's proper role in peace, which both he and King had highlighted, Blake declared, "most religious communities usually either defend the status quo, however unjust, or give divine sanction for revenge and retaliation, however long before the unjust and evil acts were done."[94]

Blake set out to answer his critics, for as he said, "changed ideas and assumptions are required to avoid world-wide disaster."[95] In the early 1950s,

---

90. Blake, "Mandeville Lecture," March 28, 1972, 995.1.05/16 Speeches (1972), WCC Archives, Geneva, Switzerland.

91. Ibid.

92. King, "A Christmas Sermon on Peace," December 24, 1967, King Center Library and Archives, Atlanta, GA.

93. Blake, Eugene Carson, "The Ambiguous Role of Religions in Relation to World Peace (revised)," address in New York, June 8, 1970, 995.1.05/12 Speeches (1970), WCC Archives, Geneva, Switzerland.

94. Ibid.

95. Blake, "Mandeville Lecture," March 28, 1972, 995.1.05/16 Speeches (1972),

a new line of argument was established suggesting that US policy was the containment of Communism. Anti-Communism became the conviction and the rallying cry of the "silent majority" of Americans. For twenty-five years, American foreign policy was based on disrupting the Soviet Union worldwide. This led the US to the most disastrous quarter century in its history, said Blake, a conclusion echoed by King.[96] Blake contended that US policy culminated in "a defeat both of arms and ideas in Vietnam, the loss of any semblance of moral leadership in the so-called free world, and the continuing confrontation now of both China and Russia."[97] Blake bemoaned the loss of America's best traditions of justice and freedom in the previous quarter century. One by one, he observed, the US had given up the principles of freedom, especially overseas, which at the outset had distinguished the "free world" from the Communists. It was now the policy to support military dictatorships' repression of their own people, if necessary, to maintain America's allies against the Communists.[98] Blake's point was that until the US gave up the policy of justifying itself in all kinds of immorality and repression on the grounds of combating Communism, it could not begin to discern right from wrong in the world. America needed to find its proper role in struggling for a peaceful world community, but anti-Communism had become an excuse for any self-interested evil.[99] Blake was aware that many of his listeners would have reservations about this message, and he addressed their fears: "The World Council of Churches is leading all the churches into areas of concern in politics and economics where they have no business. But I must argue both from Christian theology and Christian history that they are wrong. If Christian faith, especially in its organized form, continues to be a blessing not merely on the status-quo but really on the status-quo-ante, it will be increasingly rejected by men who care what is happening to man in the latter part of the twentieth century."[100]

Blake, like King, sought to do the best for mankind by putting his head above the parapet, though the slings and arrows were never far away. Interestingly, in an article by Dr. A. B. Jackson that appeared in Jefferson City, MO's *News and Tribune* on October 29 1967, the writer, obviously not an admirer of Blake's, chose to mention both leaders in his piece:

WCC Archives, Geneva, Switzerland.

96. Blake, "Mandeville Lecture," March 28, 1972, 995.1.05/16 Speeches (1972), WCC Archives, Geneva, Switzerland. See also King, "Time to Break Silence," 231–44.

97. Ibid.

98. Ibid.

99. Ibid.

100. Ibid.

We Presbyterians put up with Dr. Blake for a long time. We thought we were rid of him when he became secretary of the World Council of Churches, but he comes back to hound us. But then the Episcopalians have Bishop Pike, the Catholics have Father Groppi, and the Baptists have Dr. King. We all have our crosses to bear.[101]

---

101. Jackson, "Funny Things Do Happen," *Sunday News and Tribune* (Jefferson City, MO), October 29, 1967.

3

Challenging the Color Line
Martin Luther King Jr., the WCC, and Racism

Injustice anywhere is a threat to justice everywhere. We are caught in an inescapable network of mutuality, tied to a single garment of destiny.

—Martin Luther King Jr.

IN MY MIND, THESE words from King's "Letter from Birmingham Jail," written on April 16, 1963, neatly summarize King's philosophy. Far ahead of his peers, King glimpsed into the future to see globalization coming at breakneck speed down the tracks. Only too aware that racism had already caused untold hardship on African Americans and other minority groups in the United States, he sought a worldwide solution to this intractable problem. This chapter and chapter 5 will examine King's relationship with the WCC paying attention to their joint opposition to racism and to the Vietnam War, which some critics claim was a racist war. My analysis will concentrate on areas where King and the WCC shared common ground. As King scholar Lewis V. Baldwin observes, although King always appreciated the WCC's interest in him, "he attached far more importance to the willingness of that body to consistently raise its voice in the interest of freedom, justice, and human dignity."[1]

1. Baldwin, *Voice of Conscience*, 197.

Frank H. Joyce, National Director of the People Against Racism, offers harsh criticism of the historical Protestant ethic and liberal tradition that led slaves in the US to be considered subhuman. Once that criterion had been established, any behavior meted out to slaves was acceptable, for morality only existed between humans. Joyce argues that the same thing happened in the "settling" of the West (including Texas, Oregon, Hawaii, the Philippines, American Samoa, etc.), contending that "it was necessary for the missionaries to certify that the natives were uncivilized, heathen, savage barbarians so that generals, politicians, citizens and the missionaries themselves could sleep at night, secure in the knowledge that 'the only good Indian is a dead Indian.'"[2] Joyce maintains that this kind of double thinking was used to justify and defend racism in Vietnam. It was, he wrote, "racism and its military, political, and economic corollaries which got the US involved in the war in the first place, and which control the unprecedented brutal tactics of the war."[3]

The WCC is the chief ecumenical organization, with a membership of 345 churches, denominations, and church fellowships in more than 110 countries throughout the world, representing over five hundred million Christians. It includes most of the world's Orthodox churches, plus scores of Anglican, Baptist, Lutheran, Methodist, and Reformed churches. While the bulk of the WCC's founding churches were European and North American, today most member churches are in Africa, Asia, the Caribbean, Latin America, the Middle East, and the Pacific.[4]

The following is a brief history of the major ecumenical statements against racism in the first half of the twentieth century. In *Christianity and the Race Problem,* J. H. Oldham wrote in 1924 that "a very fruitful cause of racial bitterness is found in the feelings of superiority on the one hand, and on inferiority on the other, which are apt to be engendered by the existing political and economic predominance of Western peoples. The white man's claim to superiority is sometimes blatantly proclaimed and more often quietly taken for granted."[5] The following year at the 1925 Stockholm Universal Christian Conference on Life and Work, this assessment was made: "The modern ascendancy of the white races throughout the world is overwhelming. So often have they used their power for selfish ends and ruthless exploitation of weak and backward peoples that an ominous tide of

2. Joyce, "People Against Racism," Notting Hill Consultation 1969, 4223.1.03, WCC Archives, Geneva, Switzerland.

3. Ibid.

4. "An Introduction to the World Council of Churches," WCC, Geneva Switzerland, 4–5, http://www.oikoumene.org/en/about-us.

5. Adler, *Small Beginning*, 72.

indignation, unrest and resentment is arising among all other races."[6] The International Missionary Council, meeting in Jerusalem in 1928, adopted a statement demanding that "all Christian forces . . . are bound to work with all their power to remove race prejudice and adverse conditions due to it . . . Any discrimination against human beings on the grounds of race or color, any selfish exploitation and any oppression of man by man . . . is a denial of the teaching of Jesus."[7]

With war clouds gathering, a report by the Conference of Oxford in July of 1937, convened by the Universal Christian Council for Life and Work, included a section on "The Church and Race," which set out the fundamental concepts of Christian race relations for subsequent ecumenical gatherings: "Against racial pride, racial hatreds and persecutions, and the exploitation of other races in all their forms, the Church is called by God to set its face implacably, and to alter its words unequivocally, both within and without its own borders."[8] Lest there be any misunderstanding, the report laid out the facts clearly: "Therefore for a Christian, there can be no such thing as despising another race. Moreover, when God chose to reveal Himself in a human form, his words became flesh in One of a race, then as now, widely despised." Words directed at racial supremacists spelled out the lesson even more simply: "The assumption by any race or nation of supreme blood or destiny must be emphatically denied by Christians as without foundation in fact and wholly alien to the heart of the gospel."[9]

In July of 1939, the Federal Council of Churches of Christ in America's Department of International Justice and Goodwill organized a conference in Geneva to discuss the deteriorating international situation. Under the auspices of the Provisional Committee of the WCC with Acting General Secretary Willem Visser 't Hooft, they met "to consider what action was open to the churches and individual Christians with a view to checking the drift toward war and leading [us] nearer to the establishment of an effective international order."[10]

With the interruption of World War II, the WCC First Assembly eventually convened in the Netherlands in August of 1948, and Visser 't

6. "Report of the Commission on the Church and International Relations," quoted in Adler, *Small Beginning*, 72.

7. "WCC's Statements and Actions on Racism, 1948–1979," Programme to Combat Racism, 4223.16.3, WCC Archives, Geneva, Switzerland. See also Adler, *Small Beginning*, 73.

8. "WCC's Statements and Actions on Racism, 1948–1979," Programme to Combat Racism, 4223.16.3, WCC Archives, Geneva, Switzerland.

9. Quoted in Adler, *Small Beginning*, 73.

10. Gaines, *World Council of Churches*, 215.

Hooft declared that the new organization "will be more comprehensive in scope than any of the former ecumenical conferences. It will be the first representative post-war meeting of the churches and would therefore have to gather up the new insights which the churches have gained in the critical years."[11] Race was dealt with as a separate subject, but was included in several discussions. Some points were particularly highlighted, especially that "the church cannot call society away from prejudice and segregation unless it takes steps to eliminate these practices from the Christian community."[12] Likewise, the church took a firm and vigorous stand against the flagrant violation of human rights in discrimination on grounds of race, color, culture, or political conviction. A special committee on the "Christian Approach to the Jews" noted in its report that churches ware failing in the fight against anti-Semitism, concluding that this was absolutely irreconcilable with the profession and practice of the Christian faith.[13]

At the First Assembly in Amsterdam, 147 Christian churches from forty-four countries were in attendance. The governing body of the WCC is the Assembly, which meets every seven years. It appoints a Central Committee of 150 members that meets five times between Assemblies, and this committee in turn elects a twenty-six-member Executive Committee. The council also has a Presidium to which eight representatives are appointed. The council, which has no legislative power over its member churches, provides an opportunity for its constituents to act together in matters of common concern under their common calling "to accept our Lord Jesus Christ as God and Saviour."[14] The Roman Catholic Church is not a member of the council, but sends delegated observers to its Assemblies. It has full membership on the council's Commission of Faith and Order and on its Joint Working Group.[15] John C. Cort, in *Christian Socialism: An Informal History*, writes that the principal non-members have historically been fundamentalist churches such as the Southern Baptists in the US, and the 840 million members of the Roman Catholic Church.[16] However, in 1983, over twenty official Catholic observers attended the WCC Assembly in Vancouver, BC, and one of the preparatory documents was written by a group of Catholic theologians called to Rome by the Vatican Secretariat for Promot-

11 Ibid.

12. "WCC's Statements and Actions on Racism, 1948–1979," Programme to Combat Racism, 4223.16.3, WCC Archives, Geneva, Switzerland.

13. Ibid.

14. "Self-Understanding and Vision: The Basis of the WCC," World Council of Churches, http://www.oikoumene.org/en/about-us/self-understanding-vision/basis.

15. Ibid.

16. Cort, *Christian Socialism*, 340.

ing Christian Unity. The document made a number of significant points, which echoed similar sentiments previously expressed by King and Blake: "God shows that, in his love for all humanity and everything that is human, he is on the side of the humble and weak, the victims of the powerful . . . a church which breaches its solidarity with the poor can no longer claim to mirror the gospel."[17]

The development of policies against racial segregation continued in the WCC. The Second Assembly of the WCC was held at Evanston, IL, in August of 1954. Dr. Benjamin E. Mays and Dr. B. J. Marais, both members of the Preparatory Commission, introduced the theme of racism with a study titled "The Church Amid Racial and Ethnic Tensions," at the plenary session of the Assembly. Dr. Mays, President of Morehouse College (King's own alma mater), described the burden of segregation, which he condemned as "penalizing one for being what God made him, and as tantamount to saying to God, 'You made a mistake God, when you made people of different races and colors.'"[18] Mays argued that if the church could find no support in science for ethnic and racial tension, no backing in the Bible for segregation based on race and color, and no basis for it in Christian theologies, "How can segregation and discrimination in the Church be justified?"[19] Therefore, the WCC concluded in its report that: "As part of its task of challenging the conscience of society, it is the duty of the church to protest against any law or arrangement that is unjust to any human being or which would make Christian fellowship impossible, or would prevent the Christian from practicing his vocation."[20] And furthermore, the church is expected to take the initiative, since "the churches have a duty to challenge the conscience of society; if there is no tension between the church and society, then either the society is regenerated or the church is conformed."[21]

The Second Assembly of the WCC declared its conviction that any form of segregation based on race, color, or ethnic origin was contrary to the gospel, incompatible with the Christian doctrine of men, and in opposition to the nature of the Church of Christ. The Assembly urged churches within its membership to renounce all forms of segregation or discrimination, and to work for their abolition within their own life and within society. In doing so, the Assembly was painfully aware that many churches found themselves confronted by historical, political, social, and economic

17. Ibid.

18. Gaines, *World Council of Churches*, 661–62.

19. Ibid.

20. Ibid., 1205.

21. Ibid., 1204.

circumstances that could make the immediate achievement of this objective extremely difficult.[22] The timing of this Assembly at Evanston was critical, as it was just about a year before Martin Luther King Jr., came to international prominence in Montgomery. Although the resolution was passed in 1954, no steps were taken to implement a program of action until the Notting Hill Consultation on Racism in 1969. Nevertheless, it laid a marker for King at the very beginning of the modern civil rights movement in 1955. As this study shows, King recognized the importance of involvement with the WCC in promulgating his message for universal justice. It is noteworthy too that King saw the white church in general as an upholder of the status quo in the United States. He wrote, "called to be the moral guardian of the community, the church at times has preserved that which is immoral and unethical. Called to combat social evils, it has remained silent behind stained glass windows."[23]

In 1960, the WCC wished to intervene in what many of its representatives viewed as a dangerous situation in South Africa under apartheid. This position was exacerbated by the tragic events at Sharpeville, which also evoked sharp condemnation from King. At Sharpeville, Transvaal, on March 21, 1960, sixty-nine black South African protesters, mostly women, were shot and killed by police, and 186 or more were wounded. The victims were protesting against the discriminatory pass laws. Authorities declared a state of emergency, and thousands of black citizens were arrested and many were banned. Leaders of the ANC and PAC, including Albert Luthuli, Nelson Mandela, and Robert Sobukwe, were also arrested. There followed an exodus of blacks from the country to Europe and North America, where many participated in anti-apartheid movements in exile. Emotions were running high after Sharpeville, and Archbishop Joost de Blank[24] was furious at the Dutch Reformed Church (DRC) for its support of the apartheid regime. He demanded that the WCC expel the Cape and Transvaal synods, which, along with the Nederduitsch Hervormde Kerk, were then members. In a letter to W. A. Visser 't Hooft, de Blank argued that "the future of Christianity in this country demands our complete dissociation from the Dutch Reformed attitude . . . either they must be expelled or we shall be compelled to withdraw."[25] The DRC attitude had been established by Rev. C.B. Brink, a member of the Central Committee of the WCC and an obvious apolo-

22. Ibid., 1206.

23. King, *Strength to Love*, 21.

24. Archbishop Joost de Blank (November 14, 1908–January 1, 1968) was the Archbishop of Cape Town, South Africa, from 1957 to 1963 and was known for his courageous opposition to apartheid.

25. De Gruchy, *Struggle in South Africa*, 62–63.

gist for South Africa's status quo: "Apartheid, or segregation, or separate development, has been a feature of South African society for three hundred years. During all this time, the measure of separation between the races has become a way of life in this country."[26]

The WCC convened at the Cottesloe Church Consultation in December of 1960, and as John W. De Gruchy stated, it was a gathering of great importance for the churches in South Africa.[27] The delegation of the World Council approached the meeting on the basis of the resolution adopted by the Evanston Assembly in 1954, "that any form of segregation based on race, colour, or ethnic origin is contrary to the gospel, and . . . incompatible with the Christian doctrine of man and with the nature of the Church of Christ."[28] Dr. Franklin Clark Fry, chairman of the Central Committee of the WCC, presided over the consultation. Ten delegates from each of the eight South African member churches and five representatives of the WCC, including W. A. Visser 't Hooft, attended. Bishop Alphaeus Zulu[29] and Professor Z. K. Matthews[30] were among the eighteen black participants, in addition to eight laypeople.[31] The consultation concluded after seven days with a statement that had been adopted by at least eighty percent of the participants declaring: "we are united in rejecting all unjust discrimination. Nevertheless, widely divergent convictions have been expressed on the basic issue of apartheid . . . No one who believes in Jesus Christ may be excluded from any church on the grounds of his color or race."[32] The report concluded on a holistic note, saying, "we recognize that all racial groups who permanently inhabit our country are part of our total population . . . [and] have an equal right to make their contribution towards the enrichment of . . . [its] life . . . and to share in the ensuing responsibilities, rewards and privileges."[33] The participants also noted that in a period of rapid social

26. Gaines, *World Council of Churches*, 915.

27. De Gruchy, *Struggle in South Africa*, 65.

28. Gaines, *World Council of Churches*, 914.

29. Bishop Alphaeus Zulu (July 29, 1905–August 26, 1988) became Bishop of Zululand and Swaziland in 1968. He was elected president of the WCC and was one of the organization's leading figures in the 1960s.

30. Professor Z. K. Matthews (October 20, 1901–May 12, 1968) was an established black academic. He was a political activist who joined the ANC in 1943. Having relocated to Geneva in 1961, he became secretary of the Africa division of the WCC.

31. De Gruchy, *Struggle in South Africa*, 65.

32. "Report of the Cottesloe Church Consultation," Statements, Reports, and Memorandums from the WCC Consultation in Cottesloe, Johannesburg, December 7–14, 1960, 4223.9.4, WCC Archives, Geneva, Switzerland. Quoted in Adler, *Small Beginning*, 75–76.

33. Gaines, *World Council of Churches*, 917.

change, the church had a special responsibility "for fearless witness within society," and that although the tension in South Africa was the result of a long historical development, "all groups bear responsibility for it." Finally, the statement acknowledged the East/West power struggle in the demise of colonialism, recognizing that "the South African scene is radically affected by the decline of the power of the West, and by the desire for self-determination among the peoples of the African continent."[34]

The consultation's resolution spoke of the need for consultation between race groups on all matters. Some expressed reservations on racially mixed marriages, but such marriages were ultimately supported. Special notice was paid to the disastrous effects of apartheid on migratory workers, the low wages paid to blacks, and the inequitable distribution of jobs. Further reference was also made to urgent matters such as justice in trials, multiracial worship, freedom to preach the gospel, and future consultation and cooperation between the churches.[35] Despite admirable intentions, there was little new in the resolutions or anything unacceptable to the English-speaking churches. In fact, they did not go far enough. The question looming in everyone's mind was how the DRC synods would react to these decisions. A swift response came from Prime Minister Verwoerd,[36] who expressed deep annoyance at the actions of the DRC delegation. Reactions from conservative groups within the church soon followed, notably voiced by Dr. Koot Vorster, brother of the future Prime Minister. The DRC took immediate action, and the Cape and Transvaal synods complied with government wishes to leave the WCC. W. A. Visser 't Hooft reflected on this move in his autobiography, saying, "I have always wondered whether the majority of the delegates [i.e. to the synods] realized that they were not voting against the positions imported by the World Council of Churches and imposed on their churches, but against the convictions expressed by the best minds of their churches and submitted at Cottesloe by their own trusted leaders."[37] The first director of the PCR, Baldwin Sjollema, said that the Cottesloe Church Consultation became critically important for the future of church-state relations in South Africa.[38] Cottesloe had made a

34. "WCC's Statements and Actions on Racism, 1948–1979," Programme to Combat Racism, 4223.16.3, WCC Archives, Geneva, Switzerland.

35. De Gruchy, *Struggle in South Africa*, 66–67.

36. Hendrik Frensch Verwoerd, (September 8, 1901–Septmber 6, 1966) served as Prime Minister in South Africa from 1956 to 1966 and was known for his rigid application of the apartheid policy.

37. Quoted in De Gruchy, *Struggle in South Africa*, 68.

38. Sjollema, "Initial Challenge," 4.

lasting impact, an influence that is made clear in F. W. de Klerk's[39] reflec-
tion, "the ghost of Cottesloe would return to haunt the Afrikaner's wayward
theologizing. There was evidence that, in spite of the silencing, recantation,
bowing of heads and deep cogitation, something remained. The Church
could never be quite the same again."[40]

The Third Assembly of the WCC was held in New Delhi, India, in
1961. Participants again emphasized that churches should identify with the
oppressed in their struggle to achieve justice. The Assembly recognized that
racism led to despair and often to violence. Therefore, it urged those in power to refrain from the use of violence and to avoid provoking it. The WCC
echoed King in calling on Christians to encourage and support all efforts to
bring about change through nonviolence means in helping to construct a
society permeated by justice and reconciliation. The Assembly made clear
that because everyone has their own contribution to make to the fellowship of human society, there was no reason for separate development.[41] The
WCC statements, like King's, exposed the expression, "separate but equal,"
as a contradiction in terms, for it was "only in community with others of diverse gifts that persons or communities can give of their best."[42] Such words
were a direct indictment of US practice at the time. Acknowledging the intransigence of sections of the white population, they called on US churches
to intensify efforts to eliminate all forms of racial discrimination from every
aspect of life. Citing the two main players in the battle against apartheid,
the WCC declared, "We remind ourselves that references to South Africa
and the United States present a challenge to all our consciences, to do in
our cities and churches all that we should for racial justice and Christian
fellowship."[43] The WCC putting the US in the same category as South Africa in this way is significant. In fact, King had indicted his country for its
arrogance in refusing to learn from other nations in condemning South Africa and Rhodesia, saying, "We are arrogant in our contention that we have
some sacred mission to protect people from totalitarian rule, while we make
little use of our power to end the evils of South Africa and Rhodesia."[44]

39. Frederik Willem de Klerk (March 18, 1936) was the final State President of
apartheid South Africa. Best known for his leadership in ending apartheid, he won
the Nobel Peace Prize with Nelson Mandela in 1993.

40. Quoted in De Gruchy, *Struggle in South Africa*, 68.

41. "WCC's Statements and Actions on Racism, 1948–1979," Programme to Combat Racism, 4223.16.3, WCC Archives, Geneva, Switzerland.

42. Ibid.

43. Ibid.

44. King, Martin Luther, Jr., "The Casualties of the War in Vietnam," address at
the Nation Institute, Los Angeles, CA, February 25, 1967, SLCC Papers, Box 28.33,

From August 26 to September 2, 1963, the seventeenth meeting of the WCC Central Committee was held in Rochester, New York. The Committee addressed itself especially to racial injustice in the United States and South Africa. They acknowledged that the movement to secure full human and civil rights for black citizens "has now become a tide which cannot be turned back."[45] The timing of this statement is significant, for the WCC addressed this issue just as King led the civil rights March on Washington. In the post-war period and well into the sixties, many WCC statements echoed King's in urging member churches to eliminate racist practices in their own ranks, to recognize their involvement in racial and ethnic tensions in the world, and to denounce the violation of human rights on grounds of race, color, and culture. For example, the Central Committee adopted a statement on racial and ethnic tensions recognizing that "the struggle is approaching its climax" and asking churches, particularly in the United States and South Africa, to intensify efforts to find a peaceful solution of the race problem.[46] In spite of many such brave declarations, however, the churches and the ecumenical movement did not effectively respond to these challenges. It was not until 1959 that the WCC appointed a full-time secretary to help member churches in dealing with problems of "interracial relations."[47]

The churches' direct engagement with the civil rights movement in 1963 and 1964 was a reactivation of the early twentieth-century social gospel. Throughout the nation's history, clergy had often actively participated in political struggles, whether on issues of war and peace in colonial times or problems with slavery in the nineteenth century. Following World War II, the churches made something of a retreat during the Cold War era. Mainstream churches' deep commitment to the racial crisis in 1963 resurrected the social gospel tradition by demanding a demonstration of faith through active concern for the poor.[48] At the center of this revival in the United States stood the NCC, the principal Protestant ecumenical body and a major advocate of the social gospel. The NCC had created an emergency Conference on Religion and Race on June 7, 1963, which was headed by King, Blake, and the trade union leader Walter Reuther,[49] and acknowledged that

---

February 1967, King Center Library and Archive, Atlanta, GA.

45. "WCC's Statements and Actions on Racism, 1948–1979," Programme to Combat Racism, 4223.16.3, WCC Archives, Geneva, Switzerland.

46. Ibid.

47. Ibid.

48. Findlay, "Religion and Politics," 66–67.

49. Walter Philip Reuther (September 1, 1907–May 9, 1970) was an American labor union leader for the United Automobile Workers and a powerful political force in the Democratic Party.

King was making an increasingly significant impact on the white churches, most of which were affiliated with the WCC.[50]

By 1963, Blake had become an outspoken advocate of church activism in support of racial justice. He was now a major influence within the NCC, and was the official sponsor and financial supporter of the Conference on Religion and Race. As Findlay acknowledged, by 1963, King was without question the leading black interpreter of the civil rights struggle to white people throughout the country.[51] King's willingness to participate in direct action and to preach powerfully to white churches about the consequences of racism was compelling. Indeed, King was held in such high esteem that he was appointed to the steering committee to plan the Conference on Religion and Race in Chicago, IL, where he delivered one of the keynote speeches.[52] What I am demonstrating here is that King and Blake came into close contact on committees and at conferences, which offered both leaders ample opportunity to cooperate and influence one another. A little over two months after the conference in Chicago, King was incarcerated in Birmingham Jail, where he wrote his most famous letter. This was first published in the widely read *Christian Century*.[53] The "Letter from Birmingham Jail" received widespread international exposure, and importantly, the top echelons of the NCC were galvanized into action.

A report on the Ecumenical Consultation held at Kitwe, Zambia, from May 25 to June 2, 1964, was titled "Christians and Race Relations in Southern Africa." This consultation, held under the auspices of the WCC Church and Society Department, the South African Institute of Race Relations, and the Mindolo Ecumenical Foundation, discussed political church involvement, the rising trend from nonviolence to violence, and racial patterns in the economic structures of society.[54] The WCC highlighted black awareness of white indifference to their plight in Southern Africa, noting that "in reaction to white prejudice, many non-whites are developing a revolutionary attitude born of the realization that the white group which sets the patterns of society is oblivious to the deepest human aspirations of its underprivileged partners."[55] At the Mindolo Consultation, the question of

50. Holstein, Joanne, "National Council of Churches," Becker Bible Studies Library, http://www.guidedbiblestudies.com/library/national_council.html.

51. Findlay, "Religion and Politics," 66–69.

52. Ibid.

53. King, "Letter from Birmingham Jail," 767–73. See also King, *A Testament of Hope*, 289–302.

54. "WCC's Statements and Actions on Racism, 1948–1979," Programme to Combat Racism, 4223.16.3, WCC Archives, Geneva, Switzerland.

55. Ibid.

violence became a very serious dilemma. Many black Africans felt "that, as all peaceful measures tried by African political organizations over a period of many years to bring about an ordered change have proved abortive, only one avenue remains open—that of violence."[56]

It may well have been the case that all avenues to a peaceful ending of racism had been exhausted in Africa, but it has to be emphasized that blacks in the United States made up a small minority of the population, perhaps ten percent, whereas blacks in Africa were the clear majority. Any violent uprising in the United States would have resulted in a massacre of black protesters, but should such a violent conflagration arise in Africa, the odds for minority whites were grim. The Mindolo Consultation's observation came as a direct contrast to King, who also advocated change, but only through peaceful means. African Christian leaders maintained that violence had never been desired if any other mode of effective negotiation was available, but that if the urgency of the situation was not recognized, violence was sure to increase.[57]

By 1964, the deteriorating situation for blacks in the United States led the NCC to request the WCC's Division of Inter-Church Aid, Refugee, and World Service to list a comprehensive project in the Mississippi Delta for worldwide support. This represented a new departure for the WCC, as the Division had never before listed a project in the US. The WCC intervened because "the Mississippi Delta is a symbol of resistance to full racial equality and the race problem, which the whole Christian world must help to solve."[58] The project targeted the heart of the Southern segregation belt, where King and the SCLC were in the midst of a campaign against violent racist administrations, making timely support from an international Christian body exceedingly significant.

Because London was chosen for the Consultation on Racism in 1969, it is useful to reflect on King's earlier visit there in December of 1964 on his way to accept the Nobel Peace Prize. Although the Nobel laureate was treated like royalty, he cautioned Britain against the problem of growing racism. King warned that if housing was restricted and ghettoes were allowed to develop, this would permit "festering sores of bitterness and deprivation to pollute the national health," thus creating a serious situation.[59] King further criticized Britain's immigration policy toward commonwealth citizens: "Immigration laws based on color were totally out of keeping with the laws of

---

56. Ibid.

57. Ibid.

58. Ibid.

59. *The Times*, July 12, 1964, 6.

God and with the trends of the twentieth century. They would eventually encourage the vestiges of racism and endanger all the great democratic principles which his great country held dear."[60]

With the Nobel Peace Prize pending, King was now an acknowledged spokesman on issues of race, and he seized the opportunity the spotlight afforded to call for economic sanctions against South Africa. In calling for a boycott, he said, "more and more I have come to realize that racism is a world problem."[61] King spoke before a packed congregation in Saint Paul's Cathedral, and with every seat taken and hundreds of people standing in the aisles, in what the *Times* described as "a spellbinding performance. At times his voice was a slow, soft Southern drawl; then the tempo would increase and the words would come tumbling out in a flurry of oratory. Quotations rolled off his tongue; he was actor, poet and preacher all at the same time."[62] This was a momentous occasion, as King was the only non-Anglican to preach there in the church's 291-year history. King's enthralling sermon, titled "The Three Dimensions of a Complete Life," argued that "these are the three dimensions of any complete life. These three must be correlated, working harmoniously together, if any life is to be complete. Life is something of a great triangle. At one end stands the individual person, at the other end stands other persons, and at the top stands the Supreme, Infinite Person, God. These three must meet in every individual life if that is to be complete."[63] King was speaking to the world when he cried, "God is not interested in the freedom of white, black, and yellow men but in the freedom of the whole human race," reminding listeners "that all over the world, as we struggle for justice and freedom, we must never use second-class methods to gain our aims."[64]

Although King had always expressed deep concern for the Third World, when he was awarded the Nobel Peace Prize, he became more confident in asserting himself on the world stage. Visser 't Hooft recognized King's increasing international importance, and King replied in a letter, "May I express my deep and sincere gratitude to you for your very warm message on the announcement of my being chosen as the recipient of the 1964 Nobel Peace Prize. Your encouraging words and your genuine expression of confidence give me new determination to carry on the struggle to

60. Ibid.

61. Garrow, *Bearing the Cross*, 364

62. *The Times*, July 12, 1964, 6.

63. King, Martin Luther, Jr., "The Three Dimensions of a Complete Life," address at Saint Paul's Cathedral, London, December 6, 1964, King Papers, Box 1, September 1, 1958–December 11, 1960, King Center Library and Archive, Atlanta, GA.

64. Ibid.

make the brotherhood of man a reality."[65] King expounded on the wider applications of the nonviolent methodology used in the civil rights struggle: "This award . . . should also challenge us to work passionately and unrelentingly to discover the international implications of nonviolence; for in a real sense, there can be no justice without peace and there can be no peace without justice."[66]

The WCC Central Committee met in Enugu, Eastern Nigeria in 1965 to declare, "we support the recommendation that churches once again appeal to the Dutch Reformed Churches in South Africa to enter the struggle for human rights in South Africa, in such a way as to forbid enforced separate development."[67] On a positive note, it continued, "we note with gratitude that a considerable minority in these churches has already taken up this struggle. We express our hope that they will soon find official support by their churches, thus uniting the Christian forces in this cause."[68] The Central Committee expressed deep sympathy for the victims of unjust and discriminatory laws in South Africa, Rhodesia, and all other countries where such practices prevailed. The Committee supported appeals for funds for legal defense and aid for victims, saying, "in order that Christian witness may be genuine and effective, it is essential that the churches in all lands act to ensure that all forms of social discrimination in the churches themselves be rooted out."[69]

King and the WCC were also on parallel paths in their condemnation of the Vietnam War, and in their appeals for the eradication of racism worldwide. In October of 1965, Visser 't Hooft, wrote to invite King to be a speaker at the World Conference on Church and Society to be held in Geneva, Switzerland in July of 1966. The theme of the conference was "The Christian in the Technical and Social Revolution." It would bring together about four hundred participants from WCC member churches in a unique opportunity for worldwide Christian discussion of the social problems of the time.[70] Visser 't Hooft explained that "the aim of the conference is

65. Martin Luther King Jr. to W. A. Visser t' Hooft, November 17, 1964, WCC General Secretaries, Correspondence: Frequent 1937–1977, King, Martin Luther (1966–1970), 42.11.08, WCC Archives, Geneva, Switzerland.

66. Ibid.

67. "World Council Actions Since 1964," Programme to Combat Racism, Notting Hill Consultation 1969 (1965–1969), 4223.1.01, WCC Archives, Geneva, Switzerland.

68. Ibid.

69. Ibid.

70. W. A. Visser 't Hooft to Martin Luther King Jr., Oct. 27, 1965, General Secretaries Correspondence: Frequent 1937–1977, King, Martin Luther (1966–1970), 42.11.08, WCC Archives, Geneva, Switzerland.

to speak to our member churches about their tasks in modern society. It is planned that the Conference report should be in a form to facilitate a worldwide discussion on social questions in our churches during the period 1966–1968."[71] Visser 't Hooft further expressed his "high hopes that this Conference may result in a constructive contribution towards the solution of the urgent problems that confront our churches, the racial revolution being a major one."[72] The timing of this invitation was significant, for King was at the pinnacle of his career after the major legislative successes on civil rights in the US, and now had an opportunity, as the foremost black Christian leader in the US, to extend his international influence.

As it turned out, King did not travel to Geneva, for in mid-July he sent a telegram advising that the riots in Chicago demanded that he remain on the scene in the United States. King was disappointed that he could not attend the WCC Conference, but added that "I am sure the Council will understand the pre-eminence of my responsibility to society in these revolutionary times."[73] These were indeed momentous times, for a social revolution was taking place around the world, and decolonization was changing the old order as new states were born in Africa and Asia. In the US, "the old order of slavery and racial segregation" were being swept aside.[74] Although King remained at home, his voice was broadcast throughout Europe during the WCC Conference. In fact, Blake wrote an upbeat letter to King on June 28, advising him that this service was anticipated as one of the most important ecumenical events ever to be televised in Europe, with an expected audience of one hundred million.[75] His sermon, "A Knock at Midnight," was specially adapted for a wide-ranging European audience and so differed slightly from similarly titled speeches. It covered the role of the church in a "revolutionary age."[76] King spoke on the conflict in Vietnam, describing

71. Ibid.

72. Ibid.

73. Martin Luther King, Jr. to W. A. Visser t' Hooft, July 15, 1966, General Secretaries Correspondence: Frequent 1937–1977, King, Martin Luther (1966–1970), 42.11.08, WCC Archives, Geneva, Switzerland.

74. Martin Luther King, Jr., "Remaining Awake Through a Great Revolution," address at Oberlin College's 132nd Commencement, Oberlin, OH, August 1, 1965, King Papers, Box 14, King Center Library and Archive, Atlanta, GA.

75. Eugene Carson Blake to Martin Luther King Jr., June 28, 1966, King Center Library and Archive, Atlanta, GA.

76. King, Martin Luther, Jr., "Martin Luther King Sermon Given at the Saint Pierre Cathedral in Geneva," MCW-66-048 compact disc, recorded July 17, 1966, WCC Sound Archives, Geneva, Switzerland. This version of King's "A Knock at Midnight" sermon differs somewhat from those that appear in King, *Strength to Love*, 56–66; King, *A Knock at Midnight*, 61–78.

it as "the evil of the war still before us."[77] He proclaimed that churchmen could never endorse violence, a position that many in the WCC supported. King was driven by his conscience to declare that "we in the church must admit we have left men and women disappointed." King then turned to America, where he described eleven o'clock on Sunday mornings "as the most segregated hour in the country." Yes, he cried, "the church left men disappointed at midnight."[78] King had thoughtfully prepared his taped address, and his message was clear: the church must remember "that it is the conscience of the state." King rebuked the church for its failure to act, and he demanded that it "recover its historic mission of truth, justice and peace." King had previously reminded his listeners that "the world in which we live is geographically one. The great challenge now is to make it one in terms of brotherhood."[79] King had spoken as a Christian pastor to admonish the church's passive attitude towards the evils of war and racism.

The Conference on Church and Society in 1966 laid the foundation for the Programme to Combat Racism, which finally demanded concrete action. The Conference stated, "it is not enough for churches and groups to condemn the sin of racial arrogance and oppression. The struggle for racial change in structures will inevitably bring suffering and will demand costly and bitter engagement."[80] The Assembly urged Christians and churches everywhere to "oppose, openly and actively, the perpetuation of the myth of racial superiority, as it finds expression in social conditions and human behavior as well as in laws and social structures."[81] It further suggested changing of the structure of society through legislation, social planning, and corporate action. Considering the ongoing problems within Rhodesia, the WCC, along with the British Council of Churches and the Rhodesian Council of Churches, condemned the Smith Regime and declared it illegal, saying "we identify ourselves with the African nationals of Rhodesia in their quest for majority rule."[82] But as Blake noted, although the Conference on Church and Society laid the foundation for the Programme to Combat Racism, it had no legislative power. Even so, "this Conference condemned ethnocentrism in the churches, urged Christians to oppose the myth of

77. Ibid.

78. Ibid.

79. King, "Remaining Awake," August 1, 1965, King Center Library and Archive, Atlanta, GA.

80. "WCC's Statements and Actions on Racism, 1948–1979," Programme to Combat Racism, 4223.16.3, WCC Archives, Geneva, Switzerland.

81. Ibid.

82. Ibid.

racial superiority, and demanded equal participation of all racial and ethnic groups in the corporate life of a pluralistic society."[83]

The issue of racism was dramatically highlighted in Geneva by the refusal of the South African government to issue a passport to Anglican Bishop Alphaeus Hamilton Zulu, one of the Presidents of the Conference.[84] As Mitchell K. Hall emphasizes in *Because of Their Faith*, the majority of laypeople felt that the churches should stay out of political and social matters, disapproving of clerics who expressed views on these issues. Hall saw the predicament particularly clearly in Protestant churches, where the congregation controlled the selection of ministers such that any minister who stepped out of line in support of civil rights activities could be dismissed.[85] King did not have this difficulty with his own Baptist church. The WCC appreciated King's political activism, for 't Hooft wrote in gratitude to CBS News, New York, for broadcasting King's magnificent delivery during the service.[86] The WCC conveyed its regard for King's work, when it stated, "The strife in Chicago has weighed heavily on the hearts of us all, [sic] gathered in Geneva for the World Conference on Church and Society. The empty pulpit in the cathedral last Sunday was a vivid Word of the Lord, reminding us all that the needs of the world must take priority over the meeting of the churches."[87] The WCC confirmed that King's sermon had struck a chord at the conference, reassuring him that "we deeply respect your decision to remain in the midst of the conflict, though we regret your absence and the tragedy that necessitated it. But the stirring and sobering words of your sermon cut deeply into the key issues of our conference and have greatly encouraged us in our work. Christians from every corner of the world uphold you in their prayers."[88] King's example was inspiring, for "from your deeds and words this week we have been taught again that Christians belong in the midst of conflict and crisis."[89] This correspondence confirms the WCC's high regard for King even prior to Blake's appointment in 1966. The WCC's hope that King's successes could be replicated elsewhere was made clear by the when its representatives wrote, "we are eager to learn from the civil rights movement's work in Chicago, for many countries are struggling

83. Ibid.

84. Sjollema, "Initial Challenge," 8.

85. Hall, *Because of Their Faith*, 6.

86. WCC Board to Martin Luther King Jr., July 1966, General Secretaries Correspondence: Frequent 1937–1977, King, Martin Luther (1966–1970), 42.11.08, WCC Archives, Geneva, Switzerland.

87. Ibid.

88. Ibid.

89. Ibid.

with similar problems."[90] Consequently, King concluded that the WCC and other global agencies were the ideal platform from which to explore and resolve ethical questions concerning war.[91]

Blake also lent King some formidable support by penning a letter to Chicago's notorious Mayor Richard J. Daley explaining that King had canceled his speaking engagement in Geneva due to the riots in his city. Blake requested that Daley do his utmost with the "opening up of housing opportunities outside of the pressed-in Negro community," as this was a priority for both King and the WCC. Blake made it clear that any effort Daley made would be deeply appreciated, not only by the Christian community, but also by people of goodwill at home and abroad.[92] Here Blake was articulating WCC policy, which involved challenging the conscience of society. Blake wrote to President Lyndon Johnson with an enclosed copy of the request he had sent to Mayor Richard Daley. Drawing the president's attention to the need for worldwide advancement on the problems of racism and war, Blake wrote, "we, of course, had hoped that Dr. King would be able to make an important American contribution to the programme of this conference. The unfortunate developments in Chicago understandably required Dr. King to stay there."[93] The SCLC's Chicago Campaign, which began in January of 1966, had to contend with the rise of the Black Power movement on the one hand and with white backlash on the other. King maintained that nonviolence could work in the North, and he called for an end to gradualism: "Now is the time to have a confrontation between the forces resisting change and the forces demanding change. Now is the time to let justice roll down like water and righteousness like a mighty stream."[94]

The 1966 Conference called on churches to ratify and enforce the UN Covenant on the Elimination of Racial Discrimination that had been adopted by the Twentieth Assembly and to support the creation of the office of UN Commissioner on Human Rights to oversee the implementation of the Covenant.[95] It is interesting to reflect on how one of the most successful of these Commissioners viewed the struggle for equality. Speaking in Addis Ababa, Ethiopia, at the Celebration of International Human Rights Day in

90. Ibid.

91. Baldwin, *Voice of Conscience*, 198–99.

92. Eugene Carson Blake to Richard Daley, July 18, 1966, WCC General Secretaries, Correspondence: Frequent 1938–(1966–1970), 42.11.08, WCC Archives, Geneva, Switzerland.

93. Eugene Carson Blake to Lyndon B. Johnson, July 18, 1966, King Center Library and Archive, Atlanta, GA.

94. King, *Autobiography of Martin Luther King, Jr.*, 303.

95. Thomas and Abrecht, *World Conference on Church and Society*, 137.

December of 2001, Mary Robinson, the former President of Ireland gave credit where it was due: "It was the determination of the new African and Asian nations of the United Nations in the 1960s to end apartheid in South Africa that shaped the long UN campaign against racism. When you view the struggle for equality as underscoring the entire human rights movement—as I do—this critical role assumes yet more importance." Robinson went on to confirm the significance of this historic progress, for "it led to the International Convention on the Elimination of All Forms of Racial Discrimination of 1965, one of the cornerstones of all international human rights treaties."[96]

The WCC Central Committee convened again in 1967 in Crete, Greece, where it emphasized the 1966 World Conference on Church and Society statement on the "perpetuation of the myth of racial superiority."[97] It called for "organized efforts to eradicate from the Church and Christian community all forms of discrimination based on race, color, or ethnic origin in the selection of persons for church leadership, admission to the membership of congregations, and in adopting social and cultural values and traditions to the present."[98] The Central Committee expressed regret for the situation in Rhodesia, where successive British governments since 1951 had been unable to secure a solution to the minority Smith regime. The WCC had never been short of rhetoric in condemning racism, but the time for action was now at hand.[99]

Martin Luther King Jr.'s contribution to racial justice was brought to bear on the future WCC deliberations in London. Indeed, King was aware of racism as a growing problem in the UK during his visit to Newcastle University in 1967, when he included his host country in a speech, saying, "there is a challenge and a great one—for all men of good will to work passionately and unrelentingly to get rid of racial injustice. Whether it exists in the United States of America, whether it exists in England, or whether it exists in South Africa—whenever it is alive it must be defeated."[100] King again emphasized that we are all "caught in an inescapable network of mutuality"

96. Robinson, Mary, "Challenges for Human Rights and Development in Africa," address at the Celebration of International Human Rights Day, Addis Ababa, Ethiopia, December 10, 2001, http://www.sacc.org.za/ARCHIVED%20SACCNEWS/docs/NEPAD.html.

97. "World Council Actions Since 1964," Programme to Combat Racism, Notting Hill Consultation 1969 (1965–1969), 4223.1.01, WCC Archives, Geneva, Switzerland.

98. Ibid.

99. Ibid.

100. King, "Honorary Degree Congregation Speech," November 13, 1967, University of Newcastle Archives.

when he advised, "there can be no separate black path to power and fulfillment that does not intersect white routes, and there can be no separate white path to power and fulfillment, short of social disaster, that does not recognize the necessity of sharing that power with colored aspirations for freedom and human dignity."[101] The WCC would also later address racism at Notting Hill, admitting that because the developed Western and so-called Christian countries of the world had obtained their wealth from centuries of exploitation, they now had a moral obligation to make restitution through the transfer of these material resources.[102]

Indeed, the WCC attached such importance to King's success in the civil rights movement as a source of hope for other troubled regions that there were constant demands on his time. In October of 1967, Blake invited King to preach the opening sermon of the Fourth Assembly of the WCC in Uppsala, Sweden scheduled for July of 1968. King was considered a Biblical preacher who was sure to enjoy a rapport with an international audience. The sermon was to be based on the theme of the Assembly, "Behold, I make all things new" (Rev 21:5). The sermon was to last about twenty minutes due to the requirements of television coverage.[103] King was advised that his sermon should be theologically and exegetically sound as well as spiritually powerful. Blake explained that the invitation was not based primarily on King's role as a civil rights leader or Nobel Prize winner, but on his experiences with racial strife, poverty, and war, in which God's purpose through the church is fully realized. It was hoped that King would stay as an adviser for the duration of the Assembly, but if this was not possible "guest status" would be accorded to him during his stay.[104] Blake had outlined the relevance of the ecumenical movement in relation to the world community when he urged, "everyone in the whole world ought to be interested in any movement which gives some promise of gathering the people of our shrinking planet into one community, for if mankind is unable to find a way spiritually and politically to create a single community to match the hopes and control the dangers of the technological advance of our time, it is certain that civilization will destroy itself."[105]

101. Ibid.

102. "Towards the Eradication of Racism," Programme to Combat Racism, Notting Hill Consultation 1969 (1965–1969), 4223.1.02, Box 2, No. 6, Consultation Papers, WCC Archives, Geneva, Switzerland.

103. Eugene Carson Blake to Martin Luther King Jr., October, 13, 1967, 42.11.08, WCC General Secretaries, Correspondence Frequent, 1938–(1966–1970), King, Martin Luther (1966–1970), WCC Archives, Geneva, Switzerland.

104. Ibid.

105. Blake, "Ecumenical Movement," October 1966, 995.1.01/1, WCC Archives,

Thus it is clear that King and Blake were on a similar trajectory, for just such a "beloved community" was foremost in King's thoughts. In his sermon "The American Dream," King asserted, "in order to make the American Dream real, we must be concerned about the world dream of peace and brotherhood and therefore, every person of good will must have a world perspective."[106] There is no doubt that King's thinking held worldwide implications, and Blake showed his recognition of the potential for King's philosophy when he extended his request. In December of 1967, Blake confirmed King's acceptance of his invitation to preach in Uppsala the following July.

On March 23, 1968, ten days before King's assassination, Professor Abraham Joshua Heschel[107] described the civil rights leader in moving terms at the sixty-eighth convention of the Rabbinical Assembly, asking, "Where in America today do we hear a voice like the voice of the prophets of Israel? Martin Luther King is a sign that God has not forsaken the United States of America. God has sent him to us. His presence is the hope of America. His mission is sacred, his leadership of supreme importance to every one of us."[108]

The struggle against racism never lost its intensity for King. "Doubts and Certainties," probably the last of King's interviews, was broadcast after his death on April 4, 1968. The question was put to him that, as a figure of world importance in the struggle for human rights, whether he thought that his activities in the US constituted a world pattern? In response, King demonstrated again that any solution to racism had worldwide ramifications, saying, "I think we have to honestly admit that the problems in the world today, as they relate to the question of race, must be blamed on the whole doctrine of white supremacy, the whole doctrine of racism, and these doctrines came into being through the white race and the exploitation of the colored peoples of the world."[109]

Martin Luther King Jr.'s peaceful crusade against racism and the Vietnam War continued to the very end. *A Testament of Hope*, published

---

Geneva, Switzerland.

106. King, Martin Luther, Jr., "The American Dream," address at Plymouth Church of the Pilgrims, Brooklyn, NY, February 10, 1963, King Papers, 1963, Box 3, January 1–May 25, King Center Library and Archive, Atlanta, GA.

107. Abraham Joshua Heschel (January 11, 1907–December 23, 1972) was an American rabbi of Polish descent and among the foremost Jewish theologians of the twentieth century.

108. Heschel, "Conversation with Martin Luther King," 1–19.

109. King, "Doubts and Certainties Link," April 4, 1968, King Center Library and Archives, Atlanta, GA.

posthumously in January of 1969, reaffirmed his condemnation of the war and its racist undertones. According to King, it was all too obvious that peace would never come to America without "an integrated foreign policy. Our disastrous experiences in Vietnam and the Dominican Republic have been, in one sense, a result of racist decision-making."[110] King made his point succinctly: "men of the white West, whether or not they like it, have grown up in a racist culture . . . They don't really respect anyone who is not white."[111]

110. King, "Testament of Hope," March 22, 1968, King Center Library and Archive, Atlanta, GA.

111. Ibid.

4

The Lessons of Apartheid

Martin Luther King Jr. Looks to South Africa and
Its Struggle

KING'S INTERNATIONAL SIGNIFICANCE HAS been largely ignored by most
scholars, for the majority of research has concentrated on King's work as
a civil rights leader during the turbulent 1960s in the United States. Even
within these parameters, it appears that some whitewashing of King's civil
rights struggle has taken place. For reasons unknown, attempts have been
made in media and government circles to portray King as the great American hero who had a dream in 1963, and this memory has been consolidated
into American history as the epitome of his career. Yet there is much more
to King, for his influence extended far beyond American shores from the
mid-1950s onwards. This national amnesia has been recognized by scholars
such as Lewis V. Baldwin, who explains that most literature on King has
either explicitly or implicitly "limited him to the American context, present-
ing him as a Southern black leader, a civil rights activist, an 'American Gandhi,' or a national symbol."[1] Vincent Harding complains of the difficulty in
analyzing King's career when so much of what he represented is "rooted in
our apparent determination to forget or ignore the last years of his life."[2]

1. Baldwin, *Toward the Beloved Community*, 1.
2. Harding, *Inconvenient Hero*, vii.

On December 5, 1955, when King stepped up to the podium and addressed the first Montgomery Improvement Association meeting, he had a vision that these times were extraordinary. This was no ordinary bus dispute, but rather a major step on the road to equality for nonwhites. As King preached, when the history books are written in the future, somebody will have to say, "there lived a race of people, a black people, 'fleecy locks and black complexion,' a people who had the moral courage to stand up for their rights. And thereby they injected a new meaning into the veins of history and of civilization."[3] Downtrodden people throughout the world would soon hear about this modest black Baptist preacher who had taken on the might of America's racist diehards in the Deep South, where for two hundred-odd years, slavery, and later quasi-slavery in Jim Crow, had thrived. As far back as November 4, 1956, in "Paul's Letter to American Christians," King had thrown down the gauntlet for his brethren, saying, "but America, as I look at you from afar, I wonder whether your moral and spiritual progress has been commensurate with your scientific progress," lamenting that "through your scientific genius you have made the world a neighborhood, but through your moral and spiritual genius you have failed to make it a brotherhood."[4] King advised his fellow US Christians to "keep your moral advances abreast with your scientific advances."[5] Even early on in his public career, King's vision of freedom and equality transcended continents, where he saw the demographic reality: "We are not fighting for ourselves alone but we are fighting for this nation. Go back and tell those people who are telling us to slow up that there are approximately two billion four hundred million people in this world and tell them that two thirds of these people are colored."[6]

King spoke of the ongoing decolonization then taking place in Africa and Asia, where the masses had gotten tired "of being pushed out of the glittering sunlight of life's July, left standing in the piercing chill of an alpine

3. King, Martin Luther, Jr., "Address to the Montgomery Improvement Association," at Holt Street Baptist Church, Montgomery, AL, December 5, 1955, http://www.thekingcenter.org/archive/document/address-montgomery-improvement-association#.

4. King, Martin Luther, Jr., "Paul's Letter to American Christians," address at Dexter Avenue Baptist Church, Montgomery, AL, November 4, 1956, http://www.thekingcenter.org/archive/document/pauls-letter-american-christians-0.

5. Ibid.

6. King, Martin Luther, Jr., "A Realistic Look at the Question of Progress in the Area of Race Relations," address at Saint Louis Freedom Rally, Saint Louis, MO, April 10, 1957, http://mlk-kpp01.stanford.edu/kingweb/publications/papers/vol4/570410.000-A_Realistic_Look_at_the_Question_of_Progress_in_the_Area_of_Race_Relations.html.

November."[7] The early examples of India and Pakistan, having been freed from the yoke of imperialism and racism, gave King some optimism as he met major leaders in Asia and Africa. Ghana's Prime Minister Kwame Nkrumah, and his Minister of Finance, N. K. Gbedema, told King "our sympathies are with the free world," and they made it clear through their efforts in the UN and in other diplomatic circles around the world "that beautiful words and extensive handouts can not be substitutes for the basic simple responsibility of giving freedom and justice to our colored brothers all over the United States."[8]

King was able to draw inspiration from successful decolonization efforts in parts of Asia and Africa, and his increasing outspokenness about injustice worldwide in turn gave hope for those whose freedom movements were then in their infancy. Following King's success in the Montgomery Bus Boycott in March of 1957, he attended Ghana's independence ceremony with his wife, Coretta. King displayed outward emotion as he considered Ghana's evolution: "Before I knew it, I started weeping. I was crying for joy, and I knew about all of the struggles, and all of the pain, and all of the agony that these people had gone through for this moment."[9] The significance of King's presence at the ceremonies was further reinforced when he attended a reception with Vice President Richard Nixon and cautioned him, "I want you to come visit us down in Alabama where we are seeking the same kind of freedom the Gold Coast is celebrating."[10] Using his well-honed media skills, King told radio listeners in Ghana that "this event, the birth of this new nation, will give impetus to oppressed peoples all over the world. I think it will have worldwide implications and repercussions—not only for Asia and Africa, but also for America."[11] King seized the opportunity to reinforce his message for those still struggling against imperialism and colonialism across the globe: "It renews my conviction in the ultimate triumph of justice. And it seems to me that this is fit testimony to the fact that eventually the forces of justice triumph in the universe, and somehow the universe itself is on the side of freedom and justice. So this gives new hope to me in the struggle for freedom."[12] Considering King's stance, Baldwin writes that many in the US and overseas "considered King unique among

7. Ibid.

8. Quoted in ibid.

9. King, Martin Luther, Jr., "The Birth of a New Nation," address at Dexter Avenue Baptist Church, Montgomery, AL, April 7, 1957, King Papers, Box 4:160, King Center Library and Archive, Atlanta, GA.

10. Ibid., Box 4:163.

11. Ibid., Box 4:146.

12. Ibid.

American clergy in that he symbolized, perhaps more than anyone else, the essential unity of the civil rights movement in America and the anti-apartheid struggle in South Africa."[13]

Martin Luther King Jr. and Chief Luthuli in South Africa were also on parallel paths during the 1950s and 1960s. Although they lived and fought for freedom and equality on difference continents, they influenced one another and sought to cooperate in the fight. Both were handicapped by restrictions on travel by a hard-line racist regime in South Africa. They could not meet in person because Luthuli could not get out of the country and King could not obtain a visa to get in. Nevertheless, they were very aware of their roles as leaders in a common cause, a brotherhood of man built on equality and freedom for their people. King worked hard to bring South Africa's woes to the international community, and the civil rights movement in turn was further motivated by the winds of change taking place all over the African and Asian continents. It was an advantageous situation for both sides, as King was one of the first great leaders to recognize the importance of the interrelatedness of man and the ways in which technological advances were making the world a truly global village. Thus, King foresaw globalization's benefits and problems long before the majority of his peers.

At this point it is useful to clarify where Chief Luthuli stood in relation to nonviolent action in bringing about the demise of apartheid. Several of his contemporaries have attempted to rewrite the history of that time to suit their own agendas. Before we proceed, some details of King's attitude to nonviolence might help to contextualize Luthuli's stance. King explained how he tried desperately to respond to the reactionary elements in the Deep South by calling on people's better nature: "It is the method which seeks to implement the just law by appealing to the conscience of the great decent majority of who, through blindness, fear, pride, or irrationality, have allowed their consciences to sleep."[14] By the early 1960s, King was a seasoned political activist, but also a realist. There was no possibility that an armed revolution waged by African Americans against the might of a right wing administration—which had at its disposal the most heavily armed military and police force in the world—could win out. Regardless, the consequences of staging, never mind winning, an armed revolt alarmed King. No matter how noble their cause, how great their courage and sacrifices, those who participate in violent struggle emerge changed. The use of brutal tactics to achieve results brutalizes its users, and this characteristic is then carried

13. Baldwin, "'Coalition of Conscience,'" 57.

14. King, Martin Luther, Jr., "The Future of Integration," address at Ford Hall, Boston, MA, December 11, 1960, King Papers, Box 1, September 1, 1958–December 11, 1960, King Center Library and Archive, Atlanta, GA.

forward in the rebuilding of the social order.[15] The insight of Jesus that "men do not gather figs from thorns, nor grapes from thistles," (Luke 6:44) is applicable here. In "Nonviolence Not First for Export" James Bristol writes that "the brutality, the killing, the hatred, the desire for revenge, and the distortion of values that inevitably accompany violent revolution are apt to undermine the constructive goals of the revolution."[16] Thus freedom may be achieved, but often it is just a reversal of roles as new victims become subservient to new tyrants with new oppression displacing the old. The next section deals with Luthuli's philosophy on nonviolence and the controversy that arose surrounding his stance on the armed rebellion in South Africa, Umkhonto we Sizwe (MK), led by Nelson Mandela.

CHIEF ALBERT LUTHULI, KING, AND THE COMMITMENT TO NONVIOLENCE

Chief Luthuli was born in 1898 in Rhodesia, and he died on July 21, 1967 in South Africa. He was President-General of the African National Congress (ANC)[17] from 1952 to 1967. Resistance to apartheid led to the 1952 Defiance of Unjust Laws Campaign. Activists began to resist on June 26, 1952, and by the end of the year there had been over eight thousand arrests. Membership of the ANC increased rapidly to more than one hundred thousand, and Luthuli was seen as crucial to this success. Consequently, the South African authorities issued an ultimatum, demanding that he either resign as president of the ANC's Natal branch or as Zulu Chief of his district. Luthuli declined to choose, and he was dismissed from his position as Zulu Chief in November of 1952.[18] Luthuli issued a public statement entitled, "The Road to Freedom Is Via the Cross," at this time, remarking, "who will deny that thirty years of my life have been spent knocking in vain, patiently, moderately, and modestly at a closed and barred door? What have been the fruits

---

15. Bristol, James E., "Nonviolence Not First for Export," American Friends Service Committee, Commission of the Churches on International Affairs, 1977, Militarism, Arms Race, Development Third World TNCS, Peace Proposals, WCC Archives, Geneva, Switzerland.

16. Ibid.

17. African National Congress (ANC) is South Africa's governing political party. Founded in January 1912, it was originally called the South African National Congress but changed to ANC in 1923. The military wing, known as Umkhonto we Sizwe, was set up in 1961 by Nelson Mandela.

18. Woodson, "Albert Luthuli," 348–49.

of my many years of moderation? Has there been any reciprocal tolerance or moderation from the government, be it Nationalist or United Party? No!"[19]

One month later, Luthuli was elected President-General of the ANC. Various parties have interpreted Luthuli's statements in "The Road to Freedom Is Via the Cross" as an indication that he had seen the futility of nonviolent action, and that he may have left an opening for alternative action in the future. We will examine the years following with this interpretation in mind, for Luthuli made a lifelong commitment to a nonviolent resolution to apartheid in hopes that it might culminate in an inclusive society. The ANC convened at Kliptown, South Africa from June 25 to 26, 1955, where they adopted the "Freedom Charter"[20] with an overwhelming majority. Media coverage was extensive, and the document highlighted the nonviolent rationale of the movement, declaring "that South Africa belongs to all who live in it, black and white, and that no government can justly claim authority unless it is based on the will of the people."[21] In words reminiscent of King's plea for entry into mainstream America, Luthuli outlined the outrage felt by black South Africans who "have been robbed of their birthright to land, liberty, and peace by a form of government funded on injustice and inequality; that our country will never be prosperous or free until all people live in brotherhood, enjoying equal rights or opportunities."[22]

Back in the US, the Cold War era had produced hysteria among government agencies such that Communists and even merely alleged Communists were persecuted and deprived of their livelihoods. This panic had repercussions for King and others in the civil rights movement when the FBI, under J. Edgar Hoover, attempted to undermine them using a dirty tricks campaign and anything else that would hinder progress. South Africa was an important link in the chain to keep Communism at bay. In December of 1956, the entire leadership of the ANC was imprisoned on a trumped-up charge that the organization had been infiltrated by Communists who were planning to overthrow the state. In an affront to all right-thinking people, the "Freedom Charter," which advocated democratic changes, was the principle document used in the indictment, although a mountain of evidence followed later. It was ironic that all the ANC's leaders were incarcerated in such close quarters, for Luthuli, whose stature rose considerably during the

19. Ibid.

20. The "Freedom Charter" was a memorandum of the principles of the South African Congress Alliance, which included the African National Congress, the South African Congress of Democrats, and the Coloured People's Congress.

21. Luthuli, *Let My People Go*, 239.

22. Ibid.

Treason Trial,[23] observed, "it is extraordinary difficult in so large a country as South Africa for resistance leaders to meet together, especially since many of us do not belong to the ruling classes. Yet here we all were; met together and with time on our hands."[24] The Treason Trial was an extraordinary difficult time that lasted for four years, and by 1958, ideological differences had emerged within the ANC. Robert Sobukwe led a breakaway group to form the Pan Africanist Congress (PAC).[25] These dissidents were critical of Luthuli's strict adherence to a nonviolent revolution and his plans for a non-racialist society. During the late 1950s, widespread but often disorganized demonstrations broke out, coming to a head in March of 1960, when a PAC-organized anti-pass protest at Sharpeville resulted in a massacre. Despite worldwide condemnation, the government further tightened the noose by banning both the ANC and PAC.

Robert Sobukwe, along with many others, was arrested and imprisoned on Robben Island. Luthuli was placed under a banning order and restricted to his home in Groutville. These draconian measures forced the ANC and PAC into exile, but the military arm of the ANC, Umkhonto we Sizwe, and the PAC's POQO, led by Potlako Leballo,[26] commenced guerilla warfare in the early 1960s. Their activities continued for a number of years up until the imprisonment of Nelson Mandela, Walter Sisulu,[27] Govan Mbeki,[28] and other leaders curtailed their military campaign. There is some debate among historians as to whether Luthuli had concluded that nonviolence had run its course in South Africa, and whether he may have considered other alternatives, including armed revolt. Paradoxically, this was about the time he was notified that he had been awarded the Nobel Peace Prize for 1960. Luthuli had every reason to be despondent, for Prime Minister Verwoerd, on hearing the good news, lamented the "spirit" of enmity toward a

23. The Treason Trial was a trial in which Nelson Mandela and almost the entire executive branch of the ANC were arrested and accused of treason in 1956. The ordeal lasted until 1961, when all 156 defendants were found not guilty.

24. Luthuli, *Let My People Go*, 166. See also Woodson, "Albert Luthuli," 351–52.

25. Pan Africanist Congress (PAC) was launched on April 16, 1959. Robert Sobukwe served as the first President, and Potlako Leballo as the Secretary General.

26. Potlako Leballo was commander of the Azanian People's Liberation Army (POQO), the military wing of the PAC.

27 Walter Max Ulgate Sisulu (May 12, 1912–May 5, 2003) served as Secretary General and Deputy President of the ANC. He was jailed with Nelson Mandela and spent twenty-five years in prison.

28. Govan Archibald Mvuyelwa Mbeki (July 9, 1910–August 30, 2001) was the father of Thabo Mbeki, a South African president. He was a leader of the ANC and the South African Communist Party (SACP) and was jailed for twenty-four years on Robben Island.

country that had in no way harmed Norway.[29] However, Luthuli, not unlike the rising star that was Martin Luther King Jr., was not regarded as a most important person in South Africa, and despite all the travel restrictions, the government was left with little choice but to allow Luthuli fly to Norway. Thus, on December 10, 1961, Luthuli delivered his "Africa and Freedom" speech after accepting the Nobel Peace Prize, in which he reiterated his commitment to nonviolence: "We, in our situation have chosen the path of nonviolence of our own volition. Along this path we have organized many heroic campaigns. All the strength of progressive leadership in South Africa, all my life and strength, has been given to the pursuance of this method."[30]

In what must have been an embarrassment for Luthuli, the armed struggle known as MK was announced the day after his return from Norway.[31] Scholar Dorothy C. Woodson explains that "sadly, Luthuli now realized the futility of this nonviolent movement."[32] The raison d'être of the ANC was quite simple really, but the "embarkation on a path of violence had been the outcome of disillusionment with the ineffectiveness of nonviolent tactics."[33] The controversy over whether Luthuli abandoned the nonviolent stance has continued over the years, and it has now entered the realm of contested history. According to scholars Jabulani Sithole and Sibongiseni Mkhize, "the memory of Chief Luthuli has been and continues to be, a site of friendly contested struggle in South Africa."[34] The authors argue that as Luthuli became a major figure in South African politics, people with varying political affiliations produced alternative images and representations to suit their own purposes. Typical among these were former State Security Police (or Special Branch), Inkatha Freedom Party, the ANC, and the South African Communist Party (SACP). Luthuli's legacy was appropriated when they realized that his reputation would continue to grow nationally and internationally following his death.[35]

Sithole and Mkhize effectively demonstrate the means by which one's reputation can be hijacked to support different objectives. Luthuli's actions speak for themselves, and none more so than his purchase of two farms in Swaziland as a haven for South African refugees from the civil unrest. The purchase was financed by Luthuli's Nobel Peace Prize money, and Sithole

29. Saint Laurent, "Negro in World History," 14.
30. Luthuli, "Africa and Freedom," 267–71.
31. Mandela, *Long Walk to Freedom*, 273.
32. Woodson, "Albert Luthuli," 345–62.
33. Karis, Carter, and Gerhart, *From Protest to Challenge*, 659.
34. Sithole and Mkhize, "Truth or Lies?" 70.
35. Ibid.

and Mkhize assert that his purchase of the farms "raises questions about suggestions that he was totally opposed to what the leadership of the ANC was doing after December 1961."[36] For Scott Everett Couper, the purchase of the farms for refugees "can be seen as his approval of ANC tactics after MK's launch."[37] Couper makes the point that one would need to determine what kind of "refugees" these farms were intended to serve. The line between a "combatant" refugee and a "political" refugee was difficult to establish during the struggle. Whether the farms were used as "safe houses" or as launching pads for military operations in South Africa would clarify whether Luthuli favored the change in ANC strategy.[38] Certainly, the ANC's website "argues that Luthuli was a strategic pacifist only because he was the representative leader of a movement that had upheld a policy, a policy of nonviolence since 1912."[39] Nevertheless, a contradictory picture emerges in the ANC's interpretation of the role Luthuli played in alleged discussions to set up MK. In *Long Walk to Freedom*, Mandela recalled, "the Chief initially resisted my arguments . . . But we worked on him the whole night . . . He ultimately agreed that a military campaign was inevitable."[40] On the other hand, Joe Slovo,[41] who was a co-leader of ANC's military wing, denied that Luthuli had any part in the decision to endorse the armed struggle. Slovo agreed that it was typical of Luthuli's character, that despite his deep Christian commitment to nonviolence, he never prevented or condemned the switch to an armed struggle, as he blamed the South African government for their intransigence.[42] Mandela claimed that when Luthuli returned from Oslo, "he was also unwell, his heart was strained and his memory was poor. But the award cheered him and all of us as well."[43]

Anza Mehnert's article, "Memory and Heritage: How Memory Functions and How It Can Be Used in Heritage; Chief Albert Luthuli as a Case Study," advises that we should never feel uncomfortable about contradictory memories, since they come about because of divergent or overlapping

36. Ibid.

37. Couper, "My People Let Go," 101–23. See also http://www.anc.org.za/show-people.php?p=1.

38. Ibid.

39. Ibid.

40. Mandela, *Long Walk to Freedom*, 260.

41. Joe Slovo (May 23, 1926–January 6, 1995) played leading roles in the South African Communist Party (SACP), and a leading member of the ANC. He went into exile abroad in 1963 and lived in Britain, Mozambique, Zambia, and Angola.

42. Slovo, *Unfinished Biography*, 147. See also Sithole and Mkhize, "Truth or Lies?" 69–85.

43. Mandela, *Long Walk to Freedom*, 271.

experiences. Mehnert confirms that it is only by gathering and comparing conflicting memories that we will ever establish the truth.[44] Although it is widely recognized that Luthuli possessed outstanding qualities, Mehnert contends that even this legacy has its contentious issues, especially in the continuing debate about Luthuli's involvement in the movement towards armed struggle in 1961. Autobiographies and oral history interviews of his contemporaries offer very different accounts of these events.[45] Ismail Meer[46] in *A Fortunate Man* recalled a meeting held by the ANC National Executive Committee in August through September 1961, when as chairman Luthuli raised concerns as to whether "all means of nonviolent struggle" had been exhausted. Meer opened the meeting held near Stanger, South Africa, with an announcement that the ANC National Executive Committee had decided to permit the formation of an organization that would engage in a violent offensive.[47] Billy Nair[48] said in an interview with ZSE TV that when a decision was made to move towards violence, Luthuli was not against it, but did insist that a separate organization should be set up to engage in the armed revolt rather than ANC.[49] Nair remembered driving Luthuli to Durban, South Africa, for medical treatment and discussing the development of MK, including its launch date.[50] Couper wrote in 2005 that current South African historiography had concluded that Luthuli supported the ANC's shift to a violent struggle. Most of the evidence in support of this claim came from Mandela, Zuma,[51] Nair, and Kathrada.[52] In the 2005 documentary on Luthuli produced by the National Film and Video Foundation, Billy Nair testified that Luthuli "already knew, before he left for Oslo, to receive the Nobel, he knew that night, that Umkhonto was going

44. Mehnert, "Memory and Heritage," 85–91.

45. Ibid.

46. Ismail Meer (September 5, 1918–May 1, 2000) was a journalist, lawyer, and political activist who was a good friend of Nelson Mandela.

47. Meer, *Fortunate Man*, 223–24.

48. Billy Nair (November 27, 1929–October 23, 2002) was a political activist imprisoned on Robben Island with Nelson Mandela. He joined the National Assembly of South Africa after his release from jail.

49. Quoted in Mehnert, "Memory and Heritage," 85–91.

50. Ibid.

51. Jacob Zuma (April 12, 1942) was elected President of South Africa in 2009. He joined the ANC in 1959 and became involved in the organization's military wing in 1963.

52 Ahmed Kathrada (August 21, 1929) was imprisoned on Robben Island with Nelson Mandela. After his release from prison in 1990 he was elected to Parliament as a representative of the ANC.

to be launched."[53] Jacob Zuma, President of South Africa, revealed in the documentary "The Legacy of a Legend," that Luthuli himself had named the military wing of the ANC.[54] Yet in complete contrast to the recollections above, Moses Kotane[55] and Joe Slovo remain adamant in maintaining that Luthuli was not present at the meetings endorsing armed revolt. In fact, Kotane insisted that he was actually charged with informing Luthuli of the decision.[56] These divergent accounts demonstrate that even the individuals involved recall the events leading up to this historic decision to pursue violent resistance differently.

The controversy rumbled on over the intervening years, and in 2005, scholar Scott Everett Couper tackled the issue of whether Luthuli approved of the use of violence to achieve liberation in "My People Let Go." As Couper explains, as a leader and spokesman for fourteen million oppressed, humiliated, and exploited South Africans, Luthuli was a militant. He unceasingly fought for freedom and justice as leader of the ANC for twenty-two years.[57] For Couper, the greatest paradox of Luthuli's life was his consistent advocacy of nonviolence prior to MK and in the last seven years of his life. The former observation posed the question, was Luthuli aware of discussions concerning MK prior to June of 1961, when agreement was reached? Luthuli's testimony in the Treason Trial from 1958 to 1961 suggests that he was not aware of this development. Couper ponders on what Luthuli might have known, considering Mandela's claim that talks on armed revolt had been going on since early 1960. It may have been counter-productive for Luthuli to be informed of any armed struggle. There were also logistical hindrances and delays in communication, for Luthuli was subject to a banning order in Groutville and busy with preparations for traveling to Norway to accept his Nobel Peace Prize. Perhaps it was feared that Luthuli would veto any change in policy if it were intimated to him at an inappropriate time.[58] In fact, Luthuli was on record declaring repeatedly that he was not a pacifist. The most prominent instance came during the Treason Trial, when he responded to the judge's direct question as to whether he was a pacifist by Luthuli

---

53. Williams, Buntu, and Mandla Ngwenya, "The Legacy of a Legend," (Amman, Jordan: Amandla Communications, 2004) DVD, quoted in Couper, "My People Let Go," 115.

54. Ibid., 115.

55. Moses Kotane (August 9, 1905–May 19, 1978) was Secretary General of the SACP from 1939 to 1978 and was widely respected by even non-communist leaders.

56. Couper, "My People Let Go," 120.

57. Ibid.

58. Ibid.

answered succinctly, "No, I'm not."[59] Kader Asmal, South Africa's former Minister of Education, sought to explain how Luthuli, although favoring a nonviolent solution to apartheid, might acquiesce to such a decision but not support or approve the resolution to take up arms: "He once observed that anyone who thought he was a pacifist should try to steal his chickens. I believe that he came to appreciate—under the pressure of events—that some measure of force was inevitable, but he felt that any use of force should be done through a military formation that was separate from the political movement of the ANC."[60]

Couper makes a cogent point when he observes that from the beginning the ANC sought to utilize Luthuli's name to arouse legitimacy for the armed conflict. Oliver Tambo, the leader of the ANC in exile, justified the violent struggle using extracts from Luthuli's 1952 speech, "The Road to Freedom Is Via the Cross," which by then was almost ten years old and was never intended to defend MK.[61] It is highly unlikely that Luthuli was unaware of the building momentum for a change in tactics to topple apartheid, but his 1962 autobiography does not shed much light on his support for an armed revolt: "But the struggle goes on, bans, banishments, deportations, gaol or not. We do not struggle with guns or violence, and the supremacist's array of weapons is powerless against the spirit."[62] Some ambiguity is apparent in a later speech following the Rivonia Trial,[63] when Luthuli explained that "the [ANC] never abandoned its method of a militant nonviolent struggle, and of creating in the process, militancy in the people. However, in the face of uncompromising white refusal to abandon a policy which denies the African and other oppressed South Africans their rightful heritage—freedom—no one can blame just men for seeking justice by the use of violent methods."[64]

Couper questions whether Luthuli was providing implicit support for violent methods, though not stating so explicitly. He concludes that Luthuli remained ambiguous about violent means in "neither supporting nor

59. Ibid.

60. Ibid.

61. Ibid.

62. Luthuli, *Let My People Go*, 229.

63. In what is often called "the Rivonia Trial" (1963–1964) after the Johannesburg suburb where the military wing of the ANC had its hideout, Nelson Mandela and ten other leading opponents of South Africa's apartheid regime went on trial for their lives. The charges were sabotage and conspiracy, and Mandela was sentenced to life imprisonment along with eight others.

64. Pillay, *Albert Luthuli*, 30.

condemning [them], despite his personal faith, views and ethics."[65] Couper broached the subject again in a 2009 article entitled, "An Embarrassment to the Congresses? The Silencing of Chief Albert Luthuli and the Production of ANC History." Couper's article resonates with the ways in which King's own history has been whitewashed in the process of nationalist myth-making. Couper argues that the silence in the ANC archives was due to Luthuli's "embarrassingly persistent espousal of nonviolent methods that led to his marginalization as a leader of the ANC in the early 1960s."[66] Couper affirms that Luthuli lost political authority over the ANC following the banning of the organization on April 8, 1960. His influence eroded further with the launch of MK on December 16, 1961. Consequently, Luthuli was only the nominal head of the ANC in the seven years until his death in July of 1967.[67] For this reason, Couper questions when, precisely, Luthuli became aware of MK. It appears that most accounts written prior to Mandela's 1995 autobiography, *The Long Walk to Freedom*, indicate that Luthuli was ignorant of the establishment of MK, whereas later accounts claim that he was fully conversant with the decision. In support of this analysis, Brian Bunting, in his 1975 biography of South African revolutionary Moses Kotane, reveals that Luthuli was not consulted for fear of a "presidential veto."[68]

Similarly, Joe Slovo's 1995 autobiography explains that "the leadership of the ANC as a whole" was not consulted about the decision for fear of rejection.[69] Couper is adamant that despite current political narratives implying Luthuli's involvement in MK operational decisions, ANC's archival silence casts doubts on this assumption. However, evidence suggests that in July of 1961, Luthuli, with some reluctance, relented to the decision of the ANC and the Joint Congresses' executives to take up arms.[70] Significantly, from April of 1962 until his death in 1967, Luthuli was silent on his stance on the efficacy of violence even as MK curtailed his capacity to give leadership. This silence suggests that Luthuli did not support the commencement of the armed struggle. The June 1962 Sabotage Act prohibited any publication from quoting Luthuli but did not prevent him from issuing international statements arguing for nonviolent means of struggle. If Luthuli disagreed with the decision to pursue violence, what prevented him from opposing it? First, Luthuli had decided that he would not publicly

65. Couper, "My People Let Go," 101–23.

66. Couper, "'Embarrassment to the Congresses?'" 331–48.

67. Ibid., 332.

68. Ibid., 334–35.

69. Ibid., 335.

70. Ibid., 336.

disagree with any decision made democratically. Second, if a decision had been made to launch MK, nothing would be achieved by opposing this fait accompli.[71] On March 25, 1962, Luthuli contributed to his regular column in the *Golden City Post*, where he lamented: "I would urge our people not to despair over our methods of struggle, the militant, nonviolent techniques so far have failed the method—not the method us."[72]

The ANC has always kept quiet about Luthuli's objection to the armed struggle. After April of 1962, Luthuli no longer expressly voiced his objections to violence, thus facilitating the ANC's silence on his position until his death.[73] Luthuli appreciated that resisting the apartheid government through force was equivalent to "national suicide"[74] considering the armed forces opposed to them, as did Martin Luther King Jr. in the US. Having received the Nobel Peace Prize in recognition of his efforts, it was Luthuli's belief that nonviolent methods were more appropriate, despite the lack of initial success, because the ANC held the moral, political, and economic high ground. Luthuli refused to countenance violence because he held out hope for a peaceful non-racial society following the dismantling of the apartheid regime.[75]

Raymond Suttner, in his "The Road to Freedom Is Via the Cross: Just Means in Chief Albert Luthuli's Life," examines ambiguities relating to the ANC's use of violence. "Luthuli abhorred the harm wreaked by violence," but "like Gandhi, he was not a pacifist and all his statements on violence have an element of conditionality attached, related to the practicality of implementing the principle at a specific moment," argues Suttner.[76] Whereas violence at an abstract level could do no good, violence at a concrete level by the oppressor could force the oppressed to change tactics and renege on nonviolent methods. Nevertheless, the national liberation movement never espoused violence as a principle, choosing instead to advocate for peace: "There shall be peace and friendship," as quoted by Suttner from the "Freedom Charter." Suttner argues that although armed struggle was never a principle of the ANC, it may have been heroic at specified times. Consequently, Suttner concludes that although Luthuli had not wanted violence,

71. Ibid.
72. Ibid., 339.
73. Quoted in ibid., 338.
74. Couper, "'Embarrassment to the Congresses?'" 340–41.
75. Ibid.
76. Suttner, "Road to Freedom," 693–715.

he left the way open for debate and perhaps even an element of conditional support.[77]

By contrast, Martin Luther King Jr. was very clear when he preached that nonviolence demands that the means used to end segregation must be as pure as the ends sought: "I have tried to make it clear that it is wrong to use immoral means to attain moral ends. But now I must affirm that it is just as wrong, or perhaps even more so, to use moral means to preserve immoral ends.[78] In a similar vein, Suttner writes that Luthuli believed that the ANC's means should be worthy of its just cause, and that although he adds the notion of practicality, Luthuli considered nonviolent methods as just means. Suttner further points to any conditionality of this principle as dependent on the actions of the oppressor. Luthuli evidenced this view this in his 1953 ANC presidential address: "[we] can assure the world that it is our intention to keep on the nonviolent plane. We would earnestly request the powers that be to make it possible for us to keep our people in this model.[79] Suttner points to the ambiguity in this quote, which he contends is open to more than one interpretation. Unfortunately, quotes from a long speech can be taken out of context, and in the same speech, Luthuli seems to adhere to his previous policy of nonviolence: "So long as white South Africa denies the non-whites full democratic freedom we shall have no option but to advise and continue to lead the voteless non-whites to use extra-parliamentary nonviolent methods of struggle."[80] In support of his argument that Luthuli probably did come to terms with the armed revolt, Suttner airs views expressed by Professor Z. K. Matthews, who was said to have seen eye to eye with Luthuli. In a 1964 WCC speech in Kitwe, Zambia, Matthews said, "it is clear that Mandela and his colleagues were still inspired by the spirit of nonviolence. They reluctantly recognized that violence was inevitable, but they were convinced that if it did come, it was their duty as responsible leaders of the people, to take certain steps about it."[81] Under the spirit of nonviolence, acts of sabotage were to be directed at installations in such a manner that there would be no loss of life. Suttner takes these words as an acknowledgement of continuity within the rupture caused by MK, insofar as Matthews confirmed actions to be undertaken by those committed to

---

77. Ibid.

78. King, *Autobiography of Martin Luther King*, 202–203.

79. Suttner, "Road to Freedom," 696–97.

80. Luthuli, "Freedom in Our Lifetime," address to the 46th Annual Conference of the African National Congress, Durban, South Africa, December 12–14, 1953, http://www.anc.org.za/show.php?id=164.

81. Quoted in Suttner, "Road to Freedom," 703–704.

nonviolent struggle.[82] Suttner concludes that he himself makes no pretence at finalizing any debate on Luthuli and the use of violence as a means of resistance.[83] This interpretation will not go unchallenged and is likely to remain a point of controversy among historians.[84]

Couper has been active of late in defending Luthuli's adherence to a nonviolent philosophy. He argues that "many myths assert that Albert Luthuli as President General of the African National Congress (ANC) launched the armed struggle on his return to South Africa after receiving the Nobel Peace Prize in December 1961."[85] There is extensive archival evidence in Luthuli's own hand to support the view that he never anticipated the initiation of violence by Umkhonto we Sizwe. In arguing this position, Couper makes two important points. First, he alleges that those who dismiss Luthuli's own words are fearful of a history that drives a wedge between Luthuli and the ANC. Second, those who ignore the archives may be fearful that the Luthuli thesis undermines assumptions that ANC traditionally operates as a collective through consensus decision-making, despite the fact that decisions such as Nelson Mandela's initiation of violence and negotiations with the National Party regime were made unilaterally to avoid objections from colleagues. In support of this argument, Couper points to Mandela's *Conversations with Myself*, in which the leader recalls that "people like Chief Luthuli, like Moses Kotane, like Dr. Monty Naicker[86] . . . All of them were saying, 'Let us not embark on violence; let us continue with nonviolence.' And when they couldn't resist the argument I was putting forward, they said 'You go and start that organization. We will not discipline you because we understand why you have taken this line. But don't involve us, we are going to continue with nonviolence.'"[87]

In "Emasculating Agency: An Unambiguous Assessment of Albert Luthuli's Stance on Violence," the latest installment of Couper's efforts to uphold Luthuli's nonviolent philosophy, the author suggests that Nelson Mandela undermined Luthuli at best, and at worst committed insubordination by launching Umkhonto we Sizwe without the ANC and Luthuli's knowledge or consent. However, Couper accepts that Luthuli was not strictly a pacifist

82. Ibid., 704.

83. Ibid., 713.

84. Ibid., 697.

85. Couper, "Irony upon Irony," 339–41.

86. Dr. Monty Naicker (September 30, 1910–January 12, 1978) was an important member of the South African Indian Congress (SAIC), and the Natal Indian Congress. Although he was initially accused in the Treason Trial (1956–1961), the charges were later dropped.

87. Mandela, *Conversations with Myself*, 78.

and so did not oppose violence in all circumstances: "Publicly, [Luthuli] advocated only nonviolence and dialogue because they were what he passionately wanted South Africa to believe in; but privately he maintained that Stauffenberg[88] was right in trying to destroy Hitler . . . [Luthuli's] condemnation of violence was conditional and qualified."[89] Couper is emphatic in emphasizing that Luthuli opposed the use of violence within the South African context, and there is little if any evidence that he ever came to support it thereafter. As he sees it, the ambiguous interpretation of Luthuli's views on the arms struggle simply muddies the water while not offering any new substantive evidence.[90] Luthuli's stance was certain and concise, and he fulfilled his democratic leadership role by recognizing, allowing for, and acknowledging as valid a range of opinions.[91] Nokukhanya, Luthuli's wife, confirmed her husband's continued stance on nonviolent action in 1985: "Like my husband, I am sick and tired of violence. Albert worked towards a better South Africa by negotiation, not by the barrel of a gun, which is what the ANC of today is doing. It makes me very sad indeed. I am glad my husband has not lived to see what's happening to the present-day ANC."[92] Couper returns to the argument that Luthuli "did not stand in the way of armed struggle," according to Mandela.[93] But Couper argues that this "does not convey that he therefore supported it." Luthuli had no power to "stand in the way" other than to offer his resignation as President-General, and this option was considered.[94]

Luthuli received a very strict banning order in 1964 that restricted him to the small hamlet of Groutville. By 1967, restrictions placed on him by his own movement not to condemn their armed struggle, in addition to the 1962 Sabotage Act which prevented his words or image from being published, had rendered Luthuli almost completely silent and invisible. Couper takes a dim view of the revisionists he fears are monopolizing the history of South Africa with an agenda "to legitimize their own iconic status within

88. Claus Philipp Maria Schenk Graf von Stauffenberg (November 15, 1907–July 21, 1944) was a German army officer and aristocrat who was involved in the failed July 20, 1944 plot to assassinate Adolf Hitler.

89. Hooper, Charles, "Letter in the S. A. Press," *Sechaba*, October 1967, 7, quoted in Couper, "Emasculating Agency," 565.

90. Ibid., 568.

91. Ibid., 569.

92. Luthuli, Nokukhanya, "Albert Would Have Rejected Today's Violence," *Durban Daily News*, 1985, quoted in Couper, 569.

93. Quoted in Couper, "Emasculating Agency," 574.

94. Ibid.

the armed movement and who are willing to adulterate Luthuli's stance to validate their own legacy." For Couper, "that is a betrayal of Luthuli."[95]

Having thoroughly examined Luthuli's commitment to nonviolent action and the revisionists' interpretation of his stance, we now return to the struggle for equality in South Africa in the 1950s and 1960s, where Luthuli and Martin Luther King Jr. worked in tandem despite constraints that interfered with their efforts. The South African government was not prepared to tolerate any opposition to its apartheid regime, and Luthuli's uncertain prediction of the future came to pass in December of 1956, when he and 155 other democrats of all races were rounded up and jailed. They were incarcerated at Fort Prison in Johannesburg for one year before being released without charge.[96]

Martin Luther King Jr. was aware of the connection between the struggle of black people in the United States and the efforts of Africans, Asians, and Latin Americans to break away from their colonial masters. In 1958, he declared, "the determination of Negro Americans to win freedom from all forms of oppression springs from the same deep longing that motivates oppressed peoples all over the world. The rumblings of discontent in Asia and Africa are expressions of a quest for freedom and human dignity by people who have long been victims of colonialism and imperialism."[97] Some years before in South Africa, Luthuli spoke against the evils of apartheid at the ANC's forty-third National Conference in December of 1954. Luthuli welcomed the rejection of the Bantu Education Act of 1953[98] by the Roman Catholic Church and the diocese of Johannesburg under the Rev. Ambrose Reeves. Luthuli took heart from the unequivocal public condemnation of the policy of apartheid "by a good number of churches in the Union and overseas, especially the Church of England in Great Britain."[99] Of great significance to Luthuli was the condemnation of apartheid from such "a world-important body" as the WCC, which had recently met in Evanston, IL.[100] Like King, he recognized the importance of this international body of churches in sharing their vision of a world free of hatred and violence. De-

---

95. Couper, "Irony upon Irony," 342.

96. Luthuli, "Man of the People," 11–12.

97. King, *Stride Toward Freedom*, 191.

98. The 1953 Bantu Education Act brought African education under government and extended apartheid to church schools. The majority of African schools had previously been run by missionaries with some state support.

99. Luthuli, Albert, "Forty-third National Congress Presidential Address," at the Bantu Social Centre of the YMCA in Durban, South Africa, December 16, 1954, http://www.anc.org.za/show.php?id=154.

100. Ibid.

cember of 1955 was a groundbreaking time for both King and Luthuli. King proclaimed to his newly confident audience of the Montgomery Improvement Association: "You know, my friends, there comes a time when people get tired of being trampled over by the iron feet of oppression. There comes a time, my friends, when people get tired of being plunged across the abyss of humiliation, where they experience the bleakness of nagging despair."[101]

Luthuli likewise gave a special presidential message at the ANC's Forty-fourth National Conference on December 17, 1955, when he confidently stated, "in my judgment, this period in the national history of the African people will go down as one of the most outstanding periods in the all-round political awakening of the African people, despite the almost insurmountable obstacles put in their way by the white rulers of South Africa, who have selfishly created barriers to African progress and advancement in South Africa in order to promote their own interests."[102] Luthuli went on to explain his organization's use of nonviolent resistance, which King would soon implement in his own campaign. A nonviolent approach was no guarantee that the response from their adversaries would be equally peaceful, however, for as Luthuli cautioned, "We have been busily engaged in a laudable effort to establish a spirit of defiance against unjust laws and treatment along nonviolent lines, and in getting Africans to see that no one is really worthy of freedom until he is prepared to pay the supreme sacrifice for its attainment and defense."[103]

South Africa's apartheid laws were causing turmoil both within and outside the country. The *Anderson Herald* reported that December 10, 1957, had been set aside by the American Committee on Africa (ACOA) as a worldwide day of protest against apartheid. The paper claimed that for the first time, the rulers of South Africa would know without the slightest doubt that people everywhere would no longer be silent in the face of South Africa's attempts to crush its non-white majority.[104] In December of 1957, the *Christian Science Monitor* reported that the South African government was deeply disturbed by the ACOA's international protests against its racist policies. Mr. Eric H. Louw, South Africa's Minister of External Affairs, attempted to defend the indefensible, explaining that it had been necessary to apply "certain control measures" partly in the interests of the undeveloped and "largely uncivilized" indigenous peoples of Africa, and that these

101. King, *Autobiography of Martin Luther King*, 60.

102. Luthuli, Albert, "Forty-fourth National Conference Special Presidential Message" address at Bloemfontein, South Africa, December 17, 1955, http://www.anc.org. za/show.php?id=158.

103. Ibid.

104. *Anderson Herald* (Anderson, IN), December 10, 1957.

measures would remain in force. He added that it had not been possible to extend "democratic equality" to the non-whites of South Africa.[105] Louw tried to brand the protest against South Africa as a leftist-organized and Communist-exploited campaign. Similar charges were made against Martin Luther King Jr. and the civil rights movement by diehard racists. Describing Eleanor Roosevelt, who headed the protest, as "not a stranger in American left-wing circles," Louw further charged that Mr. George Houser,[106] executive secretary of the ACOA, was a "known leftist." All in all, he claimed the committee had a "decidedly pinkish tinge," and that leading members were associated with left-wing organizations.[107]

It is worth emphasizing that the ACOA benefited from the talents of a wide variety of American clergymen, including Martin Luther King Jr., Rev. James A. Pike,[108] and Reinhold Niebuhr.[109] The *New York Times* reported that South African Prime Minister Johannes Strijdom's[110] government protested that a United States group headed by Eleanor Roosevelt had made "false and spurious changes" against South Africa's race policy.[111] The *Oregon Journal* compared both countries in a column headed "Men of Conscience Protest," declaring, "There is a vast difference between the situation in South Africa and in the United States. There it is the official policy of the national government to keep races apart . . . Here, it is official policy of the national government to end segregation and by possible means to improve the status of the negro."[112] Nevertheless, Louw's remarks indicated government concern over this adverse international publicity, particularly insofar as it might influence American policy toward South Africa. The Minister of External Affairs gave no indication of any change in the South African

105. *Christian Science Monitor*, December 13, 1957.

106. George M. Houser (June 2, 1916) is a Methodist minister and civil rights activist who worked with the Fellowship of Reconciliation (FOR), the Congress of Racial Equality (CORE), and the American Committee on Africa (ACOA) for many years.

107. *Christian Science Monitor*, December 13, 1957.

108. James Albert Pike (February 14, 1913–September 9, 1969) was an American Episcopal bishop and writer. He was widely known for his controversial views on theological and social issues, and he used the media to promote these views.

109. Reinhold Niebuhr (May 21, 1892–June 1, 1971) was a professor at Union Theological Seminary for three decades. An outstanding intellectual and a prolific writer, he influenced King and others during the Kennedy administration. His best-known book is the bombshell *Moral Man and Immoral Society* (1932).

110. Johann Gerhardas Strijdom (July 14, 1893–August 24, 1958) was a member of the National Party and Prime Minister of South Africa from November of 1954 to August of 1958.

111. *New York Times*, December 13, 1957.

112. "Men of Conscience Protest," *Oregon Journal*, December 10, 1957.

government's racial policy following the protests.[113] Considering attack the best defense, Louw turned his attention to recent problems with school integration in the American South. He called on the protesters to examine their own consciences and devote their energies to the elimination of racial discrimination and religious intolerance still practiced in some of the "most advanced" countries concerned with the protest.[114]

King drafted a joint appeal for funds with Mrs. Roosevelt, the ACOA's International Chairman, and Rev. James Pike, US Chairman, to support the ACOA in February of 1958, declaring, "the struggle for equality among men continues in Montgomery, Alabama, in Johannesburg, South Africa. In America the battle is aided by public opinion, and to an extent federal action. In South Africa the government itself has fostered a short-sighted doctrine of apartheid."[115] King explained that the ACOA was one of the chief organizations actively helping the victims of the racist government policy, and had raised $35,000 in 1957 through its defense fund. Requesting financial support, King urged, "the struggle must continue against the forces of apartheid; it cannot be lost in South Africa and it must not be lost here."[116]

King had a broad vision for a brotherhood of man, one that became even more focused shortly after his return from India in 1959. The poverty he had seen in India touched King deeply, and as he stood watching the wretched conditions, he asked, "Can we in America stand idly by and not be concerned? The answer is an emphatic 'No,' because the destiny of America is tied up with the destiny of India. So long as India or any other nation is insecure, America can never be totally secure. Therefore we must use our vast resources of wealth to give aid to these undeveloped nations."[117] King went on to state a tenet which became an oft-repeated part of his philosophy for life: "For you see, in the final analysis this dimension of breadth means that you recognize that all life is interrelated; so no nation or individual is independent. We are interdependent. We are involved in a single process. We are caught in an inescapable network of mutuality."[118]

113. *Christian Science Monitor*, December 13, 1957.

114. Ibid.

115. James A. Pike and Martin Luther King Jr. to the Members and Supporters of the American Committee on Africa, February 25, 1958, King Center Library and Archive, Atlanta, GA.

116. Ibid.

117. King, Martin Luther, Jr., "The Dimensions of a Complete Life," address at Orchestra Hall, Chicago, IL, April 19, 1959, King Papers. Box 1, September 1, 1958–December 11, 1960, King Center Library and Archive, Atlanta, GA.

118. Ibid.

King penned yet another fundraising letter for the ACOA in 1959. He pointed out that although he was well acquainted with racial problems in the US, South Africa's difficulties were compelling. King spoke of hundreds of Africans imprisoned, their families impoverished. This fundraising exercise was part of an effort to bolster the organization's South African Defense Fund, which provided legal assistance to those detained. King reminded donors that the ACOA was the only organization actively trying to channel American aid in support of Africa's struggle for greater democracy.[119]

King further showed his support for the struggle against apartheid when he wrote to Chief Luthuli in South Africa. This followed a visit by King's good friend, Dr. G. McLeod Bryan, to that country to meet Luthuli. King said, "May I say that I too have admired you tremendously from a distance. I only regret that circumstances and special divisions have made it impossible for us to meet. But I admire your great witness and your dedication to the cause of freedom and human dignity. You have stood amid persecution, abuse, and oppression with a dignity and calmness of spirit seldom paralleled in human history. One day all of Africa will be proud of your achievement."[120] Dr. King also sent him a copy of his book, *Stride Toward Freedom,* having learned that Chief Luthuli expressed interest to Dr. Bryan. It is important to note that King wished to have confirmation that the book was received, no doubt conscious of the censorship that prevailed in South Africa.[121]

In "Pilgrimage to Nonviolence," which was published in *Christian Century* on April 13, 1960, King reflected on the factors leading to his commitment to nonviolence as both a practice and a philosophy of life. He explained that the experience in Montgomery clarified his thinking on the question of nonviolence such that "as the days unfolded I became more and more convinced of the power of nonviolence," to the extent that it became "more than a method to which I gave intellectual consent; it became a commitment to way of life."[122] Furthermore, King perceived these times as "exciting," for the old order was being discarded, or as he put it, "old systems

---

119. Martin Luther King Jr. to the American Committee on Africa, 1959, Martin Luther King Jr. American Committee on Africa Collection, Amistad Center, Tulane University. See also Baldwin, *Toward the Beloved Community,* 19.

120. Martin Luther King Jr. to Albert Luthuli, December 8, 1959, Groutville, South Africa, King Papers. Box 1, September 1, 1958–December 11, 1960, King Center Library and Archive, Atlanta, GA. See also Baldwin, *Toward the Beloved Community,* 21.

121. Ibid.

122. King, "Pilgrimage to Nonviolence," 439–41.

of exploitation and oppression are passing away and new systems of justice and equality are being born."[123]

On April 19, 1961, King delivered a speech titled "The Church on the Frontier of Racial Tension." He referred to his visit to Africa in 1957, when only seven countries had yet gained their independence, and he now marveled that this number had already increased to twenty-seven. The old order of colonialism was crumbling, but not without resistance in places like Johannesburg, in northern and southern Rhodesia, in Nairobi, Kenya, and especially in African countries that had not yet won their independence.[124] King, like Luthuli, saw that the church had a significant role to play, and not merely a political one, but moral as well. As the moral guardian of society, the church could not evade "its responsibility in this very tense period of transition."[125] King had the foresight to see that the world was rapidly becoming a global village and that decisions made at the national level could have international ramifications. A dilemma for King was that far too much of the national budget in the US was expended on military bases around the world "rather than establishing bases of genuine concern and understanding."[126]

King saw the cross-fertilization of ideas and influences between Africans and African Americans as tremendously important in establishing this kind of world understanding. As he explained, "The liberation struggle in Africa has been the greatest single international influence on American Negro students," because "if their African brothers can break the bonds of colonialism, surely the America Negro can break Jim Crow."[127] Visits by African leaders to black college campuses were greatly encouraged. King noted that "African leaders such as President Kwame Nkrumah[128] of Ghana, Governor-General Nnamdi Azikiwe[129] of Nigeria, Tom Mboya[130] of Kenya,

123. Ibid.

124. King, "Frontier of Racial Tension," April 19, 1961, King Center Library and Archives, Atlanta, GA.

125. Ibid.

126. Ibid.

127. King, Martin Luther, Jr., "Speech Regarding the Influence of African Movements on US Students," May 1962, King Papers, Box 3, January–December 1962, King Center Library and Archive, Atlanta, GA.

128. President Kwame Nkrumah (September 21, 1909–April 27, 1972) was the leader of Ghana and its former state, the Gold Coast, from 1951 to 1966 through the nation's transition from British colonial rule. He was also a supporter and founder of the Organisation of African Unity.

129. Benjamin Nnamdi Azikiwe (November 16, 1904–May 11, 1996) became the first President of Nigeria following independence from the United Kingdom in 1960.

130. Tom Mboya (August 15, 1930–July 5, 1969) was a member of the Kenya

and Dr. Hastings Banda[131] of Nyasaland are popular heroes on most Negro campuses."[132] Accordingly, many black college groups demonstrated when Congo leader Patrice Lumumba[133] was assassinated. The newspapers, King claimed, were mistaken when they interpreted these outbursts as "communist-inspired." Rather, they were largely due to black youths' impatience at seeing change taking place so rapidly in Africa and other parts of the world, yet comparatively slowly in the South.[134]

Meanwhile, in South Africa, after a successful speaking tour in May of 1959, Luthuli was confined to his village and banned from all public gatherings for five years under the Suppression of Communism Act. Later, when he was in Johannesburg giving evidence at the Treason Trial in March of 1960, the government declared a state of emergency. Chief Luthuli and two thousand other leaders of the ANC and the trade union movement were arrested in a move that coincided with the banning of the ANC after forty-eight years of legal existence. Despite this authoritarian nationalist government's systematic persecution, the Chief was not silenced. Visitors from all over the world beat a track to his isolated farm at Groutville.[135] In February of 1961, Norwegian Socialist leaders nominated Luthuli for the Nobel Prize in recognition that the Chief was more than a South African leader—he was an international statesman concerned with world peace, ending the Cold War, and freeing Africa and Asia from colonialism.[136] Luthuli's use of nonviolent methods, he said in 1959, "one is not guided by pacifist considerations but by practical considerations."[137] He went on to explain, "it is not in the nature of man to submit forever to serfdom."[138] In a foreboding warning, Luthuli added, "if the oppressed people of South Africa ever came

---

African National Union (KANU) and served as the Minister of Economic Planning and Development under Jomo Kenyatta.

131. Hastings Kamuzu Banda (February 1898–November 25, 1997) led Malawi and its former colonial state, Nyasaland, from 1961 to 1994.

132. King, Martin Luther, Jr., "Speech Regarding the Influence of African Movements on US Students," address in May 1962, King Papers, Box 3, January–December 1962, King Center Library and Archive, Atlanta, GA.

133. Patrice Lumumba (July 2, 1925–February 11, 1961) became the first democratically elected leader of the Republic of the Congo after winning independence from Belgium in 1960, but was assassinated on February 11, 1961.

134. King, "Influence of African Movements on US Students," May 1962, King Center Library and Archive, Atlanta, GA.

135. "Man of the People," 11–12.

136. "South Africa: Prize and Prejudice," 1–3.

137. Luthuli, "Man of the People," 21.

138. Ibid.

to indulge in violent rage, that would be a reaction against the policy of the government in suppressing the people."[139]

On December 5, 1961, Luthuli and his wife flew from Durban to Oslo to accept the Nobel Peace Prize, and upon his arrival he received a warm message from President John F. Kennedy: "I have been moved by the award to you of the 1960 Nobel Peace Prize, and I join with many others from all parts of the world in extending sincere congratulations to you. This high recognition of your past and continuing efforts in the cause of justice and the advancement through peaceful means of the brotherhood of man is applauded by free men everywhere."[140] On December 10, 1961, Luthuli voiced his understanding of the award: "For my part, I am deeply conscious of the added responsibility which this award entails. I have the feeling that I have been made answerable for the future of the people of South Africa, for if there is no peace for the majority of them there is no peace for any one."[141] He spoke about the threefold significance of the award, describing it as a tribute to his humble contribution to finding a peaceful solution to racism, a democratic declaration of support for those striving for liberty in South Africa, and as a genuine recognition for the efforts of African people over half a century to establish a society based on merit rather than race in fixing "the position of the individual in the life of the nation."[142]

Luthuli, like King, was prophetic in his pronouncements that Africa acting in cooperation with other nations "is man's last hope for a mediation between East and West," and that such an alliance "is qualified to demand of the great powers to 'turn the swords into ploughshares' [Isa 2:4], because two-thirds of mankind is hungry and illiterate; to engage human energy, human skill and human challenge in the service of peace."[143] It is interesting to consider how Chief Luthuli viewed the attitude of the church in South Africa towards the demands of the blacks. He asserted that "we in South Africa were way down below in our thinking, not only as nationalists but as church leaders."[144] Furthermore, similarly to King, Luthuli blamed the church for ignoring its duty to care for people throughout their lives, asking incredulously, "how can you wipe out man's political ambitions and desires

---

139. Ibid.

140. Quoted in ibid., 51.

141. Luthuli, "Nobel Lecture: Africa and Freedom" address at Oslo, Norway, December 11, 1961, quoted in Benson, *Chief Albert Lutuli*, 52.

142. Ibid., 52–53.

143. Ibid., 56–57.

144. Ibid., 13.

and say you are developing human personality—how can you?"[145] Luthuli and King were also cognizant of the role the WCC could play in the elimination of apartheid in South Africa. In his Nobel Lecture on December 11, 1961, Luthuli urged Christians to take heed of the WCC Conference decision made at Cottesloe in 1960, "which gave a clear lead on the mission of our church in our day," adding that "our progress in this field has been in spite of and not mainly because of the government."[146] The church in South Africa, he claimed, was belatedly awakening "to take seriously the words of its Founder who said: 'I came that they might have life and have it more abundantly' [John 10:10]."[147] Following this stint on the world stage, Luthuli was silenced by the South African government under the Sabotage Act in December of 1961.

Martin Luther King Jr. made a joint appeal with Chief Albert Luthuli, in "Letter to Americans" in November of 1962. The letter asserted that "as each day passes, life under apartheid grows more difficult. Our very action meets the fierce repression of the South African Government. Our people, living under appalling conditions of poverty and hunger, find their protest movements banned, their leaders in jail or exile."[148] And even more ominous was the official threat to life "under the new 'Sabotage' Act, namely, to challenge segregation is to risk the death penalty. Under such conditions it is not too much to say that twelve million of my people look to you, for we cannot win equality without the help of the outside world."[149] In their appeal for action against apartheid under the auspices of the ACOA, Luthuli and King outlined the consequences of a 1957 unprecedented "Declaration of Conscience" which was issued by more than one hundred leaders around the world. The South African government took action as follows:

- BANNED the African National Congress and the Pan African Congress, the principle protest organizations, and jailed their leaders;

- COERCED the press into strict pro-government censorship and made it almost impossible for new anti-apartheid publications to exist;

145. Ibid.

146. Luthuli, Albert, "For Freedom in South Africa," address at Oslo, Norway, December 11, 1961, text of Nobel Lecture, British Library, London.

147. Ibid.

148. Luthuli, Albert, and Martin Luther King Jr., "Letter to Americans," distributed by the American Committee on Africa with the "An Appeal for Action Against Apartheid," campaign flyer, November 4, 1962, New York, 1–4, King Center Library and Archive, Atlanta, GA. See also http://anc.org.za/show.php?id=4743.

149. Ibid.

- ESTABLISHED an arms industry, more than tripled the military budget, distributed small arms to the white population, enlarged the army, created an extensive white civilian militia;

- ACTIVATED total physical race separation by establishing the first Bantusan in the Transkei with the aid of emergency police regulations;

- LEGALLY DEFINED protest against apartheid as an act of "sabotage"—an offence ultimately punishable by death;

- PERPETUATED its control through terrorism and violence.[150]

Both King and Luthuli saw the deepening tensions leading towards two alternatives. At one level, extensive persecution could trigger violence, revolt, and racial war. However, the resulting mass racial extermination would destroy any potential for interracial unity in South Africa and elsewhere. The preferred solution for both leaders was the "chosen path of disciplined resistance," based on a "transition to a society based upon equality for all without regard to color."[151] Many prominent Americans signed Luthuli and King's joint statement as part of a public campaign for sanctions against South Africa. King and Luthuli were conscious that both internal and external pressure would be needed to force the South African government to accede to the demands of the non-white majority. Both leaders requested all men of goodwill to take action against apartheid as follows:

- Hold meetings and demonstrations on December 10, Human Rights Day;

- Urge your church, union, lodge, or club to observe this day as one of protest;

- Urge your Government to support economic sanctions;

- Write to the United Nations urging adoption of a resolution calling for international isolation of South Africa;

- Don't buy South Africa's products;

- Don't trade or invest in South Africa;

- Translate public opinion into public action by explaining facts to all peoples, to groups to which you belong, and to countries of which you are citizens until an effective international quarantine of apartheid is established.[152]

150. Ibid.
151. Ibid.
152. Ibid.

According to Lewis V. Baldwin, public response to the King and Luthuli's appeal was strong, possibly since Luthuli was a recent Nobel Prize recipient, and King a prominent international civil rights leader. Approximately 150 world leaders signed it.[153]

In what was to become one of King's most famous works, the "Letter from Birmingham Jail," he again highlighted the connection between the continents, declaring that "oppressed people cannot remain oppressed forever. The yearning for freedom eventually manifests itself." The African American, in his estimation, "has been caught up by the Zeitgeist, and with his black brothers of Africa and his brown and yellow brothers of Asia, South America and the Caribbean, the US Negro is moving with a sense of great urgency toward the promised land of racial justice."[154] King felt that life was unfulfilled without a common understanding among men. He referred to it as "the interrelated structure of reality," and he so wonderfully put it, "for some strange reason I can never be what I ought to be until you are what you ought to be, and you can never be what you ought to be until I am what I ought to be."[155]

On May 28, 1964, King spoke at the Convocation on Equal Justice Under Law hosted by the NAACP Legal Defense Fund, where, inspired in part by events abroad, he stressed the fierce urgency of the moment in making equality a reality for all Americans. Showing frustration at the lack of progress in the US, he looked to Asia, Africa, and South America with admiration, for "in India, Indonesia, Ghana, and Brazil, to mention but a few states which together contain almost a billion humans, the right to vote has been exercised even by illiterate peasants in primitive villages still ringed by jungle."[156] Furthermore, great transformations had occurred in Africa, "where Negroes have formed states, govern themselves, and function in world tribunals with dignity and effectiveness."[157] King lamented the lack of commitment in the US to freedom and equality. It probably seemed to him that the perceived "success" of the civil rights movement had a far greater impact overseas, where it coincided with the demise of colonialism.

---

153. Baldwin, *Toward the Beloved Community*, 37.

154. King, "Letter from Birmingham Jail," 771.

155. King, "American Dream," February 10, 1963, King Center Library and Archive, Atlanta, GA.

156. King, Martin Luther, Jr., "The World's March Towards Human Rights," address at the Convocation of Equal Justice Under Law of the NAACP Defense Fund, Americana Hotel, New York, May 28, 1964, King Papers, Box 6, May 30–October 30, 1964, King Center Library and Archive, Atlanta, GA.

157. Ibid.

While on route to Oslo to receive the Nobel Prize in December of 1964, King told his London audience "we feel a powerful sense of identification with those in the far more deadly struggle for freedom in South Africa."[158] Paying respect to Chief Luthuli for his leadership, King recognized that Luthuli's "nonviolence and restraint was only met by increasing violence from the state, increasing repression culminating in the shootings of Sharpeville and all that happened since."[159] King mourned the fact that great leaders like Nelson Mandela and Robert Sobukwe were among the hundreds wasting away in Robben Island prison.[160] King drew attention to the "great mass of South Africans denied their humanity, their dignity, denied opportunity, denied all human rights," to remind his American and British audience of their "unique responsibility."[161] For it was, King claimed, "through our investments, through our government's failure to act decisively, [we] who are guilty of bolstering up the South African tyranny."[162] Calling for action to bring down this monstrous government, King urged his listeners to "join in the one form of nonviolent action that could bring freedom and justice to South Africa—the action which African leaders have appealed for—in a massive move for economic sanctions."[163]

In an interview that appeared in the January 1965 edition of *Playboy* magazine, King was asked whether there was "a sense of identity between the emergence of black Africa and the Negro's struggle for freedom in America."[164] Noting slow progress at home, King saw changes overseas as far more ambitious and successful, for "the Negro across America, looking at his television set, sees black statesmen voting in the United Nations on vital world issues."[165] And to add insult to injury, King observed that "the Negro hears of black Kings and potentates ruling in palaces, while he remains ghettoized in urban slums."[166] So from the land of the free and the home of the brave, King asked for help from abroad, saying, "Africans should use the influence of their government to make it clear that the struggle of their

---

158. King, Martin Luther, Jr., "Address on South African Independence," at London, December 7, 1964, quoted in Baldwin, *Towards the Beloved Community*, 31–32.

159. Ibid.

160. Ibid.

161. Ibid.

162. Ibid.

163. Ibid.

164. Haley, "Playboy Interview," 65–78.

165. Ibid.

166. Ibid.

brothers in the US is part of a world-wide struggle."[167] This is a clear indication that King appreciated how much the American civil rights movement had to learn from tremendous strides being made in African and Asian countries that had attained their independence.

So it was that "Remaining Awake through a Great Revolution" became an apt title for King's Commencement address at Oberlin College in August of 1965, when he reminded his audience that "whenever men are assembled today, the cry is always the same, 'We want to be free.'"[168] He exhorted the graduates to remain awake through the social revolution. King had the ability to see that the tremendous changes taking place worldwide in the second half of the twentieth century required a complete change of mindset, and he was way ahead of any of his contemporaries in promulgating the message.

King condemned the South African government in no uncertain terms on Human Rights Day, December 10, 1965, when he cried out: "The South African government to make the white supreme has had to reach into the past and revive the nightmarish ideology and practices of Nazism. We are witnessing a recrudescence of the barbarism which murdered more humans than any war in history. In South Africa today, all opposition to white supremacy is condemned as communism, and in its name, due process is destroyed."[169] King further decried the fact that this "medieval segregation is organized with twentieth century efficiency and drive; a sophisticated form of slavery is imposed by a minority upon a majority which is kept in grinding poverty; the dignity of human personality is defiled; and world opinion is arrogantly defined."[170] King condemned South Africa's disregard for world opinion, explaining the government's position as "We have become a powerful industrial economy; we are too strong to be defeated by paper resolutions of world tribunals; we are immune to protest and to economic reprisals. We are invulnerable to opposition from within or without; if our evil offends you, you will have to learn to live with it."[171]

King rebuked the US for helping sustain the South African government through American investments in the motor and rubber industries, for extending forty million dollars in loans, for purchasing gold and other minerals mined by back slave labor, for providing South Africa with a sugar quota, for maintaining three tracking stations there, and for providing

167. Ibid.

168. King, "Remaining Awake," August 1, 1965, King Center Library and Archive, Atlanta, GA.

169. King, Martin Luther, Jr., "Let My People Go," address at Hunter College, New York, December 10, 1965, quoted in Baldwin, *Single Garment of Destiny*, 39–44.

170. Ibid.

171. Ibid.

them with a prestigious US nuclear reactor, fueled by uranium provided by the US.[172] King appealed to the international potential of nonviolence (something which has been overlooked in assessing his impact worldwide) to bring down the government of South Africa, saying, "the time has come to utilize nonviolence fully through a massive international boycott which would include the USSR, Great Britain, France, the United States, Germany, and Japan."[173] Calling on the moral righteousness of their cause, he urged, "millions of people can personally give expression to their abhorrence of the world's racism through such a far-flung boycott. No nation professing a concern for man's dignity could avoid assuming its obligations if people of all states and races were to adopt a firm stand."[174] King spoke as a truly international statesman when he implored a worldwide audience to take action, for "the time has come to build an international alliance of peoples of all nations against racism."[175] King went on to emphasize the ancestral connection between Africans and African Americans, arguing that by tapping into this diaspora, the nonviolent struggle for equality for all could surely be an international phenomenon. As King concluded, "the whole human race will benefit when it ends the abomination that has diminished the stature of man for so long."[176]

Needless to say, King received several invitations to South Africa, but all were contingent on obtaining a visa for the visit. On February 9, 1966, King wrote to the South African Embassy in New Orleans, LA, informing them that he had been invited to lecture in South Africa by two outstanding student groups there. The National Union of South African Students had invited him to address the 1966 Congress in July of that year, and the Student's Visiting Lecturers Organization at the University of Cape Town had invited him to deliver the T. B. Davie Memorial Lecture. King had accepted both invitations, and explained that he had a great interest in visiting South Africa in order to "exchange cultural and human rights concerns."[177] King's visit was to be solely as a lecturer, but he also expressed a wish to meet with some religious leaders. King was likely aware that he was persona non grata to the South African government. It was reported in the *New York Times*, on March 25, 1966, that King had been denied a visa to visit South Africa. Con-

172. Ibid.
173. Ibid.
174. Ibid.
175. Ibid.
176. Ibid.

177. Martin Luther King Jr. to the South African Embassy, February 9, 1966, King Center Library and Archive, Atlanta, GA. See also Baldwin, *Toward the Beloved Community*, 61.

sul General N. M. Nel. of South Africa, informed that Dr. King had reported the denial, responded with "I think you can take that as true." He declined to go into any further detail. It was reported that King regretted "South Africa's decision, as he had stressed in his application that his visit would be only as a lecturer."[178] In a special to the *New York Times*, King said the refusal was "an expression of the continuing policies of totalitarianism in South Africa. It is an expression that democracy is not alive at all in that country."[179] Indeed, Lewis V. Baldwin's research shows that in the years from 1966 to 1968, King found it more and more difficult to influence developments in South Africa from afar. Few African American intellectuals of his stature shared his interest, and the civil rights movement in the US consumed the interests of the majority of his constituents.[180]

Although King never succeeded in obtaining a visa to visit South Africa, his work with the civil rights movement was well known in that country. In July of 1966, the *Star* reported that Rev. Dale White, an Anglican priest from Roodepoort, South Africa, and Mr. Bode Wegerif, an executive of a Johannesburg publishing organization, had excited the interest of security police by distributing, at their own expense, a gramophone record of one of King's speeches. No less than twelve hundred churches and community leaders received copies of the record. It was reported that King's speech was directed to Americans who were "sleeping through a revolution." The church, he said, must take much of the blame, for "in the midst of a nation rife with racial animosity . . . the church has failed Christ miserably."[181] The speech, although delivered before an American audience and often repeated, contained an important message for mankind. The church, said King, "must urge its worshippers to develop a world perspective. Man's scientific ingenuity has made of this world a neighborhood and yet through our moral and ethical failure we have failed to make it a brotherhood."[182] King had also included one of his favorite quotes: "we are all tied in the single garment of destiny in the inescapable network of mutuality," which has great relevance in this book, for my discussion focuses not only on the civil rights leader, but also on South African activists and the WCC as well. In a move that would be hard for the South African regime to stomach, King asked the church to "reaffirm the essential immorality of racial segregation.

178. *New York Times*, March 25, 1966, 4.

179. Ibid.

180. Baldwin, *Towards the Beloved Community*, 50.

181. Walker, Martin, "What Luther King Said," *Star*, July 6, 1966, Leader Page, Newspaper Clippings, 1966, 127.28, King Center Library and Archive, Atlanta, GA.

182. Ibid.

It is not only politically untenable, not only sociologically unsound, but it is immoral, wrong, and sinful."[183] King insisted that the church must become more active in its efforts "to get of rid of the notion that there are superior and inferior races. We must see the urgency of now." Should the church fail to take action, King warned, "we will have to repent in this generation not merely for the vitriolic words and the violent actions of the bad people, but for the appalling silence and indifference of the good people who sit around and say, 'Wait.'"[184] With such rousing rhetoric, King ensured that he would remain an unwelcome visitor to the South African government.

Early in 1967, King evoked more suspicion as he spoke out more forthrightly on the Vietnam War, for he saw that the US was preoccupied with the conflict to the detriment of other issues, saying, "honesty impels me to admit that our power has often made us arrogant . . . We are arrogant in our contention that we have some sacred mission to protect people from totalitarian rule, while we make little use of our power to end the evils of South Africa and Rhodesia, while we are in fact supporting dictatorship with guns and money under the guise of fighting communism."[185]

South Africa was brought to the forefront again in "A Knock at Midnight," King's sermon at All Saints Community Church on June 25, 1967. He described South Africa as a place where "vicious inhuman apartheid practices" were sanctioned by and large by the "Dutch Reform Protestant Church," a practice that must have puzzled and incensed many in the WCC as well.[186] He then referred to his good friend Chief Luthuli, "that great black leading Christian" who had "knocked on the door of the church of South Africa" to find that the response was always the same: "Get away from the door. We don't have time to bother with you, we're busy reciting our creedal system."[187] King highlighted apartheid as the scourge of South Africa again on June 7, 1968, in a speech titled "What Are Your New Year Resolutions?" in which he called into question the lip service that Christians sometimes give to their duty to bring about a better world. He went on to castigate the church for its failings: "But the problem is that the church has sanctioned every evil in the world. Whether it's racism, or whether it's the evils of monopoly-capitalism, or whether it's the evils of militarism. And this is

183. Ibid.

184. Ibid.

185. King, "Casualties of the War in Vietnam," February 25, 1967, King Center Library and Archive, Atlanta, GA.

186. King, Martin Luther, Jr., "A Knock at Midnight," address at All Saints Community Church, Los Angeles, CA, June 25, 1967, King Papers, Box 13, June 25, 1967, King Center Library and Archive, Atlanta, GA.

187. Ibid.

why these things continue to exist in the world today."[188] Days before King was assassinated, his "Doubts and Certainties" interview was aired by the BBC in London. When asked whether his activities in the US was part of a world pattern, King paraphrased Victor Hugo[189] in replying, "there is nothing more powerful in all the world than an ideal whose time has come," and he saw that ideal as "freedom in human dignity" in tandem with a "freedom explosion all over the world."[190] King explained that the example of the civil rights movement in the US was "a part of that worldwide struggle to achieve justice and freedom and human dignity."[191] King was quite clear in his condemnation of where the blame for racism lay, saying, "the whole doctrine of white supremacy, the whole doctrine of racism . . . came into being through the white race and the exploitation of the colored peoples of the world."[192]

188. King, Martin Luther, Jr., "What Are Your New Year's Resolutions?" address at Ebenezer Baptist Church, Atlanta, GA, January 7, 1968, King Papers, Box 14, King Center Library and Archive, Atlanta, GA.

189. Victor Hugo (February 2, 1802–May 22, 1885) was a French poet, playwright, novelist, and human rights advocate during the French Romantic movement whose best-known works are the novels *Les Miserables* and *The Hunchback of Notre Dame*.

190. King, "Doubts and Certainties Link," April 4, 1968, King Center Library and Archives, Atlanta, GA.

191. Ibid.

192. Ibid.

5

Breaking the Conspiracy of Silence

Martin Luther King Jr., the WCC, and the Racial Implications of the Vietnam War

MARTIN LUTHER KING JR., together with the WCC, strongly opposed the Vietnam War. This chapter explores the buildup of King's opposition to the war beginning in March of 1965, his eventual success in persuading the SCLC to back him wholeheartedly, and his continuous condemnation of the conflict from 1965 to 1967. Beginning in 1966, the WCC under Eugene Carson Blake fought courageously to bring about a peaceful resolution, and the organization's various speeches and pronouncements resonated with King's opposition to the war, indicating that there may have been a cross-fertilization of ideas between the two leaders.

King's radicalism manifested itself clearly in his close connection to the WCC, of which the NCC was a major player. Its predecessor council, the Federal Council of Churches under the chairmanship of John Foster Dulles recommended radical proposals to bring about world peace in *Time* magazine on March 16, 1942:

> A world government . . . strong immediate limitation on national sovereignty. International control of all armies and navies. A universal system of money. Worldwide freedom of immigration. Progressive elimination of all tariffs and quota restrictions on world trade. A democratically controlled bank . . . A new

order of economic life is both imminent and imperative through voluntary cooperation within the framework of democracy or through explosive political revolution.[1]

The WCC was also quite clear in its condemnation of war from its inception in 1949, insisting that "war as a method of settling disputes is incompatible with the teaching and example of our Lord Jesus Christ. The part war plays in our international life is a sin against God and a degradation of man."[2]

Lewis V. Baldwin argues that King engaged the WCC, the World Convention of Churches of Christ, and other Christian communities worldwide by challenging them to "first discern what God is calling" them "to do in the presence of international conflict" and to make their "witness known, not merely through pronouncements but by the submission of their bodies as living witness to the truth of Christ."[3] David L. Lewis' biography on King further shows that he supported world peace among nations as early as the summer of 1959. In answer to a question put to him by the editor of an Italian magazine, King stated that if he were to add a chapter to *Stride Toward Freedom*, it would be concerned with adapting nonviolence "not merely to the local level in struggles between relatively small groups but even between nations."[4] I argue that King was an antimilitarist guided by Christian socialist principles who both influenced and was influenced by the WCC. As King once said, "I am no doctrinaire pacifist. I have tried to embrace a realistic pacifism. Moreover, I see the pacifist position not as sinless, but as a lesser evil in the circumstances. Therefore, I do not claim to be free from the moral dilemmas that the Christian non-pacifist confronts. But I am convinced that the church cannot remain silent while mankind faces the threat of being plunged into the abyss of nuclear annihilation."[5]

To put this chapter into context, let us turn to Penny M. Von Eschen, who draws our attention to the "most profound relationship" between international and domestic politics.[6] She declares that when the State Department revoked Paul Robeson's[7] passport, it clearly revealed that the

---

1. Dulles, "Religion: American Malvern," 43–48.

2. Quoted in Eskidjian and Estabrooks, *Overcoming Violence*, 6. See also "The Maldon Institute Report," June 7, 1999, 1–2.

3. King, Martin Luther, Jr., "Revolution and Redemption," quoted in Baldwin, *Voice of Conscience*, 209.

4. Quoted in Lewis, *King: A Biography*, 302

5. King, "Pilgrimage to Nonviolence," 439–41.

6. Von Eschen, "Challenging Cold War Habits," 627.

7. Paul Leroy Robeson (April 9, 1898–January 23, 1976) was an African American

government regarded anticolonialism and civil rights activities within the United States as interlocking security issues, and this act signaled a critical shift by making it clear that the US government would not tolerate criticism of its foreign policy by civil rights leaders. King was very aware of this policy, and government documents confirm that King was convinced his own passport would be revoked if he decided to make a trip to Paris for talks on the Vietnam conflict.[8]

No visible religious opposition to the Vietnam War occurred with any regularity prior to 1965. This changed with the sustained bombing over North Vietnam and the use of American combat troops on the ground. Clergy and Laymen Concerned about Vietnam (CALCAV)[9] was formed in late 1965 to help influence public opinion, limit government options in the war, and to defend the right to dissent. The Cold War played a major role in this regard, for Americans viewed their global antagonists as evil, thereby equating their own strategies with godliness, and consequently, the nation was blinded to its own imperfections.[10] In fact, the church was brought on board early in the Cold War, when President Dwight Eisenhower christened them "citadels of faith in freedom and human dignity," and "our matchless armor in the worldwide struggle against forces of godless tyranny and oppression."[11] It was during Eisenhower's administration that Asian experts were purged from the State Department, victims of "McCarthy hysteria." In the absence of their "nuanced insights," remaining advisers "badly misread China's objectives," underestimated Ho's nationalism, and failed to grasp the poor relationship between North Vietnam and China.[12] Whether one accepts this thesis or not, it certainly makes King's objections to the war all the more compelling.

---

singer and actor who embraced the civil rights movement. His public stances on controversial issues of the day, including Communism, compromised his career.

8. Edgar Hoover, Director of the FBI, to President Lyndon Johnson; Dean Rusk, Secretary of State; and Richard Helms, Director of the CIA, "Martin Luther King and Young Invited to 5/14/67 Paris Meeting of US Movement," May 13, 1967, 1986 Fiche #76 Document #000866, Federal Bureau of Investigation, http://www.aavw.org/special_features/govdocs_fbi_abstract01_full.html.

9. Clergy and Laymen Concerned About Vietnam (CALCAV) was formed in New York in October of 1965, when more than one hundred clergy members debated how they could oppose government policy on the Vietnam War. Martin Luther King Jr. was the only representative from the South and one of the few blacks in attendance. In April of 1967, King used CALCAV as a platform for his controversial speech "Beyond Vietnam."

10. Hall, *Because of Their Faith*, 6.

11. Friedland, *Lift Up Your Voice*, 13.

12. Quoted in Cuddy, "Vietnam: Mr. Johnson's?" 351–74.

King's opposition to the Vietnam War prior to 1967 has been glossed over by many authors, and his antiwar comments have been largely seen as secondary to the main civil rights campaign. For example, Peter J. Ling comments in his introduction to *Martin Luther King Jr.*, "a close examination of King's decision to speak out against the Vietnam War exposed both his initial reluctance (of which he remained deeply and disproportionately ashamed), and his limited options."[13] In *King on Vietnam and Beyond*, Henry E. Darby and Margaret N. Rowley argue that "King's speaking out against the Vietnam conflict was not spontaneous; he deliberated for two years before doing so."[14] Another example of how King's stance on the war in 1965 and 1966 has been downplayed can be found in Robert Cook's *Sweet Land of Liberty?* as well: "In early 1967 King decided to end his near public silence on the Vietnam War. It was a bold decision, for he knew that in speaking out he was bound to further alienate the Johnson administration."[15]

KING'S EARLY OPPOSITION TO THE VIETNAM WAR

King outlined his opposition to war in 1959 in an article titled "The Social Organization of Nonviolence," written in answer to a charge by Robert Williams,[16] a critic of nonviolence, "that he was inconsistent in his struggle against war and too weak-kneed to protest about nuclear war."[17] King responded, "I state that repeatedly, in public addresses and in my writings, I have unequivocally declared my hatred for this most colossal of all evils, and I have condemned any organizer of war, regardless of his rank or nationality."[18] In a point that King was to return to regularly in the coming years, he outlined his objections to nuclear weapons: "I have signed numerous statements and have authorized publication of my name in advertisements, appearing in the largest circulation newspapers in the country, without concern that it was then 'unpopular' to do so."[19]

13. Ling, *Martin Luther King*, 4.

14. Darby and Rowley, "King on Vietnam," 249.

15. Cook, *Sweet Land of Liberty?* 208.

16. Robert Williams (February 26, 1925–October 15, 1996) presided over the Monroe, NC, chapter of the National Association for the Advancement of Colored People (NAACP) in the late 50s and early 60s. He fled white mob violence in 1961 to Cuba, where he wrote *Negroes with Guns*, a book that influenced Back Panther Party founder Huey P. Newton.

17. Williams, "Can Negroes Afford to be Pacifists?" 4–7.

18. King, "Social Organization of Nonviolence," 5–6.

19. Ibid.

King's acceptance speech for the Nobel Prize in December of 1964 further registered his opposition to war. He did not mention Vietnam by name, but argued that "man was not mere flotsam and jetsam in the river of life which surrounds him."[20] King also refused to "accept the view that mankind is so tragically bound to the starless midnight of racism and war that the bright daybreak of peace and brotherhood can never become a reality."[21] King opposed the arms race, warning, "I refuse to accept the cynical notion that nation after nation must spiral down a militaristic stairway into a hell of thermonuclear destruction."[22]

King spoke at Morehouse College on January 11, 1965, about the "evil of war," and recalling World War II, he asserted, "there may have been a time that we could have argued about the relative merits of war as a sort of negative good serving to block an evil force that comes into history like Hitler or some other force. Now with the destructive weapons of modern warfare, war cannot serve any good for anybody."[23] In the Cold War era, advanced weaponry in the hands of superpowers could escalate any conflict to the annihilation of all: "We must find some alternative to war in a day when Sputniks and Explorers are dashing through outer space and guided ballistic missiles are carving highways of death through the stratosphere, no nation can win the war."[24]

It is important to put this speech into the context of events surrounding the Vietnam War in late 1964 and early 1965. In November and December of 1964, Vietnamese guerrillas of the National Liberation Front (NLF) killed seven US advisers and wounded more than a hundred others.[25] Historian Stephen B. Oates writes that that President Johnson was incensed: "He wasn't going to let them shoot our boys out there, fire on our flag. He talked obsessively about Communist 'aggression' in Vietnam, about Munich and the lesson of appeasement, about how his enemies would call him 'a coward,' 'an unmanly man,' a 'Weakling!' if he let Ho Chi Minh[26] run through

20. King, "Nobel Prize Acceptance Speech" address at Oslo, Norway, December 10, 1964, quoted in King, *Testament of Hope*, 224–26.

21. Ibid.

22. Ibid.

23. King, Martin Luther Jr., "Address Delivered at Morehouse College Convocation," at Atlanta, GA, January 11, 1965, King Papers, Box 7, November 1, 1964–February 28, 1965, King Center Library and Archive, Atlanta, GA.

24. Ibid.

25. Oates, *Let the Trumpet Sound*, 374. The National Front for the Liberation of South Vietnam, also known as the Vietcong, was an insurgent organization in conflict with the Republic of Vietnam during the Vietnam War.

26. Ho Chi Minh (May 19, 1890–September 2, 1969) was a Vietnamese

the streets of Saigon."[27] The Johnson administration saw the war as holding the line against the influence of the Soviet Union and China in Southeast Asia. Meanwhile, King called for an alternative to war, insisting that "it is no longer the choice between violence and nonviolence. It is either nonviolence or non-existence."[28] He asked for a strengthening of the UN to prevent civilization plunging into the "abyss of annihilation."[29] On the other hand, Johnson, not known for polite language, showed his lack of confidence in a UN resolution to the conflict when he roared that "it couldn't pour piss out of a boot if the instructions were printed on the heel."[30] King acknowledged the complexity of the problem of disarmament and peace, advising that it was necessary for mankind to undergo a mental and spiritual reevaluation to achieve peace. Therefore, he counseled, "we will not achieve peace merely by engaging in a negative objection of war. It is not enough to say, we must not wage war, important as that happens to be. It is necessary to love peace and to sacrifice for it. We must concentrate not merely upon the negative expulsion of war but on the positive affirmation of peace."[31] King's words at Morehouse College confirm that King took the award of the Nobel Prize to heart in speaking out so passionately against war only one month later. As Garrow observes of King's Nobel acceptance speech, "he seemed to suggest that mass action be used to let all world leaders know that people across the globe were committed to ending war," and furthermore, "beyond racial justice, and beyond economic justice, the attainment of a lasting world peace was the great goal that lay before them."[32]

King was aware that protests directed against these authorities might well bring consequences: "When you stand up against entrenched evil, you must be prepared to suffer a little more. I cannot promise you that if you stand up against the evils of our day, you will not have some dark and agonizing moments."[33] King made his first direct reference to the Vietnam

---

revolutionary leader who defeated the French at Dien Bien Phu in 1954, after which he became President of North Vietnam. He later led the North Vietnamese in their bitter fight for reunification.

27. Oates, *Let the Trumpet Sound*, 374.

28. King, "Morehouse College Convocation," January 11, 1965, King Center Library and Archive, Atlanta, GA.

29. Ibid.

30. Oates, *Let the Trumpet Sound*, 374.

31. King, "Morehouse College Convocation," January 11, 1965, King Center Library and Archive, Atlanta, GA.

32. Garrow, *Bearing the Cross*, 365.

33. King, "Morehouse College Convocation," January 11, 1965, King Center Library and Archive, Atlanta, GA.

War on March 2, 1965, at Howard University in Washington, D.C., when he spoke on a standard theme, the three evils of racism, poverty, and violence. In a follow-up statement on March 6, he said, "the war in Vietnam is accomplishing nothing, uh [*sic*] I don't think violence can solve the problem. I think that we will gain more through dialogue than we can through monologue."[34] The war was escalating at this time. In February 1965, with the Vietcong pounding American outposts at Pleiku and Quinhon, Johnson's administration became convinced that the hazard-prone Saigon government was about to collapse. The first American combat troops landed at Da Nang, South Vietnam on March 8, 1965. As Oates explains, "the Americanization of the war took place with such stealth that people at home were hardly aware of it."[35]

Throughout the summer of 1965, King kept speaking out against the escalating war. The opportunity was now available to him to apply creative nonviolence to the world theater, and as he told his SCLC audience, "I'm not going to sit by and see the war escalate without saying something about it."[36] King's aides and advisers, including Bayard Rustin,[37] urged caution in speaking out so as not to alienate President Johnson and his administration.[38] However, King would not turn his course, and at a Virginia rally on July 2, he said, "It is worthless to talk about integrating if there is no world to integrate in. The war in Vietnam must be stopped."[39] Here again, he was mindful that the Vietnam War could precipitate a nuclear conflict between the superpowers.

King took the opportunity to protest again on the Los Angeles *Newsmakers* program in July of 1965. King was subjected to intensive questioning on a variety of subjects by the show's panel. King was asked about a statement he had made earlier in the month at an SCLC rally in Petersburg, VA, calling for a negotiated settlement of the war in Vietnam. This had provoked a response from James Farmer[40] of the Congress of Racial Equality

---

34. King, Martin Luther, Jr., "Statement on Vietnam," address given in Washington, DC, March 6, 1965, Box 8, King Papers, March–July 1965, King Center Library and Archive, Atlanta, GA.

35. Oates, *Let the Trumpet Sound*, 374.

36. Ibid., 375.

37. Bayard Rustin (March 17, 1912–August 24, 1987), a close confidant of Martin Luther King Jr., was a key player in the civil rights movement. He was the principal organizer of the March on Washington in August 1963.

38. Oates, *Let the Trumpet Sound*, 375.

39. King, *SCLC Newsletter: June–July 1965*, July 1, 1965, SCLC Papers, Box 130, King Center Library and Archives, Atlanta, GA.

40. James Farmer (January 12, 1920–July 9, 1999) served as the president of the

(CORE), who argued that involving the civil rights movement in foreign policy could fracture the black coalition. Roy Wilkins[41] of the NAACP, had also criticized King on *Face the Nation*, when he remarked, "We think we have enough Vietnam in Alabama to occupy our attention. We'll leave foreign policy to the United States, and enter our objections as citizens who know very little about it . . . we don't believe in dividing our energies; we don't have that many energies."[42] The interviewer put it to King whether he had second thoughts on his call for a negotiated settlement in Vietnam in view of this strong reaction. King acknowledged that Roy Wilkins and James Farmer had made good points, but emphasized the distinction between his role as a civil rights leader and as a minister of the gospel first and foremost, citing his obligations to the pastoral wellbeing of his flock.[43] The hosts then asked King whether he was concerned that his stance might alienate people who agreed with him on civil rights but disagreed with him on Vietnam, and he replied, "I don't think that this will happen. I'm sure there are many people who will disagree with me on this and disagree with others . . . In a real sense, there can be no peace in the world unless there's justice, and there can be no justice without peace. I think in a sense these problems are inextricably bound together."[44]

King was then asked if he had any intention of organizing demonstrations against the war, to which he answered, "I never said anything about organizing demonstrations around the Vietnam situation. I merely said that I will have to speak out on the issue, because it is a burning issue of our time."[45] From King's reply, we can see that he was navigating the water carefully, making sure the he did not go beyond the SCLC mandate that allowed him to speak out personally on the war, but not in his capacity as head of SCLC. Emphasizing the importance of the issue, King recalled the President's invitation to speak out: "I think as President Johnson said in his speech at John Hopkins University on Vietnam some months ago that there

---

Congress of Racial Equality (CORE), and was known for organizing the 1961 Freedom Rides to end the segregation of interstate buses.

41. Roy Wilkins (August 30, 1901–September 8, 1981) was the NAACP's Executive Secretary. He came under severe criticism from more militant civil rights activists for his moderate approach.

42. Roy Wilkins, interview by Martin Agronsky, *Face the Nation*, CBS, July 4, 1965, quoted in Martin Luther King Jr., interview by Maury Green, Paul Udell, and Saul Holbert, *Newsmakers*, KNXT-TV Los Angeles, July 10, 1965, King Papers, Box 8, March 1–July 31, 1965, King Center Library and Archives, Atlanta, GA.

43. King, interview by Green, Udell, and Holbert, *Newsmakers*, July 10, 1965, King Center Library and Archives, Atlanta, GA.

44. Ibid.

45. Ibid.

is room for healthy debate on this issue, and I'm sure that the people who cannot quite go along with my point of view wouldn't be alienated from the civil rights struggle."[46] As the summer of 1965 rolled out, Johnson was involving the United States more deeply in Vietnam. As journalist David Halberstam later wrote, US decision-makers "inched across the Rubicon without even admitting it," and the task of their press secretaries was "to misinform the public."[47]

King had built a reputation for himself as a peacemaker on the international stage, and invitations to participate in various conferences were extended to him. For example, Professor N. Matkovsky of the International Institute for Peace (IIP) in Vienna, Austria[48] wrote King in August of 1965 to express regret that he could not attend the World Congress for Peace, National Independence, and General Disarmament in Helsinki, Finland, assuring King that "for the 1,470 participants from 98 countries it would have been an unforgettable and inspiring experience to hear and work with the leader of an American movement that is destined to infuse the whole nation with the highest principles of morality and justice."[49] Professor Matkovsky drew King's attention to their shared sentiments on the lurking nightmare in Vietnam, saying, "as a result of the dangers inherent in the war in Vietnam, the overriding theme of the Helsinki Congress was to ensure for the people of this hapless land freedom to decide their future, and achieve this before the momentum of escalation spills over into a nuclear war on a world scale."[50] Matkovsky's letter acknowledged that Dr. Carlton Goodlett, an influential liberal from San Francisco, had read out a statement from King at the conference, which had been published in the *New York Times* on July 5, 1965, declaring that "the time had come for the civil rights movement to become involved in the problems of war. The war must be stopped."[51]

Throughout 1965, King was still seeking the full cooperation of the SCLC regarding his stance on the war. A resolution was passed at the Ninth Annual Convention held on August 9–13, 1965, stating that "the primary function of the organization was to secure full citizenship rights for the Negro

46. Ibid.

47. Quoted in Oates, *Let the Trumpet Sound*, 374–75.

48. The International Institute for Peace (IIP) is an international non-governmental organization (NGO) with consultative status at ECOSOC and UNESCO. It works in the interests of peace on a nonprofit basis.

49. N. Matkovsky, International Institute of Peace, to Martin Luther King Jr., August 6, 1965, SCLC Papers, Box 4:0, July–August, 1965, King Center Library and Archives, Atlanta, GA.

50. Ibid.

51. Ibid.

citizens of this country, and that our major contribution to world peace and brotherhood is to create a truly democratic society here in America."[52] The resolution made it clear where the SCLC's leadership stood in its opposition to the Vietnam War: "Our resources are not sufficient to assume the burden of two major issues in our society, we would therefore urge that the efforts of SCLC in mass demonstrations and action movements be confined to the question of racial brotherhood."[53] Following heated discussions between King and his supporters—including Levison,[54] Jones,[55] Wachtel,[56] and Rustin—with the board, the Committee on Resolutions report left King with some hope in conceding that "in the event of perilous escalation of the Vietnam conflict, we respect the right of Dr. King and the administrative committee to alter this course in the interest of the survival of mankind."[57] Garrow's research into the board's deliberations reveal that they recognized that "King's conscience compels him to express his concern" about Vietnam and "commend him for courageously expressing these concerns"[58]

On August 12, 1965, while the SCLC Convention was still ongoing, King issued a statement in Birmingham, saying, "few events in my lifetime have stirred my conscience and pained my heart as much as the present conflict which is raging in Vietnam. The day by day reports of villages destroyed and people left homeless raise burdensome questions within my conscience."[59] King took note of the difficulties without apportioning blame, explaining, "this is indeed a complex situation. One on which even the experts are divided. There is no need to place blame, and I certainly do not intend to argue the military or political issues involved. Neither the

52. King, Martin Luther, Jr., "Annual Report Delivered at the Ninth Annual Convention of the Southern Christian Leadership Conference," August 9–13, SCLC Papers, Box 31.11, King Center Library and Archives, Atlanta, GA.

53. Ibid.

54. Stanley Levison (May 2, 1912–September 12, 1979) was a New York-based lawyer with previous Communist connections. Levison was a close confident of King's, despite his controversial past. He advised King on setting up SCLC.

55. Clarence Jones (January 8, 1931) was a delegate to Democratic National Convention from New York in 1972 and was a close friend and advisor to King

56. Harry Wachtel (March 26, 1917–February 3, 1997) was a New York attorney and adviser to King. He helped set up the "Gandhi Society for Human Rights" to raise funds for the civil rights movement.

57. King, "Annual Report," August 9–13, King Center Library and Archives, Atlanta, GA.

58. Garrow, *Bearing the Cross*, 438.

59. King, Martin Luther, Jr., "Speech to SCLC Convention about Vietnam" address at SCLC Convention, Birmingham, AL, August 12, 1965, SCLC Papers, Box 31:11, August 1–December 31, 1965, King Center Library and Archives, Atlanta, GA.

American people nor the people of North Vietnam is the enemy. The true enemy is war itself.[60] Nevertheless, King pursued his agenda for peace, reminding his audience of the pledge he had made on receipt of the Novel Peace Prize: "It is imperative and urgent to put an end to war and violence between nations as it is to put an end to racial injustice."[61] King called for all parties to come to the table in good faith, as a matter of urgency, without laying preconditions such as the demand by Ho Chi Minh and Chou En-Lai[62] for unilateral withdrawal of American forces from South Vietnam.[63]

At the SCLC Conference August 13, 1965, King gave a interview in which he outlined how progress could be made on the war front. As a demonstration of good faith, he recommended:

1. For the US to consider halting the bombing in North Vietnam.

2. It was also necessary for the US to make an unequivocal and unambiguous statement showing a willingness to negotiate with the Viet-Cong, or its political arm, the National Liberation Front.

3. Both North Vietnam and Communist China were required to express unequivocally their desire and their determination to negotiate a settlement. They have been too slow and in recent weeks had become even more recalcitrant.[64]

In laying out these preconditions for the commencement of peace talks, King sought to present a fair and balanced view. He emphasized the importance of the US as a moral force, saying that although the world was aware of America's great military power, in order to foster peace, "we must rely more on our moral power rather than our military power."[65] King was careful to show deference to the president, saying, "I think President Johnson has made it clear that he wants to negotiate a settlement, and he has said this over and over again in the last few days."[66] Whether King was authorized to speak in such detail or not, Johnson was privately both

60. Ibid.

61. Ibid.

62. Chou En-Lai (March 5, 1898– January 8, 1976) was the first Premier of the People's Republic of China, serving from 1949 until his death in 1976.

63. King, "Speech to SCLC Convention," August 12, 1965, King Center Library and Archives, Atlanta, GA.

64. King, Martin Luther, Jr., "Statement on Vietnam," address at the SCLC Convention, Birmingham, AL, August 13, 1965, King Papers, Box 9, August 1–December 31, 1965, King Center Library and Archives, Atlanta, GA.

65. Ibid.

66. Ibid.

wounded and outraged by King's comments. According to Oates, this would have come as a surprise to King, for "he had thought that Johnson respected him and welcomed his views even if they had challenged administration policy."[67] Not only was he battling with his own organization to support his stance on Vietnam, but King also had to withstand chastisement from other civil rights leaders such as Whitney Young[68] of the National Urban League, who argued that "Johnson needs a consensus. If we are not with him on Vietnam, then he is not going to be with us on civil rights."[69] King contacted President Johnson on August 20, before he left for California following the Watts Riots in Los Angeles. Johnson raised a sensitive issue when he claimed that members of Congress had "the impression that you are against me on Vietnam."[70] Johnson intimated that peace initiatives were taking place behind the scenes, and he advised that King meet with Arthur Goldberg, United States Ambassador to the UN, for a briefing.

King continued with his criticism of the war, and he appeared on *Face the Nation* in late August 1965. Lew Wood of CBS News, reminded King that the "Logan Act"[71] prevented private citizens from entering international negotiations on behalf of the US and asked if the law had influenced King's decision to write to Ho Chi Minh as well as Chinese and Soviet leaders.[72] He responded, "Well I am aware of that Act . . . I haven't had a chance to look at that Act in all of its legal ramifications . . . No, I have no desire to negotiate . . . my only concern is that there will be a negotiated settlement, and this is the basic thing that I will say in the letters, and I don't know how this will conflict with the Logan Act."[73]

Rowland Evans of the *New York Herald* inquired whether President Johnson was in agreement with his basic position on Vietnam. King said that there were differences of opinion, of course, but "President Johnson has made it clear that he feels that he is doing what he has to do in the situation,

67. Oates, *Let the Trumpet Sound*, 376.

68. Whitney Moore Young Jr. (July 31,1921–March 11, 1971) was Executive Director of the National Urban League (NUL) and worked to end employment discrimination in the United States.

69. Dyson, *I May Not Get There*, 55.

70. Quoted in Kotz, *Judgment Days*, 345–46.

71. The Logan Act was passed in 1799 during President Adams' administration in an era of tension between the US and France. It essentially forbids private citizens from involving themselves in negotiating foreign policy. The legislation originated with the efforts of George Logan, who met with French government officials in an attempt to stave off war, a move that was called treasonous by political opponents.

72. King, interview by Agronsky, *Face the Nation*, August 29, 1965, King Center Library and Archive, Atlanta, GA.

73. Ibid.

and I am not self-righteous at this point."[74] King then clarified his stance: "I can understand the moral dilemma of those who feel the need of escalating the war, so that I don't feel that I can stand with any pretence to omniscience and say that I have the answer."[75] Evans pursued this line of questioning, asking if King ever had any encouragement from the president or from Arthur Goldberg in his peace initiatives. King made it clear that "President Johnson has not urged me at any point to withhold my statements, to cease speaking at this point."[76] Martin Agronsky pressed King further when he put it to him that "many Negro and white civil rights leaders, also spokesmen of your government, have indicated their concern that by your use of your own prestige, and the civil rights movement to seek independently a Vietnamese peace, you might end in weakening, dividing, and even negating the strength of the civil rights movement in this country."[77] King again emphasized that as a minister of the gospel, he felt a responsibility to address the social evils of the day, and since he felt that war was obsolete, "it must be cast into unending limbo, and that if we continue to escalate this war, we move nearer to the point of plunging the whole of mankind into the abyss of annihilation; and I will continue to speak when I deem it timely and necessary on this issue."[78] King's conscience compelled him to condemn the escalating war by speaking the truth to his predominantly Christian audience.

On the basis of showing national solidarity in a time of war, Agronsky then invited King to comment on a statement made by a very distinguished black leader, George Weaver, Assistant Secretary of Labor, who questioned calls for peace talks as sending signals that might cause the enemy, according to Weaver, "to miscalculate our determination to fulfill our commitment to resist aggression."[79] King rebutted questions of his patriotism by calling the Constitution to his aid: "Well I think we must see that a part of the sacred heritage of our nation is the right to take a stand on the basis of freedom of speech for what conscience tells one is right, and nothing could be more tragic at this time, it seems to me, than for individuals to confuse dissent with disloyalty. I think we need creative dissent."[80]

74. Ibid.
75. Ibid.
76. Ibid.
77. Ibid.
78. Ibid.
79. Quoted in ibid.
80. Ibid.

In the United States, as in most countries, the prevailing sentiment is that when the country is at war, everyone should cease all criticism of government policies. The postponed meeting that President Johnson had arranged between King and Ambassador Goldberg was held in September of 1965. Goldberg assured King that the United States was committed to peace in Vietnam, and that a resolution was close to hand. Lewis tells us, rather skeptically, that Johnson had instructed Goldberg "to convey the impression" to King that peace was imminent.[81] He didn't succeed in convincing King, and as Young, King's companion, recalled, "we weren't sure that Goldberg even believed what he was saying."[82] The cracks were papered over at a joint press conference King and Goldberg held later, describing the meeting as "very fruitful and amicable."[83] However, King broached another controversial issue when he spoke of allowing China in from the cold: "We must seriously consider reversing our policy beyond the question of having Communist China in the United Nations. For if there is to be peace in the world, it seems to me, the largest nation in the world must be in the peacemaking machinery."[84] What King meant here was that Communist China should not only be admitted into the UN, a move the US bitterly opposed, but should also be included in any peace negotiations. As King saw it, China was the leading power in Asia, the largest country in the world, and a key player to any lasting solution in Vietnam.[85] If King was pleased with meeting Goldberg, it did not restrain him from speaking his mind: "But not only are we concerned about the immediate damage that the war is doing, but also the long-range potential damage, and there can be no gain saying that if the war in general is continually escalated, ah, [*sic*] our earthly habitat can be transformed into an inferno that even the mind of Dante could not envision."[86]

Johnson and his associates obviously saw King as an ungrateful upstart interfering in foreign affairs. It is true that King, under pressure from colleagues, decided to drop his letter-writing campaign to Ho Chi Minh and other foreign leaders.[87] On October 5, he declared, "certain factors bearing

81. Lewis, *King: A Biography*, 307.

82. Oates, *Let the Trumpet Sound*, 381.

83. Ibid., 445.

84. Martin Luther King Jr. and Ambassador Arthur Goldberg, transcript of statements on the war in Vietnam, UN Headquarters, New York, September 10, 1965, King Papers, Box 9, King Center Library and Archive, Atlanta, GA.

85. Ibid.

86. King and Goldberg, statements on the war in Vietnam, September 10, 1965, King Center Library and Archive, Atlanta, GA.

87. Fairclough, "War in Vietnam," 318.

upon the Vietnamese situation, including the UN's 'creative role' . . . indicated that at this time it is no longer necessary for me to adopt the course upon which I had decided."[88] But there was ambiguity in King's promise, for he would "continue to oppose it as an individual and as a minister."[89] Historian Adam Fairclough maintains that this climb-down caused King considerable self-reproach.[90] King began to see that the American public was not ready for his revelations on the Vietnam War, and as he explained, "we have to face the fact that sometimes the public is not ready to digest the truth."[91]

King's self-imposed silence on Vietnam only lasted one month, as he issued another statement in October of 1965. He saw the revitalization of the UN in a recent dispute over Kashmir, India, as being hopeful, and he realized that the UN might also have a role to play in Vietnam: "The settling of the right to vote question within the UN gives us all encouragement that the UN can now realize its potential as an international conciliator which should be supported by the forces of good will in every nation."[92] He then turned his attention to perceived efforts by the US government to silence free debate on foreign policy, and with a confident upbeat statement, he asserted, "I intend to fight for the preservation of this great American tradition and will continue to express the voice of my conscience to the issues of the day that a free and healthy debate over these issues might continue among our people, and that we might mature as a nation to the point where dissent not be mistaken for disloyalty, for dissent within the context of our democracy is the very cornerstone of our form of government."[93] Here was a direct challenge to Johnson to allow open debate on the Vietnam War. King was on the offensive again. As Garrow explains, when Clarence Jones told King that support was coming from Senators Ernest Gruening[94] and

88. Branch, *At Canaan's Edge*, 331.

89. Fairclough, "War in Vietnam," 318.

90. Ibid.

91. Garrow, *Bearing the Cross*, 445.

92. King, Martin Luther, Jr., "Statement Regarding Citizen Diplomacy" October 5, 1965, King Papers, Box 9, August 1–December 31, 1965, King Center Library and Archive, Atlanta, GA.

93. Ibid.

94. Ernest Henry Gruening (February 6, 1887–June 26, 1974) was a Democrat who served as Governor of the Alaska Territory from 1939 to 1955 and as a Senator from 1959 to 1969.

Wayne Morse,[95] King remarked, "as I have said all along, there is much more support for my position than the press is willing to admit."[96]

King's star as an international antiwar activist was on the rise when Dr. Benjamin Spock,[97] a spokesman for an incipient antiwar movement, met him on an airplane and urged King to make a world tour for peace so that he might return to unite the antiwar forces in a national crusade. Spock saw King as "the most important personality around whom people would rally."[98] At an award ceremony of the Synagogue Council of America in December of 1965, King, in thanking the distinguished audience, said that he was honored to receive the Judaism and World Peace Award. King spoke about the criticism leveled at the "inexperienced" commentator on foreign policy with the intention of silencing dissent: "Are we led to believe that the chairman of Senate foreign relations, Senator Fulbright,[99] lacks expertise? Is the majority leader of the Senate, Senator Mansfield,[100] a political fool? Is Walter Lippman[101] less competent in the field of international affairs than the leaders of the Pentagon? Are the editors of the *New York Times* too uniformed to make judgments?[102] King was not prepared to remain silent, despite the threat of action under the Logan Act. In what President Johnson must have seen as an affront, King charged, "it is certainly time to consider where we are going, and whether free speech has not become one

95. Wayne Morse (October 20, 1900–July 22, 1974) served as a Senator from Oregon for twenty-four years. He was a leader on a wide range of issues, including the anti-war movement and civil rights.

96. Garrow, *Bearing the Cross*, 449.

97. Benjamin Mclane Spock (May 2, 1903–March 15, 1998), an American pediatrician, was one of the founders of the Committee for a Sane Nuclear Policy. He was active in the anti-war movement against the Vietnam War.

98. Oates, *Let the Trumpet Sound*, 381.

99. Senator William Fulbright (April 9, 1905–February 9, 1995) was a Democrat from Arkansas who was elected to Congress in January 1943, and served in the Senate from 1944 to 1979. He was Chairman of the Committee on Foreign Relations.

100. Michael Joseph Mansfield (March 16, 1903–October 5, 2001), a Democrat from Montana, was elected to Congress in 1942 and to the Senate ten years later. Mansfield supported the Vietnam War in the early days, but became a trenchant critic when he learned of deception in the early reports.

101. Walter Lippmann (September 23, 1889–December 14, 1974) was born to Jewish-German parents in New York and became a socialist while studying at Harvard University. He upset leaders of both the Democratic and Republican parties when he opposed the Korean War, McCarthyism, and the Vietnam War.

102. King, Martin Luther, Jr., "Speech to the Synagogue Council of America," address at the Waldorf-Astoria Hotel, New York, December 5, 1965, King Papers, Box 9, August 1–December 31, 1965, King Center Library and Archive, Atlanta, GA.

of the casualties of the war."[103] King also recognized the horrors of war and the effects the conflict was having on the Vietnamese civilians as well as on US troops: "A war in which children are incinerated by napalm, in which American soldiers die in mounting numbers while other American soldiers, according to press reports, in unrestrained hatred shoot the wounded enemy as they lie on the ground, is a war that mutilates the conscience."[104] The strength of this December 1965 statement negates criticism that King failed to speak out forcefully against the war prior to 1967.

King contributed regular articles to the *Chicago Defender*,[105] the largest black-owned daily in the world. The paper published King's column, "My Dream," in January of 1966, in which he spoke about the disapproval directed at him by friends, fellow civil rights leaders, members of Congress, and "brothers of the cloth" for "not sticking to the business of civil rights."[106] He outlined three overriding reasons why it fell to him personally "to sue for a war-less world." The first reason he gave was that "I am a minister of the gospel," and in that capacity, "I believe that war is wrong."[107] Furthermore, King increasingly saw the connection between the perpetuation of racist policies at home and the implementation of United States policy overseas. King defended the criticism that he was not an "expert" on the "Vietnam question" by stating, "I am an expert in recognition of a simple eloquent truth. The truth is that it is sinful for any of God's children to brutalize any of God's other children, no matter from what side the brutalization comes."[108] In an early reference to the racist nature of warfare, he explained, "as a minister, I cannot advocate racial peace and nonviolence for black men alone, nor for yellow men alone. Men bass black and treble white are of equal importance on God's keyboard."[109]

King was careful to defend himself from charges of treasonous behavior by announcing, "I am an American. Despite the shortcoming of this imperfect democracy, I love America." But, he declared, "War is obsolete, no nation wins a war."[110] Lest he be misunderstood, he explained his stance: "I am as concerned about the expansion of Godless communism as any

---

103. Ibid.

104. Ibid.

105. The *Chicago Defender* was founded by Robert S. Abbott in 1905 and had become the nation's most influential black weekly newspaper by World War I. In 1956, the *Defender* became the *Chicago Daily Defender*, the world's largest black-owned daily.

106. King, "My Dream," 10.

107. Ibid.

108. Ibid.

109. Ibid.

110. Ibid.

other man,,"[111] which was a truism of the times, "Yet I believe that our guns and bombs do not prove that we love democracy. They prove that we still believe that might makes right, despite the fact that common sense and bitter experience tells us there has never been a true conqueror."[112] Quoting President Kennedy, he asked, "is not peace, in the last analysis, a matter of human rights?"[113] King insisted that if he advocated nonviolence in Montgomery, Birmingham, Albany, and in the seething cities of the North, "how can I not be consistent, and fail to say that violence is as wrong in Hanoi as it is in Harlem?"[114] Returning to the Vietnam War's racist overtones, King observed, "the Negro must not allow himself to become a victim of the self-serving philosophy of those who manufacture war that the survival of the world is the white man's business alone."[115]

King began to question the successes of the civil rights movement in the context of waging an unjust war in Vietnam, on a quid pro quo basis: "What shall it profit the Negro to avail himself of an integrated sandwich or a quality education or a good job or a desegregated home—in the midst of horrible death and falling bombs?"[116] In other words, "what shall it profit a man to gain the whole world and lose his soul?" (Mark 8:36). King saw no gain for the civil rights movement in supporting an unjust war to placate Johnson. King pleaded "that the same idealism, nonviolent spirit, and courage which brought embattled men to the conference table in the Montgomeries of the South, might well achieve identical victory with Moscow."[117] Lewis regards the *Chicago Defender* column as King's "most exhaustively reasoned argument—until his Spring Mobilization speech in New York the following year—for his opposition to the Vietnam War."[118] As Oates explains, "he had answered his pro-war critics in a recent column for the *Chicago Defender*, a Negro newspaper."[119]

In an insightful article published in the *Christian Century*, Charles Fager, a young white ex-SCLC staffer, lamented King's perilous and tortuous middle course on Vietnam. It was Fager's contention that "Vietnam is

111. Ibid.
112. Ibid.
113. Ibid.
114. Ibid.
115. Ibid.
116. Ibid.
117. Ibid.
118. Lewis, *King: A Biography*, 309–10.
119. Oates, *Let the Trumpet Sound*, 382

perhaps the gravest challenge of Dr. King's career."[120] In his turmoil over Vietnam, Fager contended, King had to answer not only to nations, but also to history, for "if in his agony he failed to lead, would world history forgive him?"[121]

An example of the paranoia prevalent at the government level was demonstrated by the Julian Bond affair. Bond was elected to the Georgia legislature in the autumn of 1965. In January of 1966, he was banned from taking his seat because he had endorsed a Student Nonviolent Coordinating Committee (SNCC) press statement attacking American policy in Vietnam and its Cold War agenda: "We question then the ability and even the desire of the United States government to guarantee free elections abroad. We maintain that our country's cry of 'preserve freedom in the world' is a hypocritical mask behind which it quashed liberation movements which are not bound and refuse to be bound by the expediency of the United States Cold War policy."[122]

At a sermon delivered at Ebenezer Baptist Church on January 16, 1966, King showed his support for Julian Bond. King again perceived the Johnson administration as attempting to stifle open debate on the war: "This was a young man who dared to speak his mind. This is a young man who dared to be different. This is a young man who dared to dissent. This is a young man who did not fear to take a view against majority opinion."[123] The "Bond-King" position was unpopular among blacks, and this was borne out by the surprising stand taken by the once pro-SNCC *Atlanta Inquirer*: "we believe the views espoused by SNCC have the potential of comforting and aiding our enemies."[124] Rev. T. J. Edwards, President of the Chattanooga, TN, branch of the SCLC, and Assistant Rev. Robert Richards went so far as to resign because they disagreed with King's recent pronouncements.[125] King campaigned for Bond's reinstatement, imploring that "we aren't doing enough to end the war in Vietnam . . . our hands are dirty in the war in

120. Fager, Charles, "Dilemma for Dr. King," *Christian Century*, March 16, 1966, 331–32, quoted in ibid.

121. Ibid.

122. "SNCC Denounces the Vietnam War," in Holt and Brown, *Major Problems*, 2:316. The Student Non-Violent Coordinating Committee (SNCC) was one of the primary institutions of the American civil rights movement in the 1960s. The organization emerged from a student meeting led by Ella Baker at Shaw University in Raleigh, NC, in April of 1960 and an $800 grant from the SCLC.

123. King, Martin Luther, Jr., "Sermon at Ebenezer Baptist Church," address at Atlanta, GA, January 16, 1966, King Papers, Box 10, January–May, 1966, King Center Library and Archives, Atlanta, GA.

124. Lewis, *King: A Biography*, 311.

125. Ibid.

Vietnam . . . Americans must hear the truth. If we are to survive as a nation, somebody has got to have vision; somebody must be willing to stand up and be criticized and called every bad name, out of love for this country."[126] King was forever conscious of the 'Red scare,' and the FBI instigated surveillance operations against both him and the SCLC. He informed his congregation, "nobody should be considered disloyal because they dissent, because it is done out of love."[127]

An interesting exchange of correspondence between King and the WCC showed how the politics of the day, in this case the Vietnam War, intertwined with pastoral roles. In February of 1966, when George D. Comnas, President of the American Club of Geneva, learned that King was to address the WCC, he invited him to speak at a luncheon meeting on King's "work in the field of civil rights."[128] Comnas detailed his constituents: "Our membership of several hundred includes both Americans, who are officials and executives in international business, international organizations, and other fields, and non-Americans who, through business and social relations, have close ties with the United States." He went on to highlight previous speakers, including Senator Hugh Scott, Knut Hammarskjold (newly appointed Director General of the International Air Transport Association), and Ambassador Clare Timberlake, US Representative to the Eighteen-Nation Disarmament Conference. On April 20, 1966, the luncheon meeting was canceled due to a change in plans with regrets to King from Ralph C. Dudrow, Chairman of the Speakers and Program Committee.[129] Then on June 2, 1966, everything was back on schedule when King received a rather apologetic letter from Comnas, who tried to extricate himself from the hole which had been dug for him by others by writing, "man seems destined sometimes to make decisions of the moment which do not in any way reflect the objective heights to which he is often capable. I believe it was Zorba (Kantazakis' book) who, replying to a question, said, 'Am I not a man—and are not all men stupid? Therefore, I am stupid.'"[130]

Unfortunately, this letter did not explain the events that led to King's invitation to speak being canceled in the first place. It was left to Visser 't Hooft to tease out the details. Comnas explained to Visser 't Hooft that

126. King, "Sermon at Ebenezer Baptist Church," January 16, 1966, King Center Library and Archives, Atlanta, GA.

127. Ibid.

128. George C. Dudrow to Martin Luther King Jr., June 2, 1966, 42.11.08, WCC, General Secretaries, Correspondence: Frequent (1937–1977), WCC Archives, Geneva, Switzerland.

129. Ibid.

130. Ibid.

he had not attended the fateful meeting which revised the offer to King. It transpired that a member of the American diplomatic mission in Geneva feared that King would make a statement on the Vietnam War and the members present agreed to rescind the invitation. "I am most glad that this stupid incident is thus closed," wrote Visser 't Hooft, "and I express the very strong hope that you will let bygones be bygones."[131] Expressing confidence that the tension surrounding the event would ensure an eager audience, he concluded, "and if, as I hope, you will speak on human rights, you will speak in an 'existential' situation, for the American Club has had to learn a lesson concerning the meaning of human rights."[132] Unfortunately, King ultimately was unable to travel to Geneva due to compelling obligations at home.

King had regularly condemned the excesses of capitalism, and it was natural that he was drawn towards the NCC's open indictment of US policies in Vietnam. While condemning the churches in general for their silence, he exclaimed, "thank God the National Council of Churches has spoken out in a beautiful way, criticizing our foreign policy and the present war, and criticizing war in general. This is marvelous."[133] The NCC was headquartered at Riverside Drive in New York, where King launched his most forthright attack on the Vietnam War on April 4, 1967, exactly a year before he was assassinated. Meanwhile, King's nemesis, J. Edgar Hoover, saw twenty million blacks, a large proportion of whom were church-going, as vulnerable to communist exploitation. Because a large swathe of American public opinion held that socialism was close enough to communism to be suspicious, Hoover warned in 1960 that "because they despised the church, Communists continually attempt to infiltrate unsuspecting organizations. What better cloak can be found for their programs than to present them as the offerings of clergymen and churches?"[134] Indeed, Hoover saw King and his civil rights movement as unwitting dupes of socialists and communists, rather than active conspirators. That King's Baptist church was a member of the NCC further exacerbated Hoover's position, giving King additional exposure on a national scale from a respected organization.

John Lewis[135] was asked in an interview in February of 1966 whether he thought King's SCLC would take a strong stand against the war, and he

131. W. A. Visser 't Hooft to Martin Luther King Jr., June 2, 1966, WCC General Secretaries, Correspondence: Frequent 1938–(1966–1970), 42.11.08, WCC Archives, Geneva, Switzerland.

132. Ibid.

133. King, "Sermon at Ebenezer Baptist Church," January 16, 1966, King Center Library and Archives, Atlanta, GA.

134. Quoted in Evans, *Apathy, Apostasy, and Apostles*, 29.

135. John Lewis (February 21, 1940) was chairman of the Student Nonviolent

replied, "I think the pressure from within the young people on the staff and Dr. King's own influence will cause the organization to take a position. I think it will be his [King's] recommendation to come out very strongly against the war in Vietnam."[136] The momentum against the war continued, and Lewis' prediction was an accurate one. At the SCLC's annual board meeting on April 13, 1966, a resolution supporting King's stance was proposed, describing the hopeless conflict as "the gangrene of Vietnam," in which "American policy has become imprisoned in the destiny of the military oligarchy. Our men and equipment are revealed to be serving a regime so despised by its own people that in the midst of conflict they are seeking its overthrow."[137] King must have been pleased that at last his opposition to the war was moving up the SCLC's agenda, since "the confused war has played havoc with our domestic destinies. Despite feeble protestations to the contrary, the promises of the Great Society top the casualty list of the conflict."[138]

The resolution also made reference to the old bugbear that one should not criticize a nation at war: "Another casualty in this war is the principle of dissent. We deplore efforts to characterize opposition to the war as disloyal or traitorous because such attacks are destructive of our most fundamental democratic tradition."[139] The resolution called on the United States government to desist from aiding the military junta in the struggle against the forces of democracy—the Buddhists, Catholics, and students of Vietnam.[140] In addition, it argued that "the war, which was rapidly degenerating into a sordid military adventure, was detrimental to urgent need, and expectations of the neglected poor at home."[141] Furthermore, there was an urgent need to reassess "our position and seriously examine the wisdom of prompt withdrawal," from a war that was "using American men and material in so

---

Coordinating Committee from 1963 to 1966. At age 23, he was the youngest keynote speaker at the March on Washington. Lewis is a member of the Democratic Party and has served as the US Representative for Georgia's Fifth Congressional District since 1987.

136. John Lewis, interview by Archie Allen, February 14, 1969, Julian Bond Papers, File 1:7, Georgia House of Representatives printed material interviews, King Center Library and Archives, Atlanta, GA.

137. SCLC Executive Board, "Resolution of the Board," minutes of Board Meeting, April 13, 1966, SCLC Papers, Box 89:6, April–June 1966, King Center Library and Archives, Atlanta, GA.

138. Ibid.

139. Ibid.

140. Ibid.

141. Ibid.

impossible and immoral a pursuit."[142] The SCLC board voiced these bold sentiments one year before King's robust "Beyond Vietnam" speech in April of 1967.

On May 16, 1966, King took a leading role when he agreed to serve as a co-chairmen of CALCAV[143] with Dr. John Bennett,[144] Rabbi Abraham Heschel, the Reverend John McKenzie,[145] and Philip Scharper.[146] Executive Secretary Richard Fernandez wrote to King requesting urgent assistance in May of 1966. He pleaded that the "emergency nature of Vietnam requires, that we get to the 'grass roots' level of our religious institutional life with our concern."[147] Efforts were being made to raise concern about on Vietnam among the clergy. Fernandez wrote that it was imperative "that we go directly to local clergy and laymen to attempt to excite, encourage, and support them as they attempt to 'address themselves' to the Vietnam issue."[148] Fernandez was made it clear that King's expertise was required to raise awareness on the issue, illustrating that in early 1966, King was not only actively engaged in antiwar activities, but was also recognized as an antiwar activist by his peers.

King appeared on *Face the Nation* again on May 29, 1966. Host Martin Agronsky grilled him on preparations for the White House Conference on civil rights, especially the recommendations of the Council conference, which called for massive public works programs estimated at two billion dollars. King responded that the estimate was on the low side, and that he foresaw a cost of ten billion dollars a year for ten years.[149] Agronsky hit the

142. Ibid.

143. Ansbro, *Making of a Mind*, 252.

144. Reverend John C. Bennett (1903–April 27, 1995) was a theologian whose opinions on religion, politics and social policy influenced public discourse over many years, especially in his opposition to the war in Vietnam.

145. Reverend John McKenzie (October 9, 1910–March 2, 1991) was a Jesuit, a Roman Catholic biblical scholar, and a professor at University of Chicago's Divinity School. His outspoken views as a Christian pacifist led him to co-chair CALCAV.

146. Philip Scharper (September 15, 1919–May 5, 1985) was Vice President of Sheed & Ward, famed Catholic publishers. After receiving various degrees while studying to be a Jesuit priest, he left the order to marry Sarah Moorman, who was a Catholic journalist. During his tenure as Editor-in-Chief of Sheed & Ward, he served for thirteen years as an advisor to the Second Vatican Council.

147. Richard Fernandez, CALCAV, to Martin Luther King Jr., May 9, 1966, King Papers, Box 6.20, May 1966–January 1968, King Center Library and Archives, Atlanta, GA.

148. Ibid.

149. Martin Luther King Jr., interview by Daniel Schorr, Haynes Johnson, and Martin Agronsky, *Face the Nation*, CBS, May 29, 1966, King Papers, Box 10, January–May 1966, King Center Library and Archive, Atlanta, GA.

target with his next question, asking King, "what about the President's contention that because of the war in Vietnam, we can't afford to spend that kind of money in these areas?" In short, King saw the waste of resources in Vietnam as one of the main reasons that these Great Society programs[150] were being downgraded. Agronsky pressed for clarification of King's view, and he obliged: "The constant escalation of this war will make it impossible for many reasons to implement the Great Society programs, because there will always be Congressmen who will say that because of the war we can't afford to allocate this kind of money. So even though the President doesn't desire it this way, it is the inevitable outcome."[151] The interview proceeded to the question of how a resolution to the war might come about. King was up to the challenge, and proffered his opinion that "it is necessary to make an unequivocal statement that we will negotiate with the Vietcong."[152] Conscious as always of the smear tactics used by the FBI and other government agencies to discredit Communist sympathizers, King qualified his reply: "I would be the first to say that I disagree with the philosophy of communism, but we have got to see it as a reality in the world, and it will be necessary to share power with the Communists, probably in the South Vietnamese government."[153]

In the course of my research in the WCC archives, I came across a previously unpublished letter sent to President Johnson in June of 1966 that was signed by twenty-eight clergymen and academics, including King and Blake. Other signatories included John Bennett, a professor of Theology and eventual president of the Union Theological Seminary, and Robert McAfee Brown, a Presbyterian minister and professor of Religion at Union and Stanford Universities. Significantly, King was associating with reputable clergymen to enhance his moderate image at a time when Stokely Carmichael and other radicals were promoting Black Power and separatism. King may have been seen in a poor light by the Johnson administration for his opposition to the Vietnam War, but now, in contrast with these more extreme elements, he was beginning to look moderate. The clergymen advocated for peace in the world in the face of different ideologies and ongoing injustices—all under the constant threat of war: "Our hopes for world peace, and our fears

150. The Great Society Programs were a set of US domestic policies backed by President Lyndon B. Johnson in the 1960s with the goal of eliminating poverty and racial injustice. Due to the huge expenditures on the Vietnam War, the promises of social reforms largely evaporated, leaving Johnson concerned for his legacy.

151. King, interview by Schorr, Johnson, and Agronsky, *Face the Nation*, May 29, 1966, King Center Library and Archive, Atlanta, GA.

152. Ibid.

153. Ibid.

of world disaster, are centered at this time on Vietnam. Here, for over five years, this nation has committed its political power, its military force, and the lives of its youth, to a struggle which each day becomes less clear in its purpose, more uncertain in its outcome, and more dangerous in its approach to the ultimate disaster of nuclear war."[154]

Fear of nuclear war was naturally exacerbated by the all too recent Cuban Missile Crisis. Hence, apart from immediate concerns about the devastation of Vietnam, the fear was that the US might precipitate a confrontation with the Communist bloc and risk nuclear war. With the intensification of the bombing of North Vietnam in July of 1966, the WCC cabled President Johnson confirming that this escalation had caused serious concern, alarm, and resentment among many Christians and WCC member churches: "The United States in fidelity to its own tradition and by virtue of its present position as a dominant power in the world today should intensify its efforts to move without delay from the battlefield to the conference table and explore every means pragmatic and imaginative towards this end."[155] The cable also noted that the continuation of the war by the US and its allies intensified racial resentments against them, and on the other side, the vast destruction of Vietnam's people and resources meant that "the end of the conflict does not justify the inevitable cost."[156]

Throughout 1966, the antiwar movement picked up momentum, reflecting the growing willingness of some Americans to challenge the nation's hawkish temperament. King continued to worry over Vietnam, and his sermons and speeches reflected his disgust with American foreign policy. He came to Jackson, Mississippi, in August of 1966 committed to persuading the SCLC board to agree to a stronger condemnation of America's military policy than it had previously endorsed. King succeeded in winning approval for a strongly worded declaration of the SCLC's opposition to American policy in Vietnam. According to Garrow, some board members such as Roland Smith were uncomfortable with King's resolution, for it "pulled no punches"[157] in declaring that "our present posture is a caricature of our professed role as an international force for responsibility and cooperation. It justifies Walter Lippman in lamenting that we are 'whoring after false Gods

154. King, Martin Luther, Jr., et al. to President Lyndon B. Johnson, June 1966, WCC General Secretariat Correspondence: Country Files, 1946–1995 Asia, Vietnam January–July 1966, 42.3.112/3, WCC Archives, Geneva, Switzerland.

155. WCC telegram to President Johnson, July 1, 1966, WCC General Secretariat Correspondence: Country Files, 1946–1995 Asia, Vietnam January–July 1966, 42.3.112/3, WCC Archives, Geneva, Switzerland.

156. Ibid.

157. Garrow, Bearing the Cross, 469.

of world domination."[158] The resolution drew attention to the oft-quoted contention that blacks were bearing a disproportionate share of responsibility in waging war: "Negroes are providing more than twice as many combat troops in proportion to their numbers in the population . . . To be expected to prove one's patriotism by accepting a disproportionate role in combat is a particularly ugly form of discrimination."[159]

At an SCLC staff retreat in South Carolina in November of 1966, King questioned the moral values upon which the United States thrived. Referring back to comments made at Howard University in March of 1965, he mentioned the three basic evils in the country, the evil of racism, the evil of excessive materialism, and the evil of militarism. He asked his staff not to be intimidated by the connection, for "these three are inseparable triplets. It is one thing to talk about dealing with racism and this civil rights issue and not getting involved with militarism, but the fact is that the two are tied together."[160] He then elaborated on the connection between the practice of racism abroad and a similar policy at work at home: "While our work must be in Grenada and Chicago we must come to see that many of our problems in Grenada and Chicago are very odd [*sic*] because we are still living in a sick nation that will brutalize unjustifiably millions of boys and girls, men and women in Vietnam, and the two issues cannot be separated."[161] Here King outlined a direct connection between the policies of the administration in their dealings with blacks in the United States and the racist policy being extended to those in the Third World—in other words, white supremacy at work. Indeed, as historian Thomas Borstelmann explains, "the tradition of white supremacy in the United States was embedded in a broader global pattern of white control of people of color, and both systems of racial inequality appeared to some to be directly related. They predicted that the two systems would survive or fall together."[162] King spoke to the SCLC staff on world peace and how it should be strengthened. He took a swipe at the various leaders in the conflict, and asserted that "Ho Chi Minh talks about peace. President Johnson is a great talker about peace, but all these people are talking about peace as an end."[163] Revealing his dissatisfaction with their

158. SCLC Executive Board, "Resolution," August 10, 1966, King Papers, Box 11, June–December 1966, King Center Library and Archive, Atlanta, GA.

159. Ibid.

160. King, "State of the Movement," November 28, 1967, King Center Library and Archive, Atlanta, GA.

161. Ibid.

162. Borstelmann, *Cold War and the Color Line*, 46.

163. King, "The State of the Movement," November 28, 1967, King Center Library and Archive, Atlanta, GA.

interpretation of how to achieve peace by waging war, King concluded, "but one day we must come to see that war is a poor chisel to carve our peaceful tomorrow. We've got to see that peace must be the means by which we arrive at the end of peace, and this is our challenge."[164] As Coretta Scott King later wrote, "by 1966 it had become apparent to Martin that not only was the Vietnam War wrong, but that it was engulfing huge sums of money that could otherwise be spent fighting poverty."[165]

THE PROBLEM OF THE VIETNAM WAR FOR EUGENE CARSON BLAKE, THE WCC, AND MARTIN LUTHER KING JR., 1966–1968.

King received support, moral and otherwise, from the WCC throughout his civil rights campaign and in his opposition to the Vietnam War. Although his name may not have been mentioned consistently, the WCC pursued policies similar to those King advocated in eradicating racism as well as ending the conflict in Vietnam. It may be helpful here to outline the WCC's view on the Vietnam War prior to 1968, which coincided with Blake's ascendancy in the organization and his interactions with King. Blake confirmed that the WCC and its Commission of the Churches on International Affairs (CCIA)[166] had long been concerned with the situation in Vietnam. In fact, ecumenical agencies had followed developments in the area closely by since 1954, when the Asian Conference met in Geneva. The WCC was concerned that any escalation of the Vietnam War involving the US and China could have devastating effects due to their nuclear capacities. A WCC report in 1966 stated, "we have repeatedly emphasized the tragic situation in Vietnam. We would suggest that the churches have a special obligation to question continually the wisdom and rightness of the present Vietnam policies of the belligerents."[167]

In correspondence with Rev. Keith Chamberlain, Blake revealed that the most comprehensive statement on the Vietnam War had been issued in February of 1966.[168] The statement sympathized with the plight of the

164. Ibid.

165. King, *My Life with Martin*, 292.

166. The Churches' Commission on International Affairs (CCIA) consists of thirty people chosen by churches and regional ecumenical organizations to advise the WCC on international affairs, including peacemaking, militarism, human security, human rights, and international law.

167. Thomas and Abrecht, *World Conference on Church and Society*, 127.

168. Eugene Carson Blake to Keith Chamberlain, March 10, 1967, Evangelische

Vietnamese people, but acknowledged the difficulties in ending the war. It was critical of the deployment of human resources for destructive ends. It acknowledged that there was no international community under the rule of law and no interest in arriving at such an understanding. This unfortunate scenario, Blake argued, only added to the Christian imperative.[169] Following consultations at Enugu, Nigeria, in January and Bangkok, Thailand, in December 1966, a ten-point plan emerged[170] that included a call for the cessation of bombing in North Vietnam by the US with reciprocal action the part of the Vietnamese.[171] Of particular significance in the Cold War climate, the WCC statement asked for an easing of tension in the US by modifying "its policy of containment of communism and Communist countries supporting wars of liberation."[172] A particular problem with this statement for the Americans was the request for recognition of the National Liberation Front (NLF), for they could not concede to Communists sharing power in South Vietnam.

Part of the difficulty in solving the conflict was the American fear of Chinese influence on the North Vietnamese. King had recognized this obstacle, and had already spoken out in favor of China's admission to the UN, which would at least bring them into negotiations.[173] The WCC concluded that China's ostracism should cease, a move that might make them more amenable in brokering a solution,[174] recommending "that every effort be made to bring the seven hundred million people of China through the government in power, the People's Republic of China, into the world community of nations in order that they may assume their reasonable responsibility and

---

Studentengemeinde in Deutshland, WCC General Secretariat, 1946–1995 Asia, Vietnam January–July 1966, 42.3.112/5, WCC Archives, Geneva, Switzerland.

169. "WCC Statement on Vietnam," February 16, 1966, WCC General Secretariat Correspondence: Country Files, 1946–1995 Asia, Vietnam August 1966–February 1967, 42.3112/3, WCC Archives, Geneva, Switzerland.

170. The Consultation at Bangkok tested a wider area of Christian opinion, and the National Council of Churches of Christ in the US discussed their differences as well as points they held in common. Over the previous twelve months, officers of the CCIA had consulted with some of the directly concerned governments and with the UN to convey the views of National Commissions, regional agencies, and other organs of the WCC.

171. "WCC Statement on Vietnam," February 16, 1966, 42.3112/3, WCC Archives, Geneva, Switzerland.

172 Ibid.

173. King and Goldberg, statements on the war in Vietnam, September 10, 1965, King Center Library and Archive, Atlanta, GA.

174. "WCC Statement on Vietnam," February 16, 1966, 42.3112/3, WCC Archives, Geneva, Switzerland.

avail themselves of legitimate opportunity to provide an essential ingredient for peace and security not only in Southeast Asia, but throughout the entire world."[175] The WCC called for all parties, including the NLF, to be accorded a place in the negotiations, asking that all agree to greater flexibility to bring about a solution. The WCC particularly noted the suffering of civilians and demanded special attention for their protection.[176] In this, the WCC made an important point: "That all parties recognize the extent to which what is happening in Vietnam is part of a social revolution and that, freed from foreign intervention, Vietnam, both North and South, ought to be in a position to determine its own future, with due consideration of the demands of peace and security in Southeast Asia."[177]

King would make a similar point in his Riverside speech in April of 1967, and it could be argued that he was influenced by the WCC statement in this regard, for as he said, "these are revolutionary times. All over the globe men are revolting against old systems of exploitation and oppression, and out of the wombs of a frail world, new systems of justice and equality are being born. The shirtless and barefoot people of the land are rising up as never before."[178] To accept this reality, it was necessary for all parties to forego military action in solving what was in effect a political, social, and economic issue for Vietnam. For this reason, the WCC called for a massive development program and a prolonged cease-fire to allow a cooling-off period, with an enlarged international control commission to police it.[179]

Blake was active in his opposition to the Vietnam War, and he adopted a high profile similar to King's. Blake was also a guest on *Face the Nation* in December, 1966. Host Martin Agronsky asked Blake if he regarded US policy and the war in Vietnam as un-Christian. He replied that any war is un-Christian, but that this war was much more controversial than many others in that the whole world was critical of US policy. Host John Benti put it to Blake that most of the criticism of the US position in Vietnam at home had come from Christian clergy, resulting in some outcry from their own congregations. But what right did church leaders have to tell the government what to do in Vietnam? Blake replied that a moral issue was always "a right for a church to comment on," and he saw it as a rather simple one.[180]

175. Ibid.

176. Ibid.

177. Ibid.

178. King, "Time to Break Silence," 231–44.

179. "WCC Statement on Vietnam," February 16, 1966, 42.3112/3, WCC Archives, Geneva, Switzerland.

180. Blake, interview by Agronsky, *Face the Nation*, December 25, 1966, 995.1.03/1 Speeches (1966), WCC Archives, Geneva, Switzerland.

Blake was asked if he thought the United States was using overwhelming technological power to win the war in Vietnam. He conceded that there was a problem because the American people feared communism, and they were aware of the difficulties Christian churches experienced in totalitarian states. Therefore, the real problem was a battle of ideologies, "that is, the ideology of communism versus the ideology of the free world."[181] Nevertheless, Blake was critical of the US because he feared their strategy was delaying the initiation of peace talks. Edward Fiske of the *New York Times* asked Blake about the "Guns and Butter" theory,[182] and whether he agreed with it. Blake claimed not to have been following the rumors of cutbacks, but said he would be surprised if the planned scale of the war on poverty had not been affected. It could only be expanded through higher taxation.[183] For Blake, it was necessary to prioritize and the "war in the center of our cities" over the long-range interests of freedom and democracy in South Vietnam.[184] Blake had a history of being very outspoken on social issues prior to assuming his post with the WCC. He expressed views similar to King's in this interview, begging the question of whether they may have coordinated their responses to the controversies of the day—namely, racism and the Vietnam War.

David Hunter, who was Deputy General Secretary of the NCC and also served on the CALCAV committee with King, wrote to Blake in early January 1967 concerning the Education Action Mobilization scheduled in Washington at the end of that month. The purpose of the letter was to request "a statement of greetings to the Mobilization."[185] Hunter explained that only two requests were being made, one to Blake and the other to Pope Paul VI, saying, "we are writing exclusively to you and his Holiness for obvious reasons but very specifically because you were each referred to in the recent statement of U Thant. The three-point proposal of U Thant will be one of the central points of this mobilization, and we would like the mobilization to have the privilege of hearing a brief message from the two world religious leaders to whom U Thant referred."[186] Throughout his tenure from 1961 to

181. Ibid.

182. "Guns and Butter" is the choice in allocating the national budget between defense and social spending as part of gross domestic product expenditure

183. Blake, interview by Agronsky, *Face the Nation*, December 25, 1966, 995.1.03/1 Speeches (1966), WCC Archives, Geneva, Switzerland.

184. Ibid.

185. David R. Hunter, CALCAV, to Eugene Carson Blake, January 5, 1967, WCC General Secretariat Correspondence: Country Files, 1946–1995 Asia, Vietnam August 1966–February 1967, 42.3112/4, WCC Archives, Geneva, Switzerland.

186. Ibid.

1971, "U Thant was deeply concerned with the question of Vietnam."[187] The US kept the debate on the war out of the UN because they could not win any moral victory in that debating chamber, and their allies in that war were thin on the ground. Therefore, "by tacit consent the question was never formally debated in the General Assembly and only cursorily touched upon in the Security Council."[188] Nevertheless, "until the opening of the Paris Peace talks in 1968, U Thant was unremitting in his efforts to persuade the parties in the conflict to initiate negotiations on their own."[189] Blake wrote a brief reply, cryptically refusing Hunter's offer: "I am forced to reply no to your request. However, if by any chance the Pope should respond positively (which my colleagues doubt), I would be glad to reconsider the above decision. My reason is not so much to do with status as to protect my international position."[190] Blake's reticence to be involved with the antiwar movement at this point may have been due to the fact that he had only assumed the role as General Secretary of the WCC that December, and he had yet to establish himself in the position.

Although the Catholic Church was not a member of the WCC, it had a close working relationship with the WCC and some clarification is required here on the Catholic Church's position on Vietnam. Pope Paul VI made specific references to the conflict in his 1966 encyclical "Christi Matri," when he called on "all those responsible [to] bring about the necessary conditions for the laying down of arms."[191] However, the assembly of American Roman Catholic Bishops supported President Johnson. They argued that "our presence in Vietnam is justified" while supporting the search for alternatives.[192] The very influential Cardinal Spellman, the military vicar of the armed forces for the Roman Catholic Church, sounded the loudest clarion call to arms. Declaring "my country right or wrong,"[193] Spellman enthusiastically supported the Johnson administration at home and abroad. On a visit to South Vietnam, Spellman asserted that American soldiers were in there "helping to defend the freedom and independence of the Vietnamese people, and, incidentally our own people, against Communist aggression."[194] It was not

---

187. Gall, "U Thant's Stand on the Vietnam War," 51.

188. Ibid.

189. Ibid.

190. Hunter, CALCAV, to Blake, January 5, 1967, 42.3112/4, WCC Archives, Geneva, Switzerland.

191. Friedland, *Lift Up Your Voice*, 174.

192. Ibid., 174–75.

193. Quoted in ibid.

194. Ibid.

only the prominent Catholic prelates who supported the war. Fr. John B. Sheerin, editor of *Catholic World* and later one of the most prominent Catholic voices within CALCAV, wrote with some exasperation in March of 1966 that "the great majority of American Catholics seem to have no particular moral convictions with regard to the war in Vietnam."[195] He added, "is it not strange that so many of our clergy who have no hesitation about making positive moral judgments week after week in confession have no opinions on the great moral problems of our generation?"[196]

The Conference of Catholic Bishops in the United States supported the government's policy on the Vietnam War in its November 1966, statement.[197] CALCAV held its Washington Mobilization at the end of January 1967, and not one Catholic bishop attended, although telegrams were sent to each one inviting them to participate or at least make public their approval.[198] Sheerin found the conflict in Vietnam unsupportable when judged by the traditional Catholic doctrine of the "just war."[199] Other representatives of the Catholic hierarchy began to speak out belatedly in March of 1967, when Archbishop Paul J. Hallinan of Atlanta affirmed that "our conscience and our voice must be raised against the savagery and terror of war."[200] It is worth noting that both Archbishop Hallinan and Martin Luther King Jr. were from Atlanta, where King's influence may have played a role in changing the Catholic hierarchy's stance. In fact, correspondence confirms Archbishop Hallinan's high regard for King, which moved him to arrange a private audience between King and Pope Paul VI on September 18, 1964. Hallinan described King's place in American life as "among the great moral leaders."[201] Arrangements were also made for King to meet with a gathering of American bishops at the Ecumenical Council in Rome. Further evidence of King's good relationship with Archbishop Hallinan is found in a letter dated from June of 1964, in which he thanked King "for your Christian witness, your courage, and your nobility. The nation, white and Negro, owes you a tribute, not so much of acclamation (for the Christian is not too concerned about that), but of following you in the Christian virtues that your life exemplifies. History will pay that tribute even though it may be clouded

---

195. Hall, *Because of Their Faith*, 39.

196. Ibid., 39–40.

197. Ibid., 39.

198. Friedland, *Lift Up Your Voice*, 179.

199. Hall, *Because of Their Faith*, 39–40.

200. Ibid., 39.

201. Paul Hallinan to Martin J. O'Connor, September 4, 1964, King Papers, Box 12.17, June–October 1964, King Center Library and Archive, Atlanta, GA.

today."[202] Two weeks after Hallinan's address, Auxiliary Bishop James P. Shannon of Saint Paul and Minneapolis joined with ten Roman Catholic college presidents calling for a "reassessment of American involvement in Vietnam."[203] Despite its moderate tone, the message marked a significant departure from the statement Catholic bishops had made the previous November.[204] Friedland makes the point that the majority of Catholic bishops mistrusted CALCAV's aims, believing it to be too left of center on the political spectrum.[205] This perception persisted despite CALCAV's careful avoidance of organizations that were not religiously oriented. CALCAV represented, as McAfee Brown points out, "the American middle class. It is here that the voters are found, and it is from here that must come the kind of pressure that can make a difference."[206]

The Executive Committee of CALCAV, which King co-chaired, prepared a position paper for distribution at the Washington Mobilization in January of 1967. The introduction was later used in King's Riverside speech, "Beyond Vietnam," and in fact the content was very similar. The group regretted that it had not spoken with a clearer voice, and it now wished to join with Pope Paul VI, the WCC, the Synagogue Council of America, the NCC, the National Conference of Bishops, and other religious bodies in urging a reappraisal of US policy in Vietnam. The group stated that their allegiance to the nation was held under a higher allegiance to the God "who is sovereign over all the nations."[207] Thus, it was obvious to CALCAV's members where their duty lay: "'You shall have no other Gods before me' [Exod 20:3], we must obey God rather than men. Each day we find allegiances to our nation's policy more difficult to reconcile with allegiance to our God."[208] CALCAV explained that the exercise of their faith and of democratic privilege obliged them to speak out. The lifeblood of democracy depended on responsible expressions of disagreement and dissent, and thus loyalty compelled them to speak on in condemnation of a national policy that could lead the world toward disaster.[209] As with King's antiwar speeches, CALCAV

---

202. Ibid.

203. Hall, *Because of Their Faith*, 39.

204. Ibid.

205. Friedland, *Lift Up Your Voice*, 182.

206. Quoted in Hall, *Because of Their Faith*, 49.

207. Executive Committee of CALCAV, "Vietnam: The Clergymen's Dilemma," position paper presented at the Washington Mobilization, January 31–February 1, 1967, WCC General Secretariat Correspondence: Country Files, 1946–1995 Asia, Vietnam, 42.3.113/5, WCC Archives, Geneva, Switzerland.

208. Ibid.

209. Ibid.

was concerned about maintaining their patriotism despite their criticism of US foreign policy. They felt entitled to articulate their condemnation of an unjust war because "at home we find the war threatening the very goals we claim to be defending in Vietnam . . . a spurious type of patriotism is challenging the right of dissent and the open debate of public issues."[210]

Speaking of their ongoing anguish over the "immorality of the warfare," CALCAV condemned a war in which "civilian casualties are greater than military; in which whole populations are deported against their will; in which the widespread use of napalm and other explosives is killing and maiming women, children, and the aged; and in which the combatants are systematically destroying their crops and production capacity of a country they profess to liberate."[211] This quotation contains the very sentiments expressed by King in his escalating antiwar speeches, which began around this time in February of 1967. CALCAV and King also campaigned relentlessly on the erosion of the Great Society program. Both argued that "financial and psychological preoccupation with the war is destroying creative plans to alleviate poverty, overcome disease, extend education, replace city slums, and exalt human dignity."[212] The position paper emphasized the necessity for more openness and urged that it is "our duty to magnify the moral voice of the nation" by asking for clarification of real alternatives to war.[213] This was a sharp rebuke to the Johnson administration, the implication being that he had been less than frank about peace initiatives. King, as co-chair of CALCAV, may have been aware of the content, for it was released just two months before his sensational Riverside speech. But, as Harold E. Quinley argues, the record of the church in wartime was hardly one of militant pacification. Not only have some of the bloodiest wars in history been fought primarily on religious grounds, but even more worryingly, virtually all recent military conflicts have been carried out in the name of a deity.[214]

The WCC was consistent in its opposition to the war, and in August of 1967, issued a definitive antiwar statement. The WCC cautioned that the situation had deteriorated and that greater dangers lay ahead. Positions had hardened, for the continued military escalation was opening up "an apparently endless vista of horror."[215] Despite the gloom, the WCC felt that new

210. Ibid.

211. Ibid.

212. Ibid.

213. Ibid.

214. Quinley, "Protestant Clergy," 43–52.

215. "Statement on the Middle East," adopted by the WCC Central Committee at Heraklion, Crete, Greece, August 15–26, 1967, WCC General Secretariat Correspondence: Country Files, 1946–1995 Asia, Vietnam, 42.3.112/3, WCC Archives, Geneva,

opportunities for negotiation may be emerging. Pleading for action, they implored, "peace cannot be made by either side alone. We therefore urge all parties, in the interests of greater justice, no matter for what reasons they are still fighting, to take steps now to test the worth of negotiation rather than warfare."[216]

The Vietnam War had become so controversial by 1967 that Johnson and his supporters were increasingly sensitive to any criticism. A typical example was directed at Blake by William Tucker Dean of the Cornell Law School, who objected to the former's comments in the *New York Times* urging that the US stop the bombing of North Vietnam. Dean said that he did not begrudge the clergy's right to their opinions, but when a minister takes to the pulpit, he "may appear to be speaking for the millions of church members," and it is a step too far when the minister "takes what might be termed an official position on a political matter on which honest Christian men may reasonably disagree."[217] It is worth remembering that Blake and King, along with the Berrigan brothers,[218] were among the relatively small number of prominent clergymen who spoke out consistently on major issues such as the Vietnam War prior to 1967.

King attended the Pacem in Terris II Convocation in Geneva in May of 1967, where he welcomed the opportunity to speak out on the "costly, bloody, and futile war in Vietnam."[219] King made it clear that he loved America, but spoke critically "because I want to see her stand as the moral example of the world." King expressed his fears that this war had the potential to spread far and wide: "The war in Vietnam is more than a local conflict taking place on Asian soil. It is a nightmarish struggle that involves and threatens the whole world. I cannot help but feel that the present crisis in the Middle East is indirectly related to the US involvement in Vietnam. War anywhere intensifies the possibility of war everywhere."[220] King spoke of major nations flouting the authority of the United Nations by embarking

---

Switzerland.

216. Ibid.

217. William Tucker Dean to Eugene Carson Blake, May 3, 1967, WCC General Secretariat Correspondence: Country Files, 1946–1995 Asia, Vietnam, 42.3.115/5, WCC Archives, Geneva, Switzerland.

218. Philip Berrigan (October 5, 1923–December 6, 2002) was an internationally renowned American peace activist and former Roman Catholic priest. Berrigan, along with his brother Daniel, conducted anti-war campaigns to the considerable annoyance to the authorities.

219. King, Martin Luther, Jr., "Statement at Pacem in Terris II Convocation," address at Geneva, Switzerland, May 29, 1967, King Papers, Box 3, May–July, 1967, King Center Library and Archive, Atlanta, GA.

220. Ibid.

on "unilateral courses of action" and opening the door for other nations to follow suit. King felt that the war in Vietnam had played havoc with the "destiny of the entire world" and that the consequences of the conflict had been disastrous for international relations: "It has torn up the Geneva Agreement, it has seriously impaired the United Nations; it has exacerbated the hatreds between continents and, worse still, between races."[221] This misguided foreign policy also had repercussions in the US, said King, for "it has frustrated our development at home, telling our underprivileged citizens that we place insatiable military demands above their most critical needs," and moreover, "it has greatly contributed to the forces of reaction in America and strengthened the military industrial complex, against which even President Eisenhower solemnly warned us." Finally, King proclaimed, the war had "practically destroyed Vietnam and left thousands of Americans and Vietnamese youth maimed and mutilated and exposed the whole world to the risk of nuclear warfare."[222]

Blake also delivered a speech on the Vietnam War in October of 1967 in Saint Louis. He believed that the United States, due to its great economic and military power, had the right and the duty to resist the spread of communism by force. He expressed his belief in the sincerity of President Johnson's administration "when they say that this is our chief reason for being in Vietnam."[223] But Blake was of the opinion that no state had the right "to solve its social and economic problems by liquidating the opposition and ignoring individual human rights in the process."[224] As Blake had previously argued, it was obvious that the military side of the war could be won. In fact, all of Vietnam could be bulldozed to the ground, but that would not constitute victory. It had to be recognized, Blake told his listeners, that "the Vietnamese are fighting a war of independence, and overwhelming force won't make them seek peace."[225] King, in his Riverside speech earlier that year, had preached that the war in Vietnam was a social revolution and that "a true revolution of values will lay hands on the world order and say of war: 'This way of settling differences is not just' . . . A nation that continues year after year to spend more money on military defense than on programs of social uplift is approaching spiritual death."[226] Blake criticized US policy

221. Ibid.

222. Ibid.

223. Blake, Eugene Carson, "Vietnam," address at Kiel Auditorium, Saint Louis, MO, October 15, 1967, 995.1.03/36 Speeches (1966–1968), WCC Archives, Geneva, Switzerland.

224. Ibid.

225. Ibid.

226. King, "Time to Break Silence," 231–44.

in Vietnam for its unilateral rather than multilateral approach. With the possible exception of South Korea, he claimed, "there is no government that would dare risk a free vote of its people to go all out in our support."[227] Again, in this speech we hear Blake echoing King's views from a liberal Christian standpoint.

In February of 1968 the NCC adopted a resolution on Vietnam that included a number of observations. The NCC noted that British Prime Minister Harold Wilson[228] had spoken in the House of Commons on February 13 concerning the prospect of negotiations, saying, "there is a very narrow gap to be bridged now, very narrow indeed."[229] The *New York Times* also observed that "Secretary General U Thant believes that if the United States unconditionally stopped the bombing of North Vietnam for as long as about two weeks, Hanoi would begin meaningful negotiations."[230] The NCC welcomed these statements and considered it time for the government do its utmost in the search for a peaceful settlement.[231] U Thant was further reported to have said that there was "a not unhopeful prospect for negotiations despite bloody military developments of the last few weeks."[232] U Thant was referring to the Tet[233] Offensive, a maneuver that had caught the Americans off guard in an intelligence failure ranking with Pearl Harbor. In view of these hopeful statements, the NCC was dismayed to hear Johnson say, "the search for peace appeared to be exhausted, and therefore the time for debate had come to an end while brave Americans made their stand in battle."[234] Thus, 1968 had arrived with little progress on the peace front.

After King was assassinated on April 4, 1968, Blake consoled a grieving Mrs. King by telling her that he had counted her husband as a friend and

227. Blake, "Vietnam," October 15, 1967, 995.1.03/36 Speeches (1966–1968), WCC Archives, Geneva, Switzerland.

228. Harold Wilson (March 11, 1916–May 24, 1995) was a British Labour Party politician who served as Prime Minister of Great Britain from 1964 to 1970 and from 1974 to 1976. Wilson's government supported the US position in Vietnam.

229. "National Council of Churches of Christ in the US Resolution on Vietnam," February 22,1968, WCC General Secretariat Correspondence: Country Files, 1946–1995 Asia, Vietnam, 42.3.112/6, WCC Archives, Geneva, Switzerland.

230. Quoted in ibid.

231. Ibid.

232. Ibid.

233. On January 30, 1968, the Viet Cong and North Vietnamese launched a military assault against South Vietnam, the United States, and their allies. Known as the Tet Offensive, the attacks against military and civilian control centers throughout South Vietnam came as a dangerous surprise.

234. "National Council of Churches of Christ in the US Resolution on Vietnam," 42.3.112/6, WCC Archives, Geneva, Switzerland.

colleague. Even more importantly, he stated, "I want you to know that in my judgment he was the outstanding Christian minister in our nation."[235] Numerous church bodies issued tributes following King's death. Below is the text of an appreciation of the life of Martin Luther King Jr. from three international Christian organizations based at the Ecumenical Centre in Geneva, including Dr. Eugene Carson Blake, General Secretary of the World Council of Churches; Dr. Marcel Pradervand, General Secretary of the World Alliance of Reformed Churches; and Dr. Andre Appel, General Secretary of the Lutheran World Federation:

> But it is not as statesman and prophet we think of him first. We mourn him most as a man; a brilliant, valiant, beloved man . . . By international consensus Dr. King was a first citizen of the world. In the United States he was a main hope for a tormented nation. To the church, he was the leading minister of Christ. For the unjustly used everywhere, he was a prime mover in the nonviolent campaign for justice, the peaceful way to peace . . . We missed him then, we miss him now; but we heard, we hear.[236]

From Nairobi, Kenya, J. Lowrie Anderson, a fraternal worker under the United Presbyterian Commission on Ecumenical Mission and Relations, wrote, "perhaps nowhere was the impact of the assassination greater than in Africa . . . Africans identified themselves with the civil rights movement in America, and with Dr. King. They felt that in his fight for equality for the disinherited in America, he was fighting for black men everywhere."[237] Anderson went on to share how he and a colleague sat down to tea with an African friend who said "We hate you Americans. You killed our Martin Luther King." The colleague replied, "Yes, I was ashamed of being an American—until I remembered that Martin Luther King was an American also. Then I was proud."[238]

Thus, the 1960s came to an end with the loss of Chief Luthuli in July of 1967 under suspicious circumstances, followed on April 4, 1968, with the assassination of Martin Luther King Jr., leaving a lacuna in both South Africa and the United States that would be impossible to fill. As Luthuli

235. Eugene Carson Blake to Coretta Scott King, April 1968, WCC General Secretariat, Correspondence: Frequent (1937–1977), 42.11.05, WCC Archives, Geneva, Switzerland.

236. "Churchmen Open Memorial Fund for Dr. King," *Catholic Herald*, April 19, 1968, 2, http://archive.catholicherald.co.uk/article/19th-april-1968/2/churchmen-open-memorial-fund-for-dr-king. See also, Approach, *The Mission Education Newsweekly*, April 22, 1968, Philadelphia, 42.11.08/2, WCC Archives, Geneva.

237. Anderson, "Foreign Tributes to Dr. King," 629–30.

238. Ibid.

had wisely pronounced, "apartheid in practice is proving to be a monster created by Frankenstein. This is the tragedy of the South African scene."[239] Fortunately, King's legacy survived, and the powerful impact he made on the WCC was brought to bear when its Programme to Combat Racism convened in London in May of 1969, a development which we will discuss later.

This chapter and chapter 3 have shown how King's growing opposition to the Vietnam War and racism followed a similar path to that adopted by the WCC. King made a significant contribution to Christian attempts to address both of these problems, which he saw as being related. We have seen the high esteem that Willem Visser 't Hooft and his successor, Eugene Carson Blake, had for King. The WCC' invitation to attend the Fourth Assembly in Uppsala illustrated that they saw his nonviolent policy as a solution to some of the major issues of the day. The significant shift in the WCC's position at Uppsala was certainly influenced by the changed composition of the Council's constituency. The WCC was becoming a truly world council. In 1948, forty-two of the 147 churches that formed the Council were from Third World countries, with ten from African churches in South Africa, Egypt, and Ethiopia. Some twenty years later at Uppsala that number had increased to 103 out of 253. Among the forty-one African churches the majority were not from independent Africa. The presumed assassination of Chief Albert Luthuli and the life imprisonment of Nelson Mandela had a strong impact on the life of the ecumenical movement, which called for action by the WCC in South Africa. The Assembly, for the first time in WCC history, used the terms "racism" and "white racism," which it called "a blatant denial of the Christian faith."[240]

239. Luthuli, "For Freedom in South Africa," December 11, 1961, British Library, London.

240. "Preface by Dr. Eugene Carson Blake," in Vincent, *Race Race*, ix–xii.

6

A Tribute to a Peaceful Crusader

The WCC, Martin Luther King Jr., and the
Resolution at Uppsala

KING'S CLOSE RELATIONSHIP WITH the WCC, together with the organization's appreciation of his successful campaign against racism in the United States, resulted in the WCC adopting a program to deal with worldwide racism and the resolution of disparate conflicts by nonviolent means. In words consistent with his maturing global vision, King had insisted, "the philosophy and strategy of nonviolence [should] immediately become a subject for study and serious experimentation in every field of human conflict, including relations between nations."[1]

The WCC and King influenced one another in their efforts to bring an end to the Vietnam War and to racism worldwide. The WCC considered the Vietnam War to be racist, and was concerned that it was adversely affecting its outreach to Asia. Members agonized over the very thought of "white people killing people of color; noting that this is not helping us in terms of our position in Asia."[2] King denounced the racist overtones of the war in a similar fashion when he preached, "there is something strangely

1. King, Martin Luther, Jr., "Dreams of Brighter Tomorrows," Chicago, *Ebony*, March 1965, 34–35, quoted in Baldwin, *Voice of Conscience*, 190.

2. Blake, interview by Agronsky, *Face the Nation*, December 25, 1966, 995.1.03/1 Speeches (1966), WCC Archives, Geneva, Switzerland.

inconsistent about a nation and a press that would praise you when you say," be nonviolent towards Jim Clark,[3] but will curse and damn you when you say be nonviolent toward little brown children."[4]

Blake referred to the racist nature of the Vietnam war in Norwalk, CT, on April 26, 1967, when he spoke of the weakening of America's best ideals: "the picture of a great and wealthy nation mobilizing each month more and more of its unparalleled technological might to bring a tiny, long suffering, dark-skinned nation to capitulation means clearly that the more we win the more we lose."[5] No doubt, Blake, in contemplating the upcoming Assembly, was concerned about how deliberations on these two majors issues would proceed.

In early 1968, Blake was interviewed for the International Christian Union of Business Executives (UNIAPAC) in connection with the forthcoming Assembly in Uppsala, Sweden. He explained that delegates of some 230 churches, which together represented 350 million Christians, would concentrate on six groups of questions on the subject of unity, mission, social development, political affairs, worship in secular society, and the style of life Christians were searching for in the second half of the twentieth century. Blake added that they would consider difficult questions of world peace and international economic justice, along with the consequences of rapid social change on Christian lifestyles. It was accepted that the national churches were often divided on these questions, and that the fundamental differences between the churches of the rich Western nations and the new nations of Africa, Asia, and Latin America had to be acknowledged. Blake cautioned, "the polarization of opinion on such social questions within the church and the secular world is a special challenge to the ecumenical movement, and tests the ability of the church to work for reconciliation with its own life."[6] The challenge for the Assembly, said Blake, was that in order for the churches to view these problems from a universal perspective, it was necessary for them to overcome their rather narrow national and regional outlook. This kind of unity was very much in keeping with King's rationale for an

3. James Gardner Clark, Jr. (September 17, 1922–June 4, 2007), was a sheriff of Dallas County, Alabama, from 1955 to 1966 and was involved in the violent arrest of civil rights protestors.

4. King, Martin Luther, Jr., "Why I Am Opposed to the War in Vietnam," address at Ebenezer Baptist Church, Atlanta, GA, April 30, 1967, Box 12, January–April 1967, King Center Library and Archive, Atlanta, GA.

5. Blake, Eugene Carson, "The Vietnam War," *Newsletter of the International Fellowship of Reconciliation*, May 1967, WCC General Secretariat, 1938–1993 Asia, 42.3.112/6 Vietnam (1949–1967), WCC Archives, Geneva, Switzerland.

6. Blake, Eugene Carson, "Interview for UNIAPAC," *UNIAPAC International*, January–February 1968, 995.1.01/5 Works (1968), WCC Archive, Geneva, Switzerland.

end to racism and war. The alternative, Blake claimed, could at best achieve "some partial compromise of different hard positions." He concluded, that the Assembly was more than a test of the health of the church, it was "a test of the readiness of nations and peoples to tolerate new opinions, and accept outside judgments on their new policies."[7]

Speaking at Uppsala in July of 1968, James Baldwin[8], whom King had admired greatly, delivered a speech titled, "White Racism or World Community." Baldwin spoke on the quest for civil rights in the 1960s, and he criticized how the official response made him a special target of the FBI. That alone had resulted in a 1,750-page FBI file on him, equating Baldwin with King as a threat to government stability.[9] Baldwin talked of the historical confrontation between the Christian church and those who could not accept black people as their equals. For Baldwin, it was quite simple; the Christian church had betrayed its own principles as far as black people were concerned, for it had sided with the white power structure in support of the status quo. King had held a similar view, and in 1963, had supported Baldwin's criticism of the church, describing the author as one of the nation's most perceptive writers in his scathing indictment of the Christian church. King wrote of Baldwin, "he made it clear, that particularly in the area of race and color prejudice, the religious forces of America in many ways aided and abetted the ills of injustice and inequality in race relations."[10]

It is noteworthy that King himself had first embraced Baldwin, and now the WCC had invited him to speak following King's death. Undoubtedly, Baldwin was right in criticizing the white church for their discriminatory practices against people of color and for their general implied endorsement of the status quo by silence, which facilitated the perpetuation of white superiority. By inviting Baldwin, the WCC perhaps acknowledged the accuracy of his indictment of white Christian churches in the US and in other states practicing apartheid, particularly South Africa and Rhodesia. Therefore, in the absence of King, Baldwin was an appropriate substitute. Baldwin, like King, saw the injustices in society and told the churches that they should use their power and resources to influence states claiming to act

---

7. Ibid.

8. James Baldwin (August 2, 1924–December 1, 1987) renowned author and playwright, and considered one of the greatest writers of his time. Baldwin was very active in the civil rights movement.

9. Baldwin, James, "White Racism or World Community," Programme to Combat Racism, Notting Hill Consultation 1969 (1965–1969), 4223.1.01, WCC Archives, Geneva, Switzerland.

10. King, "Segregation in the Church," *New York Amsterdam News*, February 2, 1963.

with a Christian imprimatur: "the Christian church still rules this world, it still has the power, if it will do it, to change the structure of South Africa. It has the power, if it will, to prevent the death of another Martin Luther King Jr. It has the power, if it will, to force my government to cease dropping bombs in Southeast Asia. These are crimes committed in the name of the Christian church."[11]

Baldwin spoke passionately about the exploitation of blacks by their white masters, especially in South Africa: "Until at last the Christian church has got to pretend that black South African miners are pleased to go into the mines and bring out the diamonds and the wealth which belongs to Africa, to dig it up for nothing and give it to Europe."[12] Indeed, King was equally pained by the exploitation of blacks in South Africa under the apartheid system. As he explained, "go to South Africa today, and there you will see some fourteen million black men and women, boys and girls segregated on 2 percent of their own land . . . having to use passes to walk the streets."[13]

Baldwin castigated the white church for its hypocrisy in transporting slaves from Africa and conspiring with itself "to say I preferred slavery to my own condition," for wherever the white man colonized, exploitation followed.[14] Baldwin contended that the white church opted for power in betraying its own first principle "that all men are the sons of God, and that all men are free in the eyes of God, and are victims of the commandment given to the Christian church, 'Love one another as I have loved you.'" As a result, he suggested that the church was in great danger "when they know something, know what they should do, and refuse to act on what they know." Baldwin drew attention to allegedly radical black men such as Malcolm X and Martin Luther King Jr., who was "the most popular man in his country," both of whom had been silenced.[15]

In his article, "Eugene Carson Blake, Apostle of Christian Unity," Paul A. Crow states that "it was the Uppsala Assembly, under Blake's direction, which in the turbulence of 1968, began to respond to the changing world scene."[16] The world scene had become one through global communications technologies along with economic and political independence. But as

11. Baldwin, "White Racism or World Community," Notting Hill Consultation 1969 (1965–1969), 4223.1.01, WCC Archives, Geneva, Switzerland.

12. Ibid.

13. King, "Knock at Midnight," June 25, 1967, King Center Library and Archive, Atlanta, GA.

14. Baldwin, "White Racism or World Community," Notting Hill Consultation 1969 (1965–1969), 4223.1.01, WCC Archives, Geneva, Switzerland.

15. Ibid.

16. Crow, "Eugene Carson Blake," 228–36.

Crow explains, the fellowship and community of the world were awfully fragmented. However, under the biblical theme, "Behold, I make all things new" (Rev 21:5), he wrote that the WCC addressed two questions: "Could the world discover and establish its unity and community in time to prevent its imminent nuclear self destruction? Does faith in God revealed in Jesus Christ, which has drawn the churches together in the WCC, have enough power to contribute to the unity of human community?"[17] Crow writes that Blake understood those questions and would help the WCC find suitable responses. Blake had described racism as, "the new divisive issue," and as he wrote in *Christianity and Crisis*, "unless the churches can move forward to the actual and voluntary establishment of a new pluralistic nondiscriminatory pattern of race relations here and abroad, they will have failed at a crucial moment in history."[18] Blake concluded, "conversion to color blindness is the number one challenge to Christian evangelism. Any other evangelism is a betrayal of the gospel."[19]

The Fourth Assembly of the WCC expressed confidence that the causes for which King stood would triumph. The deep feelings against racism and economic exploitation would find expression in the actions of the Assembly. King had condemned the Vietnam War and its racial and economic underpinnings since the early sixties, and the resolution adopted by the Assembly would have pleased him: "The World Council of Churches declare that the mortal suffering of the Vietnamese people should at once be ended. The restoration of peace in Vietnam is of paramount importance to our member churches, concerned as they are that mankind shall live reconciled in justice and peace."[20] The WCC resolution welcomed the fact that both sides of the conflict had come to the conference table in Paris. In order to create the proper climate for constructive negotiations, the WCC urged all parties to refrain from building up their military strength. As with previous resolutions, it was imperative that the US bombing of North Vietnam cease along with the cessation of military activities in the south. The WCC recognized that a political solution could not be achieved by military might. Peace could only come about through the self-determination of the Vietnamese people, as King had often said. Reproving the US for exacerbating a tragedy through the political, social, and economic problems triggered by unilateral intervention, the WCC saw a solution in the involvement of a strengthened

17. Ibid.

18. Blake, "Church in the Next Decade," 17.

19. Ibid.

20. "Resolution on Vietnam," adopted by the Fourth Assembly of the WCC, Uppsala, Sweden, July 4–20, 1968, WCC General Secretariat Correspondence: Country Files, 1946–1995 Asia, Vietnam, 42.3.115/5, WCC Archives, Geneva, Switzerland.

UN in the peace process. The resolution insisted that it was intolerable that Vietnam was the "symbol for our time of the misery of a developing people caught in world conflict."[21]

In view of the years that passed before the Vietnam War ended, the Assembly's resolution, in retrospect, seems to have been overly optimistic about the provision for post-war aid: "These considerations make it all the more timely to begin immediately the preparation for post-war aid. These problems, particularly as they relate to the homeless, may well be of unprecedented proportions. The planning by the churches for programs expressing their concern must be pushed forward as quickly as possible."[22] Perhaps the lack of open debate on the Vietnam War in the US, as King constantly highlighted, contributed to the scarcity of hard facts on the actual progress, or lack of it, in bringing the conflict to a speedy conclusion.

When the delegates met at the Uppsala Assembly, the WCC did not yet have an organized program to combat racism. James Baldwin questioned their intentions: "I address you as one of God's creatures whom the Christian church has most betrayed . . . I wonder whether there is left in the Christian civilization the moral energy, the spiritual daring, to atone, to repent, to be borne again."[23] This is not to say that the ecumenical movement or the WCC had ignored the issue of racism, nor is it a simple coincidence that the Programme to Combat Racism was prompted at Uppsala. The decisions taken at Uppsala and subsequent meetings of the Central and Executive Committees came almost at the end of a process of decolonization in Asia, Africa, and the Caribbean, and therefore must be seen as a reaction to the aspirations of the masses to be free of foreign domination. The WCC report, "From Uppsala to Jakarta," noted that racism was not confined to certain countries or continents, but that it was a "world problem," adding that white racism was not the only form of racism and ethnocentrism. But the major problem was confined to countries where the whites had colonized: "It is the coincidence, however, of an accumulation of wealth and power in the hands of the white peoples following upon their historical and economic progress during the past four hundred years, which is the reason for a focus on the various forms of white racism in the different parts of the world."[24] While it was widely accepted that whites in general exploited people of color

21. Ibid.

22. Ibid.

23. Baldwin, "White Racism or World Community," Notting Hill Consultation 1969 (1965–1969), 4223.1.01, WCC Archives, Geneva, Switzerland.

24. "From Uppsala to Jakarta," Report of the Commission to Combat Racism, Programme to Combat Racism, Masterfiles–Statement, No. 5 (1–6), 4223.16.1, WCC Archives, Geneva, Switzerland.

throughout the world, the WCC made a very important admission as part of the rationale for an Ecumenical Programme to Combat Racism: "We have also sadly to confess that churches have participated in racial discrimination. Many white northern religious institutions have benefited from racially exploitative economic systems. Many church members are unaware of the facts of racism and of the involvement of their religious and secular institutions in its perpetuation."[25]

It has to be emphasized that King also shared the WCC's concerns over the global inequities that led to war, poverty, and injustice: "Yet, in spite of these spectacular strides in science and technology, and still unlimited ones to come, something basic is missing. America today suffers from a kind of poverty of the spirit which stands in glaring contrast to her scientific and technological abundance . . . We have learned to fly the air like birds and swim the sea like fish, but we have not learned the simple art of walking the earth like brothers."[26] King's message was clear: the churches had a responsibility to solve the problem of racial injustice on a world scale.

At its Fourth Assembly at Uppsala, the WCC, in recognition of the potential for King's methodology to bring about change through peaceful means, adopted a resolution which proposed a Martin Luther King Institute for Nonviolent Social Change:

> *Whereas* Dr. Martin Luther King's untimely death prevented him from addressing this Fourth Assembly of the World Council of Churches;
>
> and *whereas* Dr. Martin Luther King bore witness in his own life, ministry and action the new testament of love and nonviolence as the appropriate Christian means for social change;
>
> and *whereas* the Christian Church is today the legitimate bearer of this gospel of love and nonviolence in a world fraught with injustice, war, poverty, revolution and violence;
>
> *Be It Therefore Resolved* that the Fourth Assembly of the World Council of Churches, as a fitting memorial to Dr. Martin Luther King, initiate all in its member churches a two year study of "Christian nonviolence methods for effecting social change," and that this study culminate in an ongoing program of research,

25. "WCC's Statements and Actions on Racism, 1948–1979," 4223.16.3, WCC Archives, Geneva, Switzerland.

26. King, "Beyond Discovery Love," September 25, 1966, King Center Library and Archive, Atlanta, GA.

study, training and action to be known as "The Martin Luther
King Institute for Nonviolent Social Change."[27]

This was a fitting tribute to the life and work of King, who as a Christian minister, was one of the greatest proponents for change through nonviolent means.

The proposal for implementation of the resolution spoke of the WCC's repeated affirmation over the previous decade that it was part of the Christian vocation to be involved in the struggle for social change. It referred to the 1966 World Conference on Church and Society in Geneva, where it was decided: "This struggle raises the crucial issue of the methods of opposition which a Christian may validly use. The clear Christian teaching regarding the respect for persons and love of one's enemy requires the Christian to seek all possible peaceful and responsible nonviolent means of action in society. He is called to familiarize himself with the forms of nonviolence which have been used effectively in other situations."[28] It was advised that the proposed study of nonviolent action could be a significant part of an expanded program of study and research envisioned by the working group of the World Conference on Church and Society, with a mandate to "concentrate especially on problems in which research is needed, and which are not being tackled by government or other agencies, e.g., international peace and conflict resolution. Here the church could establish and support its own research institutions."[29]

Under the "Definition and Scope" of the study, it was accepted that "nonviolent methods of social change" were obviously many. "Social change" was described as "the slow but far-reaching transformation of cultures through the dissemination of new ideas and the spread of technology."[30] Significant changes had taken place in some countries through parliamentary democracy, but normally this required some pressure from outside the electoral system, but the proposal acknowledged that some existing "political machinery" was not responsive to the demand for justice. The proposal described King's success in this way: "The distinctive contribution of Martin Luther King was his leadership in the use of nonviolent action as a means of struggle for morally necessary social change beyond the limits of con-

---

27. Blake to Cooper, October 28, 1968, WCC Archives, Geneva, Switzerland.

28. "A Proposal for Implementation of the Martin Luther King Resolution," adopted by the Fourth Assembly of the WCC, Uppsala, Sweden, July 4–20, 1968, WCC General Secretariat, Correspondence: Frequent (1938–1970), 42.11.08/2, WCC Archives, Geneva, Switzerland.

29. Ibid.

30. Ibid.

ventional political processes." It was suggested therefore, "that the Martin Luther King Resolution be implemented by a program focused on non-violent action, as it may be relevant to conflicts with national (or smaller) societies."[31]

The initial stages of resolution's implementation included gathering material "which bears on nonviolent action," for examination from "a Christian perspective." The following steps would then be taken to expand the program:

1. Sponsor research on aspects of nonviolence of particular relevance to the concerns of the churches.

2. Arrange for studies of action projects in progress and make evaluations.

3. Offer training in nonviolent action, which can greatly increase the effectiveness of campaigns for justice. There are a variety of training programs in existence in several countries. The ecumenical program should study these to see what approaches are most relevant to the needs of the churches.

4. Support nonviolent action projects aimed at goals which have been defined in ecumenical discussion of social change (as the World Council supported the Delta Ministry in the US).[32]

Zolile Mbali asserts that delegates at Uppsala realized that the issue was not just the problem of negative feelings between races but of "racism as it reinforces contemporary political and economic arrangements, and the way in which in turn these structures bolster racism."[33] Mbali makes the point that it would be naïve to attack racism without acknowledging its political and economic dimensions, or indeed, to assume that racism could be eradicated simply by moral exhortation. Baldwin Sjollema argues that racism has its roots in the economic, political, and social relations between people. In order to maintain their domination, biological and other theories were developed to provide justification for the continuance of racism.[34] Studies have shown links between colored and economic domination and institutional racism, South African apartheid being an extreme example of this connection. The regime could only survive with strong support from Western interests, and constantly adapted itself to the growing threat of radicalization by the majority black population allied to the increasing outspokenness of the churches.

31. Ibid.
32. Ibid.
33. Mbali, *Churches and Racism*, 16.
34. Sjollema, *Isolating Apartheid*, 100.

Reflecting on Uppsala, Anwar M. Barkat, Director of the Programme to Combat Racism, said that the World Conference of 1966 had a considerable impact on the Assembly in 1968. The WCC had reiterated the need for revolutionary change to deal with "unjust situations," adding that the churches had a special contribution to make in developing "effective nonviolent strategies of revolution and social change."[35] Barkat argues that this was a considerable step forward in ecumenical social thought, "because it made a valid distinction between revolution and violence, aspects of social change equated in the past." He did caution that "it meant polarization within the churches," which was a feature of the later history of the WCC. But for now, "the WCC was ready to translate this morally ambiguous distinction into concrete actions to make change possible."[36]

This discussion deals with the practicalities involved in implementing the WCC's "Martin Luther King Resolution on Nonviolence." Dr. Beverly Woodward, a staff member with the International Fellowship of Reconciliation, argues King's assassination led the WCC to pass the resolution in 1968. Although King and his movement clearly provided only partial answers to the question of achieving significant social change, Woodward claims that King "had furnished a challenge."[37] The concluding paragraph of the "Martin Luther King Resolution on Nonviolence" adopted by the Fourth Assembly of the WCC asked "the Central Committee to explore means by which the World Council could promote studies on nonviolent methods of achieving social change, bearing in mind that the issue of violent or nonviolent methods of social change has been raised in the reports of Sections III, IV, and VI."[38]

Peace activist James E. Bristol observed that many of the dispossessed people of the world believe, as most people do, that only armed violence can gain liberation from oppression and freedom from hunger and want. He added, "brave men and courageous patriots have fought and died in many corners of the world from high ideals, to break the yoke of tyranny and to smash the mailed fist of the oppressed."[39] As Bristol commented, America

35. Barkat, Anwar M., "Personal Reflections, 1980–1990," 1994, Programme to Combat Racism, History of the Programme to Combat Racism, 4223.17.1/1, WCC Archives, Geneva, Switzerland.

36. Ibid.

37. Woodward, Beverly, "Violence, Nonviolence, and Human Struggle," July 25, 1976, CCIA Archives 1977, Box P.354, International Fellowship of Reconciliation, WCC Archives, Geneva, Switzerland.

38. "Proposal for Implementation," July 4–20, 1968, 42.11.08/2, WCC Archives, Geneva, Switzerland.

39. Bristol "Nonviolence Not First for Export"

itself came into being through a violent revolution and later endured an even more violent civil war. It followed that millions of people throughout the world saw violence as essential to the achievement of rapid social, political, and economic change.[40] However, Rev. Michael Scott, writing on Africa, gave grounds for hope when he observed the accelerated forces of change at work there: "The liberation of thirty African states from imperialism was not always a bloody and painful process. Sometimes it was, in Algeria and Kenya. But some African countries proceeded by comparatively peaceful and constitutional means, first towards self-government and then to independence, like Tanzania and many others."[41] Beverly Woodward's article, "Violence, Nonviolence and Human Struggle," offers useful insights into the challenges for the WCC resolution: "To institutionalize nonviolence is to create a framework in which fear and ignorance have a chance of being replaced by appreciation—appreciation for the reality of life, the diversity of creation, the irreplaceable quality of each person as a subject of experience, and the joys as well as the difficulties of human interdependence—who among us can think that such a framework actually exists?"[42]

The question of violence and nonviolence had occupied the modern ecumenical movement for some time, going back to Archbishop Söderblom[43] and the Life and Work Conferences of 1925 and 1937. It cannot be said that the ecumenical movement ignored the problem of violence. But violence had been discussed almost exclusively in terms of international conflicts between sovereign states, addressing the scale of the problem indicated in the writings of Karl Marx and the Russian Revolution. However, the use of nonviolence as an instrument for achieving great social justice had been ignored. It was not until the Third Assembly of the WCC in New Delhi in 1961 that progress was made, particularly on nonviolence. This resulted in a statement on violence and nonviolence at the 1966 Church and Society Conference in Geneva:

40. Ibid.

41. Scott, Michael, "Christianity and War," Programme to Combat Racism, Notting Hill Consultation 1969 (1965–1969), 4223.1.01.2, WCC Archives, Geneva, Switzerland.

Reverend Michael Scott (July 30, 1907–September 14, 1983) was an Anglican priest dedicated to ameliorating the harsh apartheid policies of South Africa in South West Africa.

42. Woodward, "Violence, Nonviolence, and Human Struggle," July 25, 1976, WCC Archives, Geneva, Switzerland.

43. Lars Olof Jonathan Söderblom (January 15, 1866–July 21, 1931) was Archbishop of Uppsala, Sweden, and was awarded the 1930 Nobel Peace Prize before becoming a professor of Religious Studies at Leipzig University.

Violence is very much a reality in our world, both the overt use of force to oppress and the invisible violence perpetrated on people who by the millions have been or still are the victims of repression and unjust social systems. Therefore the question emerges today whether violence which sheds blood in planned revolution may not be a lesser evil than the violence which, though bloodless, condemns whole populations to perennial despair. Christians who have, in fact, participated in revolutionary process which involve violence and defiance of law with an uneasy conscience look to the church for understanding and guidance. Still others are complacent as long as "law and order" prevail.[44]

The statement went on to debate violence versus nonviolence, adding that it could be said that the only possible position for the Christian was one of absolute nonviolence. However, violence could only be justified in extreme situations. The use of violence required a rigorous definition of the circumstances in which it might be resorted to, with a clear recognition of its inherent evils, and should always be tempered by mercy. It had to be recognized that there was no guarantee that violence would achieve its intended end, for its consequences could not be controlled. But there are certain basic ethical principles that a Christian must relate to the specific situation in which he finds himself, and a final decision must be based on these two elements.[45]

In September of 1968, Wilmer A. Cooper of the Earlham School of Religion, one of the three members of the Ad Hoc Committee on the King Resolution, wrote to Blake urging action to explore ways in which the WCC could promote studies on nonviolence. Cooper was aware that any program required funding, and in that regard he wrote, "Already some efforts are being made in this direction, and I am informed that James Lawson[46] who was present at the Fourth Assembly, is contacting SCLC to solicit the support of the King forces in such an effort."[47] A memorandum was issued on January 18, 1969, to the Central Committee of the WCC on the implementation of the Martin Luther King study on nonviolent methods of social change. A few points were raised, including:

44. Quoted in Mbali, *Churches and Racism*, 22–23.

45. Ibid.

46. James Morris Lawson, Jr. (September 22, 1928) is still active in nonviolent training. As a leading theologian, he worked alongside King and invited him to Memphis during the sanitation workers strike in 1968. King saw the visit as preparation for the Poor People's Campaign

47. Blake to Cooper, October 28, 1968, WCC Archives, Geneva, Switzerland.

1. There is a growing urgency of the need for such a study. This is because of the growing cynicism around the world among youth.

2. Any implementation of the Uppsala decision should have a specific identity, and not be crowded out or submerged under other WCC projects or studies.

3. The study should ultimately include or correlate with action,

    a. As a device for testing Christian nonviolent methods in practice.

    b. As the way to teach Christian nonviolent methods of social change.[48]

Blake replied to Cooper in October, explaining that the WCC had been struggling to determine the kind of study and program of action that could do justice to the many decisions made at Uppsala, including the resolution in memory of King.[49] The new WCC Programme to Combat Racism, of which Blake was the chairman, would include study, education, and action to effect social change through nonviolent Christian means. These recommendations were to be ready by January of 1969. Blake assured Cooper that the WCC had passed the resolution with the "memory of King very much in mind."[50] In conclusion he wrote, "there is every reason for us to find ways of calling attention to the ecumenical significance of what he did."[51] By his words and actions, King had proven that he sought justice for all men, but as a Christian minister, he made it clear that "I must be true to my conviction that I share with all men the calling to be a son of the living God. Beyond the calling of race or nation as creed is the vocation of sonship and brotherhood. And because I believe that the Father is deeply concerned especially for his suffering and helpless and outcast children, I come today to speak for them."[52]

John H. Yoder, Associate Consultant to the Mennonite Board of Mission and Charities, offered advice to Blake for the implementation of the resolution: "I would suggest that maximum utility would come from focusing not on the national level 'alternatives to war' (with reference to the United Nations, atomic proliferation, the Near East problem, etc.), but rather on the lower levels where structures within a society can be dealt

---

48. "Memorandum," January 18, 1969, WCC General Secretaries, Correspondence: Frequent (1938–1970), 42.11.08/2, WCC Archives, Geneva, Switzerland.

49. Blake to Cooper, October 28, 1968, WCC Archives, Geneva, Switzerland.

50. Ibid.

51. Ibid.

52. King, "Why I Am Opposed," April 30, 1967, King Center Library and Archive, Atlanta, GA.

with: 'alternative to guerrilla' or 'alternatives to coup d'état' or 'alternatives to a riot.' This is the level which Martin Luther King himself made the most original and effective contribution."[53]

The Swedish Ecumenical Council proposed to the WCC on May 12, "that the World Council, possibly in cooperation with the Pontifical Commission of Justice and Peace, organize a consultation during 1970 on the issue of coordination among scholars and movements concerned with nonviolent methods of achieving social change."[54] A reply was sent to Archbishop Ruben Josefson on May 20 confirming receipt of the letter and stating that the contents had been shared with Dr. Blake's colleagues.[55]

Wilmer Cooper wrote again to Blake in July in connection with a study by their Ad Hoc Committee for the Martin Luther King Resolution. He expressed his satisfaction with the communication from the Swedish Ecumenical Council and urged the WCC to take action on the King Resolution.[56] The WCC saw nonviolent methods as having potential for action relevant in three types of conflict situations:

1. To achieve social change in countries in Africa, Asia and Latin America;

2. To achieve social change in Europe and North America;

3. As a means of national defense against foreign aggression.

Furthermore, studies of nonviolent methods may be divided into three types:

a. a) Studies of the ideological tradition and aspects of nonviolence;

b. Studies of historical cases of the use of nonviolent methods (within different disciplines, such as history, political science, sociology), including field research;

c. Experimental research in laboratory situations, i.e., "simulations."[57]

53. John H. Yoder to Eugene Carson Blake, May 5, 1969, WCC General Secretariat, Correspondence: Frequent (1938–1970), 42.11.08/2, WCC Archives, Geneva, Switzerland.

54. Ruben Josefson and Bo Wirmark, Swedish Ecumenical Council, to WCC Central Committee, May 12, 1969, WCC General Secretariat, Correspondence: Frequent (1938–1970), 42.11.08, WCC Archives, Geneva, Switzerland.

55. Eugene Carson Blake to Ruben Josefson, May 20, 1969, WCC General Secretariat, Correspondence: Frequent (1938–1970), 42.11.08, WCC Archives, Geneva, Switzerland.

56. Blake to Cooper, October 28, 1968, WCC Archives, Geneva, Switzerland.

57. "Nonviolent Methods of Social Change and National Defense," WCC General Secretariat, Correspondence: Frequent (1938–1970), 42.11.08, WCC Archives, Geneva, Switzerland.

Cooper was aware that the WCC was having difficulty in acquiring sufficient financing to get a program up and running, and he made some observations to facilitate the proposal:

a. a) Some of the work could be "farmed out" to regional study centers or groups like Bangalore or Rio Plate.

b. The timeliness of the study might well bring WCC new respect and support from other quarters than those now open or being tapped.

c. The suggested "expansion" after the "first steps" might well be able to get local support.

d. There are some potential sources of support in peace-agency circles, but the study would not be valid if all the support were from such groups.[58]

On behalf of the Ad Hoc Committee for the King Resolution, Cooper submitted the proposal and requested a report after the Central Committee acted on it. On July 23, the Joint Committee on Society, Development, and Peace (SODEPAX) issued a memorandum to Blake on the Martin Luther King Resolution. The question of nonviolent strategies for effecting social change was discussed at the meeting of SODEPAX in Bossey, France, in early July. Some difficulties arose, and the work group wished to refine the title of the proposed study. It observed that violence and nonviolence were not simple alternatives, as there was an infinite gradation between them. The group believed that cases existed where necessary social change could not be effected without some measure of violence, and so preferred that the subject of the study be defined as "the organization of power to effect social changes in the direction of greater justice, which is at the same time effective and also least violent in terms of human life and bloodshed."[59]

The Department of Church and Society issued a draft report on November 7, 1970, giving details of the August 1969 Central Committee meeting in Canterbury, England, where it was decided "that the Department on Church and Society, in consultation with other interested units of the World Council of Churches, be asked to follow closely the discussion of the issue of violence and nonviolence in rapid social change already taking place in various departments of the World Council of Churches, in view of the Martin Luther King Resolution of Uppsala and related discussion

---

58. Blake to Cooper, October 28, 1968, WCC Archives, Geneva, Switzerland.

59. "Joint Committee on Society, Development, and Peace Memorandum to Eugene Carson Blake," July 23, 1969, WCC General Secretariat, Correspondence: Frequent (1938–1970), 42.11.08, WCC Archives, Geneva, Switzerland.

by other organizations."[60] It urged the WCC to seek financial resources to address key theological and ethical issues in the areas of power, violence, nonviolence, and social change. The draft report also emphasized the Gandhi Centenary Year, recommending that "the teaching and leadership of Mohandas K. Gandhi in encouraging nonviolent political and social change be considered in these studies, in view of his influence on Martin Luther King, and the way in which they both sought to make real the teaching of Jesus about love and justice."[61]

The report concluded that the ecumenical debate in the previous decade had shown increasing openness to violence as a Christian option to overcome situations of extreme social, racial, and economic injustice. Many had spoken of the overt or covert "violence of the status quo."[62] Others had argued that nonviolence might have had a more violent long-term impact than some of its advocates recognized. Consequently, critics had grown reluctant to frame the issue as "violence" versus "nonviolence," searching instead for a more flexible "Christian criteria for evaluating alternative coercive strategies appropriate to particular situations of social injustice."[63] The Baden Formula, which considered, "strategies for social change which will foreshadow as nearly as possible that more humane society towards which the struggle is directed,"[64] was one example of this kind of approach.

In taking up the Uppsala Martin Luther King Resolution, the Central Committee entrusted the Department on Church and Society with the study on violence and nonviolence. After visits to North America, Africa, and Europe, together with communications with interested groups and churches throughout the world, the working Committee of Church and Society presented a statement to the Central Committee meeting in Geneva in August 1973. The paper did not discuss violence and nonviolence as abstractions, but instead set them out in a specific context: Christian engagement in the struggle for justice, including the struggle for racial justice. There was no single or simple answer given to the age-old debate between pacifism and non-pacifism. The paper concluded that although Christians might reasonably disagree on the means to be used, they could not disagree on the side Christians must take—the side of the oppressed.[65] The paper discussed the

60. "Department of Church and Society Draft Report," December 4, 1970, Uppsala Assembly Resolution of Martin Luther King, WCC General Secretariat, Correspondence: Frequent (1938–1970), 42.08.11/2, WCC Archives, Geneva, Switzerland.

61. Ibid.

62. Ibid.

63. Ibid.

64. Ibid.

65. Adler, *Small Beginning*, 32–33.

legitimate use of power by governments in the interests of justice for all and the dangers of open or hidden misuses of power. The paper described the methods of resistance to unjust and oppressive political and economic power. Christians could take one of three options:

1. Nonviolent action is the only possibility consistent with obedience to Christ.

2. Violent resistance is acceptable as a Christian duty under extreme circumstances.

3. In situations of violence, Christians are obliged to participate in the struggle for justice.[66]

66. Ibid.

7

Keeping King's Dream Alive

The WCC and the Notting Hill Consultation on Racism, 1969

JOHN VINCENT ARGUES IN *The Race Race* that it would certainly not be fair to give the impression that up until 1969 the WCC had been unaware of the problem of race. However, it was in 1969 that awareness became a burning conviction that action was necessary. Shortly before the Notting Hill Consultation, the Fifth Summit Conference of East and Central African States met in April of 1969 in Lusaka, Zambia, where they published a "Manifesto in Southern Africa," which declared: "In Mozambique, Angola, Rhodesia, South-West Africa and the Union of South Africa, there is open and continued denial of the principles of human equality and natural self-determination . . . For the principle of human equality, and all that flows from it, is either universal or it does not exist. The dignity of all men is destroyed when the manhood of any human being is denied. Our objectives in Southern Africa stem from our commitment to this principle of human equality."[1]

The Programme to Combat Racism Consultation at Notting Hill in London in May of 1969 invited approximately forty-five participants (including four Roman Catholics) to meet with a group of twenty-five

1. Vincent, *Race Race*, 5, 39.

consultants ranging from radical to conservative, all of whom were experts in racial conflict around the world. The participants were all committed members of Christian churches, while the consultants were mostly critics of the churches and not necessarily affiliated with Christian faith.[2] Blake concluded that the report would include attitudes and positions that challenged Christian assumptions and even Christian faith at its depths.[3]

The PCR was begun to commit Christians:

- To end discrimination based on race.

- To end the exploitation of man by man, based on feelings of superiority in some people toward other people.

- To help the churches in the understanding of their Christian mission.[4]

Blake wrote in a foreword to the report that although it was clear that promoting positive race relations and racial understanding was a local responsibility everywhere, the WCC had a world responsibility for two reasons:

1. Race relations are part of the international problem of justice and peace.

2. A world perspective can make a contribution to specific local racial confrontations and is required especially in those mono-racial communities or nations where it is often thought there is no problem of racism.[5]

The Consultation was chaired by George McGovern, a US Senator who was moved by "a memorable and significant experience in human dynamics marked by love and anger, hope and despair, bitter realism and sweet pieties, succinct insight and rambling oratory."[6] McGovern reported that the highlight of the Consultation came from the least expected quarter. At the midpoint in the Consultation at Church House in Westminster, the group gathered to hear an address by Bishop Huddleston[7] of London and Oliver

2. "Programme to Combat Racism," May 19–24, 1969, Notting Hill Consultation 1969, 4223.1.02, WCC Archives, Geneva, Switzerland.

3. Ibid.

4. "Programme to Combat Racism," History of the Programme to Combat Racism, 4223.17.1, WCC Archives, Geneva, Switzerland.

5. Blake, Eugene Carson, "Report on the Consultation on Racism," Canterbury, England, August 12–23, Notting Hill Consultation 1969, 4223.1.03, WCC Archives, Geneva, Switzerland.

6. Blake, "Report on the Consultation on Racism," August 12–23, 1969, 4223.1.03, WCC Archives, Geneva, Switzerland.

7. Archbishop Trevor Huddleston (June 15, 1913–April 20, 1998) lived a life

Tambo, a South African ANC activist. After Bishop Huddleston began to speak, a sizeable group of right-wing National Front supporters began to heckle him: "They taunted first the Bishop and then Mr. Tambo with racial eipthets [*sic*] and crude jests that left one sick at heart. Indeed, the sickness of racism pervaded the sanctuary."[8] McGovern concluded that the central theme running throughout the group's deliberations was that if racism was to be eliminated, it would require more than the private commitment of individual Christians: "Indeed, the entire church must become committed to an action program on a broad social, economic, and political front aimed at the eradication of institutional racism in the society of man."[9]

In his report on the WCC Consultation on Racism, Blake accepted that Notting Hill was itself a racial trouble spot. He explained that due to the direct confrontation with National Front demonstrators at the public meeting, and later with a group of Black Power representatives, that a number of reports were only read and not discussed. These included "The Realities of Racism" and "The Struggle to Eradicate Racism."[10]

South Africa was accorded particular attention in the Programme to Combat Racism because of the ruthless reputation apartheid had earned. A position paper by the NCC declared, "Southern Africa requires a high priority because the denial of human rights there threatens the achievement of human rights elsewhere. Southern Africa is a subcontinent where political, economic, legal, and social rights of the overwhelming majority are either limited or denied outright by a minority."[11] The NCC criticized white nations of the West for resisting change and for issuing only ambivalent statements on the regime. With the odd exception, they had used their military and political power to strengthen the white status quo in Southern Africa.[12] The Department of Internal Affairs of the NCC asked why US churches should be involved in this crisis. Part of the problem stemmed from the international nature of the economy, particularly in relation to the US and Great Britain.[13] Indeed, this issue was further considered at the Consultation on Racism, where it was recorded that international finance had a role

dedicated to helping the oppressed fight for liberation and equality in Southern Africa.

8. Blake, "Report on the Consultation on Racism," August 12–23, 1969, 4223.1.03, WCC Archives, Geneva, Switzerland.

9. Ibid.

10. Ibid.

11. "A Position Paper Concerning Southern Africa," Department of International Affairs, National Council of Churches, Programme to Combat Racism, Notting Hill Consultation 1969, 4223.1.02, Box 2, No. 3, WCC Archives, Geneva, Switzerland.

12. Ibid.

13. Ibid.

in reinforcing racist regimes in Southern Africa by affording them a false sense of power and security through trade, investments, bank loans, and the importance of gold in the international monetary system[14]

The position of blacks in South Africa was not unlike the reality for blacks in the slums of American cities, where they were disenfranchised socially, politically, and economically. In fact, in his analysis on the Chicago campaign, the Rev. James Bevel[15] described these American slums as an "internal colonial system," ghettos in which the majority of the exploited community's resources go out and even fewer come in.[16] The Consultation on Racism turned its attention to the heavy involvement of the US in South Africa: "It is involved by virtue of its deep alliance with Great Britain, by its NATO partnership with Portugal. It participates heavily in South African business. With other nations it relies upon South African gold, which in turn virtually underwrites the South African economy. It uses South Africa for military purposes."[17]

The Consultation at Notting Hill in May of 1969 was an attempt to draw together people involved in situations of racial tension to be heard before the church. The US was strongly represented both by white theologians and churchmen, including:

- Professor John Deschner

- Professor Charles Glock

- Mr. J. Irwin Miller

- Professor J. Robert Nelson
  Prominent black clergy were also in attendance:

- Miss Jean E. Fairfax

- Rev. Channing E. Phillips

- Dr. Charles S. Spivey

Consultants also included many well-known names in the racial struggle in the UN, among whom were:

---

14. "Eradication of Racism," 4223.1.02, Box 2, No. 6, Consultation Papers, WCC Archives, Geneva, Switzerland.

15. James Luther Bevel (October 19, 1936–December 19, 2008) was a civil rights leader in the 1960s who was involved in three important campaigns: the 1963 Birmingham Crusade, the 1965 Selma Voting Rights Movement, and the 1966 Chicago Open Housing Movement.

16. Bevel, James, "Direct Action Report, Chicago," April 12–13, 1966, SCLC Papers, Box 131.10, 1966, King Center Library and Archive, Atlanta, GA.

17. "Eradication of Racism," 4223.1.02, Box 2, No. 6, Consultation Papers, WCC Archives, Geneva, Switzerland.

- Mr. Eddie C. Brown

- Fr. James Groppi

- Dr. Nathan Hare

- Mr. Roger A. Harless

- Rev. Henry H. Mitchell

- Rev. C. Herbert Oliver

- Mr. Philip Veracruz[18]

The milieu within which the Programme to Combat Racism was held was intense. In South Africa, Nelson Mandela and the others convicted at the Rivonia Trial had been sentenced to life imprisonment. In the US, civil rights legislation was now on the books, but in South Africa, apartheid was more severe than ever before. The Consultation intended to put into action a program to eliminate racism worldwide, particularly in Africa and Asia. The obstinacy of diehard racists in the fight for equality in the US had already been well documented. The WCC had followed the progress of Martin Luther King Jr. in the American civil rights movement, and it was hoped that those notable achievements might inspire further successes throughout their campaigns. As John Vincent remarks in *The Race Race*, "there is no doubt that the present black revolution in the USA had a considerable influence on the outcome of the Notting Hill Consultaton."[19] In order to come to grips with the enormity of the task before them, the Consultation reviewed numerous submissions and presentations. Some historical insights provided a grim reminder of how "superior" and "inferior" racial constructs had been used in the expansion of the New World and in founding the capitalist economies that had shaped and sustained it, all with the blessing and acquiescence of the Christian church.

A WCC participant's "Background Statement on White Racism" acknowledged that the struggle for racial justice had moved into a new and revolutionary phase. The dangerous precedent of "color with rank" threatened to divide the world "into two hostile alienated groups transcending national boundaries," setting a white, affluent minority determined to remain in power against a non-white, impoverished, disenfranchised majority determined to overthrow the structures of racism and exploitation.[20] This trend had been evidenced by developments in the US, where massive re-

18. Vincent, *Race Race*, 81–89.

19. Ibid., xii.

20. "Background Statement on White Racism," Notting Hill Consultation 1969, 4223.1.01, File 1, WCC Archives, Geneva, Switzerland.

sentiments against injustice had surfaced regularly since the mid–twentieth century despite years of experimentation with various forms of nonviolent struggle for racial equality based on the Christian principle of love and the promise of reconciliation of the races. This struggle received a stunning set-back with the assassination of its leading proponent, Martin Luther King Jr. However, even before that terrible tragedy there had been clear indicators that some militant black civil rights activists conceived of nonviolence as a strategy to be used only so long as it produced effective and immediate results.[21] The background paper goes on to invoke King in the continuing struggle for a nonviolent solution wherever racism exists. Christians are called by their faith to play a vital role in the midst of disunity, discontinu-ity, disorder, and violence. The paper calls upon Christians to act in fulfill-ment of their religious mission to find new and creative ways of thinking about racism to help build new structures out of which reconciliation might develop. As the author recalls, "Martin Luther King's great contribution to the Christian community was his embodiment of the essence of this faith and his gospel of hope and love in the vortex of racial war."[22] The author goes on to advise that King's death should not obscure the long-term effects of his mission on earth. King's role was universal, for he was not only a leader of black Christians, but "of Christian and non-Christian men and women throughout the world, irrespective of their color or faith," and most importantly, "his life reflected the possibilities of the unity of mankind even though his death was ultimately the way of the Cross."[23]

PRESENTATIONS FROM THE NOTTING HILL CONSULTATION

The Consultation could only hear reports from a small representative body with experience in racial segregation and injustice. A paper presented by Gayraud S. Wilmore Jr.,[24] Chairman of the United Presbyterian Church's Division of Church and Race, looked back at the history of slavery in an attempt to unravel the present crisis. Wilmore noted the ease with which seventeenth and eighteenth-century American Christians had used the institution of religion to protect a double standard of human justice that

21. Ibid.
22. Ibid.
23. Ibid.
24. Gayraud Stephen Wilmore Jr. (December 20, 1921) is a historian, writer, and theologian who is active in the civil rights movement and an acknowledged expert on the African American church.

benefited their economic self-interests. He asserted that no amount of scholarly research or eloquence by white historians about the "deep sympathy and solicitude" the Christian slave holder had for his slaves, or about the enthusiasm with which the churches had applied themselves to the task of evangelizing the slave population after the revolution "can make us forget that the churches themselves excluded the black man from the very freedom which they justified for white men on the basis of Christian faith."[25] Wilmore added that "therein lies the core of moral corruption in the American churches today and the kernel of American racism."[26]

The original attitude of the churches separated love and justice where black people were concerned, and that attitude prevailed in the end. Wilmore added that church integration had historically been a one-way street. Wilmore asserted that the white church, to accommodate the prejudices of the white middle-class, attempted to convert the black man and his church to its own image and make him beholden to a white society where "the white church had always been in bondage and which it conceived to be the nearest thing on earth to the Kingdom of God in Heaven."[27] Wilmore distinguished these from the black churches that split from the white Methodist and Baptist denominations in the latter part of the eighteenth and early nineteenth centuries, for these faith communities were able to develop "their own styles of life and their own institutions" such that "an authentic black culture and religion were germinated."[28] The black churches that remained a part of the mainstream white denominations, on the other hand, were excluded from participation in the church culture. They were required to subordinate their own values to white cultural and religious values. The end result for the black church and the black community was an imitation of the "real" thing—a second-class culture for second-class Christians.[29] Wilmore described the latter as "whitenized black churches, and they had to recover their own self-respect by demythologizing the white cultural bag through which the faith was transmitted to them" and in which they had made themselves comfortable.[30] In the final analysis, Wilmore perceived a dilemma in the possibility "that the essence of the Christian faith not only transcends ultimately the ethnocentric culture of the white man, but that of the black man as well," and in their enlightenment, "this Christ in whom there is neither Jew nor

25. Wilmore, "New Black Church Style," 18–22.
26. Ibid.
27. Ibid.
28. Ibid.
29. Ibid.
30. Ibid.

Greek, bond nor free, male nor female, is also neither black nor white."[31] Wilmore's message for white Christian brethren was that the time had come to jettison "a religion devoid of an ethic relevant to our real situation and a culture in which we were never permitted to participate on equal terms." Exhorting black people to reassess their relationship to a white church which perpetuated a hostile society to accommodate white Christians, he said: "We must stand back and be in a strategic exodus from this unequal engagement, this degrading debilitating embrace, until we have recovered our own sense of identity, our true relationship to the people we serve, and until the white church is ready to enter into that partnership in life and mission which is able to renew the whole church of Christ."[32]

Another insightful paper, "The Role of the Churches and the World Council of Churches in the Elimination of Racism," was delivered by Fr. James Groppi,[33] a Roman Catholic priest and American civil rights activist who questioned the importance of Christ's skin color. He proposed a change of emphasis, arguing that "the portrayal of Christ as a black man is needed by white people as well as by black people in order to combat the superiority complexes that are present in the white community."[34] Recalling the violence that had erupted in the city of Milwaukee, WI, in the summer of 1967, Fr. Groppi noted that the authorities had called it a riot, as did the white church and the white community, talking of theft and the destruction of property. But the black community had interpreted events differently, viewing it instead as a righteous revolutionary act. He recalled that as the young people walked past the parish carrying food and furniture they shouted, "Black Power Father," and he replied "Black Power, Jo . . . Don't get caught." In the black community, the police were viewed as an oppressive "occupation army." Groppi complained that at one point he was suspected of encouraging some youths he was working with to start a riot. The police subjected him to intensive surveillance over a period of three months at the church and the freedom house, where he worked with the Milwaukee NAACP Youth Council. Young men and women who attended social events were followed constantly and harassed by the police, and when they ques-

31. Ibid.

32. Ibid.

33. Father James Edmund Groppi (November 16, 1930–November 4, 1985) was a Roman Catholic priest and renowned civil rights activist. He participated in the 1963 March on Washington and the Selma to Montgomery marches in support of the Voting Rights Act.

34. Groppi, James, "The Role of the Churches and the World Council of Churches in the Elimination of Racism," Programme to Combat Racism, Notting Hill Consultation 1969 (1965–1969), 4223.1.02, Box 2, No. 5, WCC Archives, Geneva, Switzerland.

tioned this obnoxious behavior, police responded with "get off this street or you'll be arrested." In desperation, the young men took action, saying, "Look Father, the next time the police follow you, drive past this alley and we will brick the squad car as you drive by."[35] Groppi observed that he had only one prayer in those days: that the boys would not be caught. Those prayers always went unanswered.

Groppi did not find it reasonable to expect black people to worship a God identified with white oppression. He emphasized that whites could not imagine what it was like to be black in Great Britain or in the US. As an American, he said that when "one speaks of the church one is speaking of two churches. One is black and one is white." He spoke of black reality and the necessity to accommodate black culture with "a relative interpretation of the Gospel." Fr. Groppi asked that churches be renamed "after black heroes such as Dr. Martin Luther King Jr., Mrs. Rosa Parks, Harriet Tubman, and others." In general, he advised that the church in black communities and in white communities had to be concerned with Christian social action—in other words, "the implementation of Christian principles in society."[36] Unfortunately in Milwaukee, there was not a single church in the entire white community—Catholic or Protestant—that had any meaningful program on inter-group relations. Groppi questioned whether they were even capable of it. On one occasion, a teacher in a Catholic parochial school put up a picture of Martin Luther King Jr. on the wall, and when the Mother Superior and the pastor objected, the picture was removed and the teacher fired. Groppi called this an "overt act of racism" on the part of the church. The Archbishop of Milwaukee had labeled the incident a "misunderstanding," and nothing was done. It was difficult to be optimistic under such circumstances, and as Groppi observed, "this, I believe, is an excellent example of institutional racism. It was the toleration of a racist act in order to keep the peace. It was the silence of the church speaking thunderously to black people."[37]

American civil rights leader Channing E. Phillips felt somewhat overwhelmed by the limits of the time and topic he was to speak on before the Consultation. As he said, "looking at the cast of the characters who were scheduled to appear before this group; I assumed that my input was to be that of transferring the horrible taste or stench of racism from a recipient to perhaps perpetrators (conscious or unconscious)."[38] The system of institu-

35. Ibid.

36. Ibid.

37. Ibid.

38. Phillips, Channing E., "The Colour of Poverty: Political and Economic Dimensions," Programme to Combat Racism, Notting Hill Consultation 1969 (1965–1969), 4223.1.02, WCC Archives, Geneva, Switzerland.

tional racism was so enormous and so complicated in the US that it was only possible to concentrate on one area: "The paper therefore moves rapidly to the questioning of the economic system of capitalism, and the requirements of that system for a 'Nigger class,' a group of people to be exploited—initially as slaves, later as consumers." Phillips argued that the decision to transport blacks from Africa and the Caribbean was not a political decision, not a social decision, certainly not a religious decision, but an economic decision. This was based on the need for slave labor in the rapid development of the capitalist economy. Now, Phillips saw that "the problem of overcoming, breaking in, or radically altering the profit-centered and exploitative system, and thereby overcoming racism, its by-product, was a problem of power." He saw the "Black Manifesto" as an attempt to acquire power predicated on the awareness that "blacks will have to wield economic power before racism can be rendered impotent, if not abolished."[39] However, Phillips argued that although the manifesto was theologically sound, the compensation of fifteen dollars per "nigger" was offensively small. As he said, "a cursory reading of Tawney's[40] *Religion and the Rise of Capitalism* ought to inform us that blacks are knocking on a proper door." Furthermore, despite the theological and moral justifications for such reparation, "the church has a penchant for letting economic factors silence moral requirements, and therefore no miracles ought to be expected."[41] Phillips saw that the persistence and strength of the profit motive and the puritan work ethnic in the US required a difference approach: the development of black political power to influence economic policies. He argued that both economic power and political power were developed against a background of potential violence, which was power in itself. Ominously, he warned that "a profit-oriented, possessions-centered, compact society is especially vulnerable to the power of violence."[42] Phillips revealed that black dissidents had discovered "that the quickest way to bring attention to a problem of injustice or inequity is to destroy the oppressor's property."[43] The church had an important role to play in preventing wholesale destruction of property and death by providing leadership towards a peaceful resolution to inequality. Phillips asserted that if the church was to take its mission of reconciliation seriously, to at-

39. Ibid.

40. Richard Henry Tawney (November 30, 1880–January 16, 1962) was the author of *Religion and the Rise of Capitalism*, published in 1926, which established his reputation as an historian exploring the relationship between Protestantism and the rise of capitalism.

41. Phillips, "Colour of Poverty," 4223.1.02, WCC Archives, Geneva, Switzerland.

42. Ibid.

43. Ibid.

tack racism significantly, "it had to be not only an institution of love, but an institution of power, making economic and political inputs into society to effect new equilibria of power."[44]

In another statement by the Board of Directors of the National Committee of Black Churchmen, the white church and its institutions came under considerable criticism for maintaining the status quo in favor of the white ascendancy with few exceptions. Having considered the "Black Manifesto" delivered by American civil rights leader James Forman[45] in April, 1969 at the National Black Economic Development Conference in Detroit, MI, the Consultation agreed that the American religious establishment, along with almost every other institution in society, had been the conscious beneficiary of one of the most inhuman forms of chattel slavery the world has ever known.[46] They concluded that white churches and synagogues "have been the moral cement of the structure of racism in this nation, and the vast majority of them continue to play that role today."[47] However, the statement makes a very important distinction in where liability lies, adding that "the black church does not stand in the same dock as the white church before the bar of justice," because "black churches were the victims rather than guardians and perpetrators of racism in America."[48] The statement finishes with a call to action for "the demands of our brothers," by which "a radical challenge has been placed before us on the threshold of a summer of unmitigated discontent and crises. That challenge must be met with an equally radical commitment to undo, as much as we are able, the injustices of the past and to eliminate the injustices of the present. The means are available, but the will to use them must not be withheld."[49]

Oliver. R. Tambo's contribution to the Consultation was titled "Racism as a Major Obstacle to World Community." He began with a quote from W. E .B. Du Bois: "The problem of the twentieth century is the problem of the color line—the relation of the darker to the lighter races of men in Asia and

44. Ibid.

45. James Forman (October 4, 1928—January 10, 2005) was Executive Secretary of the SNCC in 1961. He took part in the Black Economic Development Conference in Detroit in 1964, where his "Black Manifesto" demanding $500 million in reparation from white churches was adopted.

46. "Statement of the Board of Directors of the National Committee of Black Churchmen," minutes, Programme to Combat Racism, Notting Hill Consultation 1969 (1965–1969), 4223.1.02, WCC Archives, Geneva, Switzerland.

47. Ibid.

48. Ibid.

49. Ibid.

Africa, in America and the islands of the sea."[50] Tambo referred back to his title, claiming that "obstacle" was too mild a term for racism: "it is a menace, a threat to the survival of man himself."[51] Tambo was concerned that racism was a "virulent, aggressive, and violent ideology which would sooner destroy millions of people than accept the universal truth that racial origin is a fact of natural birth, not a measure of human worth."[52] In Southern Africa, racism was running amok "in all its naked reality."[53] Racism was being opposed by revolutionary forces that some might call terrorists or Communists, but that Tambo referred to as "the true leaders of the crusade for a world community," and "the vanguard of Christian or other soldiers 'marching as to war' against man's inhumanity to man."[54] Tambo argued that South Africa's Prime Minister Vorster was second only to Hitler in his approach to racism and military expansionism. The triplets in the continuing catastrophe in Southern Africa included Vorster, Ian Smith of Rhodesia, and Marcello Caetano, defender of Portugal's colonial empire in Angola and Mozambique. Tambo viewed racism as no longer a "mere impediment to world community," but as a danger to its security.[55] He warned that time had run out for pleading caution or advocating patience—if a resolution was not forthcoming, violence was inevitable, and he quoted President Kenneth Kaunda of Zambia's address to the United Nations Committee on Decolonization in Lusaka: "We are determined to avoid violence where this is possible, but we cannot and will not do this at the expense of the tremendous sufferings, oppression, and exploitation of the majority in Southern Africa." Finally, Tambo cautioned against the use of force in maintaining racist governments: "We will not permit the existence of a situation in which the few are given sanction to use violence against the majority. Enough violence has been employed by the minority regimes against the majority to cow them into silence."[56]

Tambo went on to cite the "disturbing alliance in action" between exploitation and Christianity. This alliance was especially apparent in the "pious, devout, God-fearing 'Christians' of the Dutch Reformed Churches in South Africa," who differed from the rest of the church because they not

50. Quoted in Tambo, Oliver R., "Racism as a Major Obstacle to World Community," Programme to Combat Racism, Notting Hill Consultation 1969 (1965–1969), 4223.1.02, WCC Archives, Geneva, Switzerland.

51. Ibid.

52. Ibid.

53. Ibid.

54. Ibid.

55. Ibid.

56. Ibid.

only "preach racism but also act it," whereas others "preach against racism but refrain from acting against it." Tambo alleged that the "bulk of Christendom allied itself with the big financial interests of the West, which criticized racism as morally abhorrent, but nevertheless resisted any attempt to dismantle it.[57] Tambo drew to mind the phony "wicked Communist" war in Vietnam for inspiration, declaring, "we shall fight on, inspired by the unconquerable people of Vietnam who, through their dauntless endurance, have proved to all the world that a united people determined on their freedom will overcome every obstacle."[58]

In "Christianity and War," Rev. Michael Scott stressed that in some parts of the world the responsibility for the initiation of "violence" in the struggle for freedom was debatable, but in general the struggle for freedom is part of the struggle for peace. However, South Africa left no room for doubt, said Scott, for the "outside world" had been examining, debating, and passing resolutions against apartheid for twenty years.[59] The future, he argued, lies with the states of a free and independent Africa and the shape of development they were striving to create, often against powerful lobby groups in the South African establishment. It is worthwhile noting that King met Scott, an Anglican priest, on his trip to Ghana in 1957. Lewis V. Baldwin confirms that they began a dialogue on how the church might best fulfill its moral obligation in addressing world problems "related to issues like racism and colonialism and their impact on Africa."[60] Britain had significant influence there, as South Africa exported 30 percent of its external trade to that country. Scott stated that "British investment in South Africa amounted to between £1,200 million and £1,600 million, and in Rhodesia up to UDI [Unilateral Declaration of Independence from Great Britain in 1965] about £200 million, while investments in Commonwealth Africa, though rising, did not amount to more than £1,000 million."[61] Scott advised that an independent Africa must work out its own politics of freedom, both in relation to the West and to Russia.

On a foreboding note, Scott warned that the highly developed industrial and military complex in the South had to be recognized, for its existence had led some to the conclusion that a race war was inevitable, considering the resentment brewing under the apartheid system and "its British

57. Ibid.

58. Ibid.

59. Scott, "Christianity and War," 4223.1.01.2, WCC Archives, Geneva, Switzerland.

60. Baldwin, *Voice of Conscience*, 194.

61. Scott, "Christianity and War," 4223.1.01.2, WCC Archives, Geneva, Switzerland.

imitation in Rhodesia."[62] Scott saw the danger of a future war in Africa leading to another, worse Vietnam. He requested that both sides in the great African controversy should "weigh up the full probable consequences of the policies they are pursuing."[63] Scott emphasized that he was not arguing for the overthrow of the oppressive apartheid regime in South Africa by force, although there were precedents from the history of liberation in America, Europe, Asia, and Africa. His argument was instead "for a frank confrontation of views before an otherwise seemingly inevitable race war is forced upon us by events and forces which get beyond the control of reason."[64]

Mrs. Rita E. Hauser,[65] US Representative to the UN Commission on Human Rights, issued a statement at the London meeting on racism in which she commented on the changing times: "The world has been witnessing a revolution in human relations, whereby the modern-day human person moves to free himself from mistaken racial beliefs which were born in the prejudices and fears of our ancestors, and handed down to oppress the lives and spirits of succeeding generations."[66] Hauser particularly targeted Southern Africa, where some of the worst excesses of World War II were being reenacted: "The terrible oppressive system of apartheid in South Africa, the racial conflicts which are continually worsening throughout Southern Africa, the vestiges of the Nazi racial doctrines which remain in Europe and elsewhere in the world."[67] She stressed that the United Nations' struggle against racial discrimination was entering a new phase. The International Convention on the Elimination of All Forms of Racial Discrimination had been passed. An important, unique feature of that Convention was the implementation of an impartial committee, which was expected to bring added effectiveness to the United Nations efforts to end racial discrimination. Hauser confirmed that these problems required the continuing close attention of the UN and the enlightened effort of organizations everywhere.[68]

62. Ibid.

63. Ibid.

64. Ibid.

65. Rita E. Hauser (July 12, 1934) served as United States Ambassador to the United Nations Commission of Human Rights from 1969 to 1972. President George W. Bush appointed her to the President's Intelligence Advisory Board in 2001, and President Barack Obama reappointed Hauser again in 2009.

66. Hauser, Rita E., "Statement for London Meeting on Racism," Programme to Combat Racism, Notting Hill Consultation 1969 (1965–1969), 4223.1.02, Box 2, No. 4, Consultation Papers, WCC Archives, Geneva, Switzerland.

67. Ibid.

68. Ibid.

The WCC's "Background Statement on White Racism" painted a glum picture for participants with a few bleak truths:

> The explosive potential of this deepening conflict cannot be adequately understood unless we bear in mind that we are now witnessing the result of a racial ideology developed and institutionalized over several centuries of European expansion, colonialism, and imperialism which included a protracted period of the most violent form of exploitation short of genocide—the dehumanizing features of the international slave trade in which most western European countries participated, and three centuries of racial slavery in the Americas.[69]

King would certainly have been saddened by the course of events in Southern Africa reported by WCC: "For in face of intensified oppression and expansionist aggression, the oppressed people of Southern Africa have formed armed resistance movements to fight against white supremacy. The forces of freedom and white supremacy face one another all over Southern Africa, in Mozambique, Angola, South-West Africa, Rhodesia, and South Africa."[70]

Daisuke Kitagawa,[71] the WCC's Secretary for Urban and Industrial Mission, presented another paper for the Programme to Combat Racism titled "Black Power, White Racism, and the Church: USA 1968." He included some of the findings of the Kerner Report, which had documented what social scientists had known for a long time, "namely that the USA is today, as it has always been, a racially stratified society."[72] Kitagawa explained that "it is a society dominated by those who are identified as White Anglo-Saxon Protestants (WASP)," the implication being that those of the "colored" race were virtually "foreigners in their own country" and tolerated as "second class citizens" only if they conformed to what the WASP community dictated.[73] Kitagawa observed that white America's attitude to all different racial

69. "Statement on White Racism," 4223.1.01, File 1,WCC Archives, Geneva, Switzerland.

70. Ibid.

71. Reverend Daisuke Kitagawa (October 23, 1910–March 27, 1970) was born in Taikoku, Japan, and immigrated to the US in 1937, where he attended General Theological Seminary. In 1968 he was appointed the Executive Secretary of the Unity and International Mission program in the Division of World Mission and Evangelism of WCC.

72. Quoted in Kitagawa, Daisuke, "Black Power, White Racism, and the Church: USA, 1968," Programme to Combat Racism, Notting Hill Consultation 1969 (1965–1969), 4223.1.02, WCC Archives, Geneva, Switzerland.

73. Ibid.

groups had one thing in common: it was intrinsically racist. Within this racially stratified society, it was almost inevitable that members of the dominant group (WASP) "think white" because "they find themselves always in 'their element,' and they have no reason to step outside of it in order to find happiness or anything else they need or want."[74] On the other hand, few black Americans had been able to "think black," because doing so would have jeopardized their chances for survival in American society. Kitagawa argued that the only "salvation" for members of minority groups within this social framework of a racially stratified society was survival by conformity to the demands, however unreasonable, placed upon them by the dominant group. According to Kitagawa the result was that many brilliant members of racial minorities had been alienated from the church by the church.

With some exceptions, self-respecting people of high caliber within most minority racial groups in the US were unwilling to subject themselves to the inferior type of ministry "their own" clergy provided, but were either barred from or made to feel unwelcome by the white churches. In the final analysis, the ordained ministry, he argued, would be the vocation least desired by the "cream of the crop" of the racial minorities in the US. The end result, he said, is that African Americans, Native Americans, and Latino Americans, and Asian Americans have all been compelled to espouse middle class white America as their "preference group," thus "paying the high price of internationalization of their self-degradation and self hatred."[75] Kitagawa observed that the Black Power movement was revolting against this price. African Americans were collectively standing up to be counted as equal citizens in their own right. Kitagawa saw that white Americans were afraid of this new phenomenon. And why are they afraid? "To put it bluntly, they are afraid black Americans might retaliate—they might do to white people what white people have done to them in the past."[76] It was revealing in this context that so many white Americans were pathologically preoccupied with interracial marriage. One consequence of this was the phenomenon of white backlash. Kitagawa called into question the church's role in this dilemma, especially in encouraging "white" and "black" churches: "In almost all communions it was tacitly assumed that Amerindians, Negro Americans, Japanese Americans, etc. would continue to have "their own" congregations, and that they would need ministers from among "their own" people."[77] The white congregations did very little to promote race relations.

74. Ibid.
75. Ibid.
76. Ibid.
77. Ibid.

Like King and Blake before him, Kitagawa likened them to "a little more than private social clubs of one type or another, whose predominant ethos is best depicted as the cult of congeniality." Kitagawa urged the churches in the US to "be humble and admit frankly their ignorance of the predicament of black people, and their inability to cope with the racial conflict," recommending that they hurry to "get off the high horse of crusader syndrome, and dig down deep with tough-minded realism and rigorous intellectual discipline, to comprehend what the crux of the whole matter is."[78]

Southern Africa was brought to the fore again in a paper submitted by the National Council of Churches of Christ that asked, "What are the most fundamental reasons why the situation in Southern Africa should have priority attention by the United States and the international community?"[79] Troublesome areas were identified as Angola and Mozambique, Rhodesia and South-West Africa, at that time illegally occupied by South Africa. The bright spots on the horizon were Botswana, Lesotho, and Swaziland; all were politically independent by the end of 1968. The NCC pointed to South Africa as the "the hard core of the problem" in the region, anticipating that if this could be resolved, the ripple effects throughout the continent would be enormous. Four aspects of South African society, taken together, were seen to constitute its strength as well as its danger. The first was the economic growth and prosperity of the white economy. The second was the international economy, particularly the connections with Great Britain and the US that had considerably weakened those nations' moral and political stances towards South Africa. The third was the nature of apartheid, the official and deeply rooted racial policy for the exploitation of black labor at the expense of property rights and political rights. Finally, the fourth element was that totalitarian police state based on arbitrary "laws" and the ruthless exercise of police power.[80]

The NCC posed another important question to the Consultation: "Why should United States churches be involved in the Southern Africa crisis?" It was argued that a large-scale crisis involving broad denials of human rights was a legitimate concern for Christians anywhere for two reasons. First, the human values embodied in the Christian gospel are compromised by such a situation. Second, the mission of the church is universal, and each part of the church shares this universal mission.[81] The NCC emphasized

78. Ibid.

79. "Position Paper Concerning Southern Africa," 4223.1.02, Box 2, No. 3, WCC Archives, Geneva, Switzerland.

80. Ibid.

81. Ibid.

that two aspects of the situation in Southern Africa demanded attention: race discrimination and the police state. The churches of the ecumenical movement had responded with an absolute "No" to the police states of Nazi Germany and Communist countries, objecting to all police states on principle. US churches were, without question, a vital part of the ecumenical movement, and so must participate in the decisive "No" on these two issues.[82]

Further reference was made to the theology, tradition, and practice of the Dutch Reformed Churches, which constituted a particular difficulty for churches elsewhere. In South Africa, the theology of the Dutch Reformed Churches had justified apartheid. Although the official line had changed, support for apartheid was still widespread, and traditional practices still gave succor to the existing systems. These churches' behavior posed a challenge to churches throughout the world.[83] The NCC's position paper acknowledged that the relationship between the US churches and the churches in Southern Africa were failing under increasingly severe strain. The US churches and the NCC needed to forcefully press the US government with the question, "Is present policy in relation to the components of Southern Africa morally right and in the true national interest?"[84]

The US was heavily involved in South Africa through its alliance with Great Britain and with Portugal through its NATO partnership. American business ties to South Africa were extensive. Along with other countries, the US relied on South Africa's gold, a mainstay of their economy, and American military commitments to the country were significant. South Africa could rely on support from the US on any contentious debates in the UN. The similarities between apartheid and racism in the land of the free gave both governments compelling reason to cooperate in the search for a *modus vivendi*. In conclusion, the paper accepted that different church agencies and individuals would formulate their own approaches to specific strategies in response to the complexities of Southern Africa. The NCC proposed a three-point plea for all: first, to move Southern Africa to a high place on the agenda; second, to make social change and the achievement of human rights the primary objective of all; and third, because resources were limited at best, to act with cooperation and coordination.[85]

Reverend Francis House saw the Programme to Combat Racism as a call to action. As he perceived it, "through the challenge of the time the

82. Ibid.
83. Ibid
84. Ibid.
85. Ibid.

ecumenical fellowship of the churches heard the voice of their Lord calling them to stand with him on the side of the oppressed."[86] He described racism in Western-dominated society as a race or group of people in power justifying their position by expounding claims of cultural and biological superiority and "expanding their own identity by diminishing that of their fellows, and consolidating their power in structures of economic exploitation and political oppression." House saw hope in the gains made by liberation movements in Southern Africa, notably in Guinea Bissau, whose independence was then recognized by eighty-four nations. But he urged caution, for reactionary forces had also intensified. The ruthlessness of the white minority regimes of Southern Africa had increased along with their military capacity. House explained that with the assistance of Western allies, including NATO, the US, and some Latin American countries, white minority regimes of Southern Africa were "building up an arsenal of destructive power which could plunge the world into a wider and catastrophic race war."[87] The reasoning was alarmingly simple, House explained: "Those who benefit from the unequal acquisition and distribution of the world's resources, faced with the inevitable challenge from the deprived peoples of the world, may unleash their destructive power in ways—and on a scale—not yet witnessed by mankind." House then articulated how progress could be made. It was no longer sufficient to deal with the race problem at the level of interpersonal relationships. Institutional racism, as reflected in racial, economic, and political structures, had to be challenged. Moreover, the power structures that drew on racism for authority most required changing. Therefore, said House, combating racism "entails the struggle to achieve the redistribution of social, political, and cultural power from the powerful to the powerless."[88] House recommended that the major thrust of the Programme to Combat Racism should continue in Southern Africa, for the aggressive and expansive policies of the white regimes, particularly in South Africa, posed a serious threat to the peace and security of independent African states.

J. Robert Nelson,[89] Professor of Systematic Theology at Boston University, presented a paper on "Racism and Its Theological Significance for the Church." Nelson described a fresco attributed to Giotto at the Basilica of

---

86. House, Francis, "The Origins of the WCC Programme to Combat Racism," Programme to Combat Racism, History of the Programme to Combat Racism, 4223.17.1, WCC Archives, Geneva, Switzerland.

87. Ibid.

88. Ibid.

89. Reverend J. Robert Nelson (1921–July 6, 2004), born in Houston, was a renowned United Methodist ecumenist, theologian, and bioethicist who worked for the Commission on Faith and Order of the World Council of Churches in the 1950s.

Saint Francis of Assisi that depicted the raising of Lazarus from the tomb. A young man is shown assisting Jesus with this miracle, and Nelson notes that he "is not pale. He cannot be. He is black."[90] In reading Nelson's paper, I am reminded that Martin Luther King Jr. preached that it may well be the black man who will save us all from self-destruction.[91] For Nelson, the church had in some ways died, and "like Lazarus they await a vivifying call back to life from the Lord, who alone has the word of life." Nelson, like King, thought that the agent to be used "by Christ for this resurrection is the black person, the black person [*sic*], the black community." Nelson believed that the words of men, the rhetoric of church, and the statements of the WCC all had a limited potency, for although they gave "respect to the much condemned sin of racism, words can only decry and diagnose, they cannot cure." Acknowledging that the WCC called for words of rebuke against "racist churches," he reminded the Assembly "that actions, not words, have power."[92] Nelson pointed out mysterious blind spots in Christian vision, oversights that could only be seen in retrospect once the failure to discern and act upon mandates of the gospel could be measured. How else, he asked, have individuals and official church bodies at various times condoned slavery, warring crusades, and the burning of heretics and witches to the detriment of the true mission of the gospel? Again and again another generation had risen to condemn the sins of their predecessors under the criteria of the very same faith. Nelson expressed hope that the revolutions of the present time were at last making it "evident to Christians that racism in all overt and subtle forms is a blatant denial of the Christian faith."[93]

Nathan Hare,[94] Chairman of the Department of Black Studies at San Francisco State College, underscored the confusion amongst oppressor and oppressed over the directions the struggle should take, its proper goals, and how liberation should come about. Hare spoke of white Europeans' imposition of their own culture onto "kidnapped and enslaved black Africans in

90. Nelson, J. Robert, "Racism and Its Theological Significance for the Church," Programme to Combat Racism, Notting Hill Consultation 1969 (1965–1969), 4223.0.02, WCC Archives, Geneva, Switzerland.

91. King, "American Dream," February 10, 1963, King Center Library and Archive, Atlanta, GA.

92. Nelson, "Racism and Its Theological Significance," Notting Hill Consultation 1969, 4223.0.02, WCC Archives, Geneva, Switzerland.

93. Ibid.

94. Nathan Hare (April 9, 1933) is often called the "father of black studies," in recognition of his forty years as a black academic and activist in the struggle for social transformation.

America."[95] This impulse arose through white ethnocentrism, "unconscious feelings of superiority cemented by the cake of custom and social practice and its resulting cultural imperialism." But whereas white immigrants could eventually assimilate into mainstream society, "black slave captives" and their descendants, along with other nonwhite minorities, cannot. This impediment to progress arose as a result of institutionalized color discrimination. Hare pointed to extensive studies evidencing the importance of education for black social mobility in an industrialized employee-society that grouped more than 90 percent of people in the employee category. The function of education in any society is to transmit the skills, loyalty, and deportment deemed necessary for full participation in that society. In order to make good previous mistakes, "revolutionary change" was needed in American society, which "we have already seen as racist," and therefore, "black education must be revolutionary or, at the least iconoclastic in order to be relevant."[96]

Hare castigated the intransigent white racists who held conferences regularly and spouted rhetoric "as an unconscious substitute for action." There were three basic responses to this situation, psychologists claimed: acceptance (conformity), aggression (revolutionary action), and avoidance (withdrawal). Hare argues that "a society cannot change itself . . . a society with its institutions, rituals, customs, traditions, and belief systems exist to self-perpetuate. It can only be reformed by people, acting to destroy antiquated institutions, norms and values, and to reconstruct them again."[97] Due to underlying feelings of white supremacy, whites as a group, concluded Hare, "are not capable—without exterior motivation—of significantly reversing the racist thrust of their society."[98]

Thus, the Consultation at Notting Hill, which lasted from May 19 to 24, 1969, was presented with many papers, only some of which have been discussed here. These documents covered the causes and consequences of white racism and the ongoing struggle to eradicate it. The Consultation was marked by two unforeseen events: One was the attempted racist demonstration by right-wing National Front supporters. The other was the interruption by black militants when Mr. George Black, an African American left-wing activist, presented a "Declaration of Revolution" demanding reparations from the churches: "The Catholic Church has been a dominant

95. Hare, Nathan, "The Struggle to Eradicate Racism and the New American Dilemma," Programme to Combat Racism, Notting Hill Consultation 1969 (1965–1969), 4223.1.02, WCC Archives, Geneva, Switzerland.

96. Ibid.

97. Ibid.

98. Ibid.

economic power in Europe for two thousand years; today it controls the economy of Italy. Catholic families control the economic and political destiny of twenty-four hundred million South Americans. In the United States, the yearly revenues from the Protestant churches alone (3.6 billon dollars) is more than three times the yearly profits of General Motors, the world's biggest corporation."[99] Indeed, Black saw, as did King, that the only way to achieve objectives was through the acquisition of power. Black went on to demand various cash donations to alter existing power relations, including five million pounds as a defense fund for various Black Panthers, including Huey P. Newton, Eldridge Cleaver, and twenty-eight others. He called for sums to be donated to liberation movements in Africa, Asia, America, Australia, and Europe, including five million pounds each for the NLF in South Vietnam, the Zimbabwe African People's Union-African National Congress (ZAPU-ANC), and the People's Movement for the Liberation of Angola (MPLA). Black also called for the establishment of an international publishing house to document the liberation struggles of all oppressed peoples, demanding another twenty million pounds for this cause.[100]

The WCC issued a response to the "Declaration of Revolution," and the following paragraph was approved for their report to the Central Committee meeting at Canterbury: "It was also clear to us that the notion of 'reparations' as used in our discussions, included not only the emphasis on large unmet needs requiring large sums of money, but also the connotation of acknowledged guilt for part exploitation, and especially, the repudiation of any shred of paternalism in meeting these needs in as much as reparations are intended to be wholly controlled by those whom they are given."[101]

Along with the accumulation of vast wealth, the churches were also accused of supporting a "religion in which the greatest black Christians are martyrs and saints, the greatest white Christians, the imperialist conquistadores and administrators who put them to death."[102] As Adler notes, these events certainly underlined the urgency of the situation, showing both the horrible reality of racial prejudice and the determination of the oppressed to demand justice.[103] The Notting Hill Consultation had done its job—it now presented a challenge to the Central Committee Meeting at Canterbury in August of 1969 to decide on a definite program of action.

99. Blake, "Report on the Consultation on Racism," August 12–23, 1969, 4223.1.03, WCC Archives, Geneva, Switzerland.

100. Ibid.

101. Ibid.

102. Ibid.

103. Adler, *Small Beginning*, 12.

The WCC statement on the Consultation clearly revealed that the church and the world "were filled with the insidious and blatant institutional racism that was producing increased polarization, and threatening an escalation of the struggle for power between white and colored races into violent conflict."[104] It was found that the Consultation itself "was exposed to the pervasiveness of stereotypes, paternalism, and attitudes of racial superiority that had developed over centuries." Unfortunately, the church also reflected the world. Hence: "The identification of the churches with the status quo means today as before, that it has remained, in effect, part of the racial problem and not a means of eliminating it."[105] If the churches were to have any relevance in those critical times, it was imperative that they no longer concentrate their attention on the individual actions of individual Christians in fighting racism. For the majority of Christians, the church was a community—maybe even a movement—and thus issues of racism needed to be addressed as a group. It was agreed that although individual commitment was commendable, it was not enough.

The patterns of racism had a frightening universality. It had become clear at Notting Hill that racism was in large part an outgrowth of the struggle for power that afflicts all men. Racist ideologies and propaganda were developed and disseminated as tools in the economic, political, and military struggles for power. Once developed, they often took on a life on their own, finding a place in the tradition and culture unless stringent controls were taken to exorcize them.[106] Another fact that became clear was that the church was not using its position to eradicate racism itself, even within its own institutions. If the church was charged with a serious ministry, then it must attack racism's origins as well as its symptoms. With this in mind, the church needed to be not only an institution of love, but also an institution of action, seeking to impact society by changing the balance of power to render racism impotent.[107] The WCC's Consultation on Racism recognized that the International Convention on the Elimination of All Forms of Racial Discrimination had recently come into force. It expressed hope that more governments would ratify the Convention and that its full implementation would support the struggle against racism at both the international and national levels.[108]

104. Blake, "Report on the Consultation on Racism," August 12–23, 1969, 4223.1.03, WCC Archives, Geneva, Switzerland.

105. Ibid.

106. Ibid.

107. Ibid.

108. Ibid.

It was imperative that the churches confess their involvement in the perpetuation of racism. In order to show the seriousness of their commitment, and the genuineness of their confession, the churches would be required to make open and public disclosure of their assets, income, investments, landholdings, and financial investments. Analysis would follow as to how the churches' financial practices, both domestic and international, contributed to the support of racially oppressive governments, discriminatory industries, and inhuman working conditions. With these facts exposed, Christians could develop strategies to enable the churches' disengagement from racial oppression. As a consequence, the Consultation endorsed the principle of reparation.[109] The WCC adopted a resolution concluding that religious institutions of the white northern world had acquired enormous wealth both in collusion with and as a consequence of racially exploitative economic systems. The WCC urged religious institutions to divest themselves of their excessive material wealth by allocating a significant portion of their total resources to organizations representing the racially oppressed. The WCC also called upon American and other member churches to consider seriously the demand for reparations.[110] Baldwin Sjollema describes how multinational corporations led to exploitation and alienation of his people in South Africa under the apartheid system: "Under new laws, rules, and regulations or more rigorous application of existing ones, thousands of black people have been harassed, arrested, sentenced, banned, tortured, or killed. Black people are systematically turned into foreigners in their own country; an estimated one-third of the total black population is forced to live in the so-called homelands."[111] According to Sjollema, the South African government had, since World War II, systematically attracted foreign capital, know-how, and highly qualified personnel. This coincided with the expansion of the large corporations in the US, Europe, and Japan. South Africa, with its stable military regime, its racially structured economy, low-cost labor, and dominant role in Southern Africa, provided an ideal climate for these multinational companies.[112]

The consequences of colonization and the extent of the exploitation of the native populations were clarified when Rt. Rev. Colin O'Brien Winter,[113]

---

109. Ibid.

110. Ibid.

111. Sjollema, *Isolating Apartheid*, 11–12.

112. Ibid., 3.

113. Reverend Colin O'Brien Winter (October 10, 1928–November 11, 1981) was an Anglican bishop in South Africa who opposed apartheid and championed the cause of migrant workers. He was eventually expelled from South Africa, but he continued to speak out while in exile.

Bishop-in-exile of Damaraland, delivered the Martin Luther King Memorial Lecture on November 15, 1972, at Wesley Theological Seminary. Winter started off on this note: "I must confess that my first reaction, after I had agreed to give this lecture, was a feeling of total ineptitude. How could I attempt to get across to a largely American audience the sufferings, the courage, zest, and the noble capacity to love, to endure, and to forgive that characterizes the black peoples of Namibia and South Africa, those who are relegated by white men's laws to be the lowliest positions in society?"[114] He then went on to talk about how the students of history and law would wince to see the "systematic stripping away" of human freedoms by whites in South Africa over the previous century coupled with the shocking exploitation of black labor. Winter said that statistics were just not enough, because behind the numbers were human beings, and they were the most important factor in the whole struggle. As he said, "Martin Luther King was so right in emphasizing that the garbage collectors of the world do matter whether we see them as the napalm victims in Vietnam or the black South African peasants, young and old huddled together in the wastelands of the bare veld in South Africa, removed from their homes by the laws of the Pretoria government."[115]

Winter explained that the Western world was very interested in Southern Africa, for Namibia boasted one of the largest diamond mines in the world, while Tsumeb had one of the largest copper mines in Southern Africa operated by American Metal Climax and Newmont Mining Corporation, in addition to abundant lead, zinc, silver, and uranium deposits to be mined.[116] Total foreign investments in Southern Africa in 1969 amounted to 3,502 million rands, of which Britain's share was 2,403 million rands compared to the US contribution of 596 million rands. South Africa received 91.5 million dollars in loans, and the profits made by three hundred US corporations between 1960 and 1970 averaged 18.6 percent (compared to 11 percent) from all other American overseas investment).[117] This led Professor W. F. J. Steenkamp of the University of South Africa to remark, "we have learnt that our large economic international relationships are our best shield in a war which has chosen us a scapegoats."[118] As Winter said of Steenkamp's

---

114. Winter, Colin O'Brien, "Martin Luther King Memorial Lecture," address at Wesley Theological Seminary, Washington, DC, November 15, 1972, Programme to Combat Racism, Masterfiles–Statements, No. 3 (1–6), 4223.16.1, WCC Archives, Geneva, Switzerland.

115. Ibid.

116. Ibid.

117. Ibid.

118. Kirby and the WCC, *Bank Loans to South Africa*, 7.

words, "put in the language of a black African: apartheid is propped up by the dollar and the pound."[119] Winter confirmed that he had fought racism for thirteen years in South Africa, and that in its worst form it was one of the greatest evils in the world. Now that he was exiled, he increasingly felt that apartheid had allies in high places throughout the Western world. He felt that the church needed to lead a moral crusade against those hypocritical societies who "beat their breasts in horror over the indignities caused by South Africa's apartheid" but then walked "home laughing from banks which are yearly increasing their investments there." Winter then concluded with a quote similar to King's sentiments on the relevance of the church in our times: "The judgment of God is upon the church as never before. If today's church does not recapture the sacrificial spirit of the early church, it will lose its authenticity, forfeit the loyalty of millions, and be dismissed as an irrelevant social club with no memory for the twentieth century."[120]

Up until 1969, the WCC's resolutions in relation to the ongoing crisis in Southern Africa centered on appeals to all Christians to acknowledge the contradiction between the Christian gospel and how white supremacists had interpreted it to perpetuate apartheid. The WCC seemed to assume that by working within the limitations prevailing in Southern Africa, white racism would somehow disintegrate. This would open up the possibility to create pluralistic societies in South Africa, Namibia, Rhodesia, Mozambique, and Angola. Perhaps naively, this belief remained the position of many Christians still struggling in their commitment to nonviolent resistance, and had to be respected by outside observers who were not faced with these difficult choices.[121]

In view of its own historic commitment to the gospel, the WCC could not tolerate the existence of a society built upon racism. It was now incumbent on the WCC to call upon its member churches to engage in coordinated action for the destruction of racism in Southern Africa. The WCC wished to bring about a situation where all the people of these territories negotiated their common future. The task before them was monumental, and would require multiple strategies for action at the international, national, and local levels. These included diverse political, economic, cultural, and religious action. WCC strategies must include recognition of the crucial role Christians played in South Africa, Namibia, Rhodesia, and the Portuguese colonies in the struggle for all the peoples of Southern Africa. This responsibility had

119. Winter, "Memorial Lecture," November 15, 1972, No. 3 (1–6), 4223.16.1, WCC Archives, Geneva, Switzerland.

120. Ibid.

121. "Eradication of Racism," 4223.1.02, Box 2, No. 6, Consultation Papers, WCC Archives, Geneva, Switzerland.

to be exercised with particular sensitivity to the conviction and needs of particular groups or individuals, which included:

a. The victims of oppression, particularly non-white victims, who are far more numerous than many suppose, and whose needs are extremely diverse.

b. Those whose convictions have led them to join movements of resistance and liberation, and who because of the evil nature of the powers that they oppose, are not granted prisoner of war status when they are captured.

c. The oppressors themselves who are victims of their own propaganda and tools of their own twisted interpretations of history.[122]

Responsibility also fell to Christians outside Southern Africa, both collectively as members of nation-states as well as individually, for having profited from the fruits of racial injustice in Southern Africa, particular responsibility lay with Christians in Great Britain, the US, France, Germany, Belgium, Holland, Switzerland, Italy, Portugal, and Japan because of their close links with the countries of Southern Africa. These links included trade, economic investments, bank loans, the international monetary system's reliance on gold, and cultural and educational ties.[123] The WCC identified areas where attention was particularly urgent, including the activities and needs of liberation movements as well as to military alliances between racist regimes in Southern Africa and Western powers. These alliances had important consequences for the strategic power alignments that made the escalation of racial war a likely possibility. Cultural links also played a role between Southern Africa and Western nations in reinforcing racism, for example in how non-white Africans' right to participate fully and equally in sports were disregarded in South Africa. The racial policy of the South African government was strengthened by overseas sports bodies, which allowed tours under conditions that implied the right of white South Africans to exclude non-white sportsmen. The WCC saw an instant and practical way for Christians to combat racism by refusing to participate in reciprocal sports tours with South Africa until racial restrictions were removed. Similar problems existed in other areas such as the performing arts, academic links, tourism, and so on.

Namibia, otherwise known as South-West Africa, demanded urgent attention. South Africa continued to defy the UN by refusing to relinquish its illegal administration of that area. A call was made for Great Britain and

122. Ibid.
123. Ibid.

the US to bring the case before the International Court of Justice, because there were special legal and moral obligations to secure indemnities and reparations for the African population dispossessed of lands and property. Furthermore, South Africa needed to terminate its expansionist policies and improve its relations with independent nations on its border, including Lesotho, Botswana, Swaziland, Rhodesia, Malawi, and Zambia.[124]

The WCC report confirmed that racism leads to oppression, domination, and injustice, concluding that the struggle against racism in every country and society was a responsibility laid upon the church by the gospel of Jesus Christ. The PCR, although a special program, is thus an integral part of the WCC. The PCR at Notting Hill resulted in well-attended, informative sessions that laid the groundwork for future action. It was agreed that if the churches were to have any relevance at this critical time, it was imperative that the churches be seen to operate as a community, a group, even a movement: "individual commitment is commendable—but not enough."[125]

The WCC also noted a UNESCO[126] finding that even when there were laws to discourage racism, the concentration of power, wealth, and status in the hands of one racial group worked in favor of de facto discrimination.[127] Not only was the WCC compelled to tackle these inequalities, they also had to solve the in-house problem of racism within their own institutions. As the report explained, the church had to realize that in the institutional world, "the closest approximation to love is justice."[128] With that understanding in mind, the Consultation called on the WCC to take action through economic sanctions against corporations and institutions that practiced blatant racism. It was agreed that WCC members should lobby governments to take similar action.[129] It was also necessary for the WCC to encourage reparations to exploited peoples and countries in recognition of the churches' historic involvement in racial exploitation.[130] A special unit was to be established by the WCC to deal with the eradication of racism. The UNESCO report was

124. Ibid.

125. Blake, "Report on the Consultation on Racism," August 12–23, 1969, 4223.1.03, WCC Archives, Geneva, Switzerland.

126. The United Nations Educational, Scientific, and Cultural Organization (UNESCO) is an agency charged with preserving peace and security by promoting international collaboration through education, science, and culture to further human freedom as proclaimed in the UN Charter.

127. Blake, "Report on the Consultation on Racism," August 12–23, 1969, 4223.1.03, WCC Archives, Geneva, Switzerland.

128. Ibid.

129. Ibid.

130. Ibid.

to be circulated among member churches to enlighten them on the evils of racism, and the WCC made a special commitment through its Commission of the Churches on International Affairs to coordinate multiple strategies against racism in South Africa.[131]

King had certainly been aware of this changing world order, and he told his audience at the International Convention of Christian Churches where their responsibilities lay: "The church is also challenged to instill within its worshippers the spirit of love, penitence, and forgiveness as we move through this transition. This is necessary for both oppressor and oppressed alike. Those who have been on the oppressor end of the old order must go into the new age, which is emerging with a deep sense of penitence, love and understanding. They must search their souls to be sure that they have removed every vestige of prejudice and bigotry, and that they moved away from the deadening idea of a white supremacy."[132] The Consultation at Notting Hill covered issues King had raised over the years, and like King, the WCC agreed that the solution to racism was not to be found in the US alone.

The next chapter deals with the implementation of PCR in Southern Africa through the 1970s. Ending apartheid was of particular interest to King and the WCC, for both saw the similarities between racism in America and in South Africa as well as how it was encouraged and sustained by white supremacist philosophy. King called for resolute action:

> It is in this situation, with the great mass of South Africans denied their humanity, denied their dignity, denied opportunity, denied all human rights; it is in this situation, with many of the bravest and best South Africans serving long years in prison, with some already executed; in this situation we in America and Britain have a unique responsibility. For it is we, through our investments, through our government's failure to act decisively, who are guilty of bolstering up the South African tyranny.[133]

131. Ibid.

132. King, "Beyond Discovery Love," September 25, 1966, King Center Library and Archive, Atlanta, GA.

133. King, *Autobiography of Martin Luther King*, 259.

8

Activism in the Kingian Mode

Implementing the WCC's Programme to Combat Racism

SOUTH AFRICA WAS THE only country in the world that was entirely governed on the basis of racism. Apartheid was a system of legalized and institutionalized racism defended in theological terms and in the name of "Christian civilization."[1] According to Blake, the international community, through the United Nations General Assembly, felt apartheid to be "a crime against humanity."[2] Reflecting on the previous lack of a proactive stance from the church, Blake went on to argue: "As a rule, the church doesn't have the courage of its convictions. The World Council has simply decided to take black Christians as seriously as white ones. Obviously for the latter, it is easier to advocate a gradual peaceful solution rather than a violent revolution; but there they are in a comfortable and wealthy situation."[3]

Following the successful Consultation at Notting Hill, the WCC quickly met at Canterbury some four months later, where it adopted a five-year mandate, appropriately named the Programme to Combat Racism, to mobilize the churches in the worldwide struggle against racism and "to

1. Blake, Eugene Carson, "Laymen Have a Ministry to Fulfil," *UNIAPAC International*, 995.1.02/4, Works (1971), WCC Archives, Geneva, Switzerland.

2. Ibid.

3. Ibid.

express in word and deed solidarity with the racially oppressed, and to aid the churches in educating their members for racial justice."[4]

The South African Council of Churches (SACC) responded to the Notting Hill Consultation and the Canterbury meeting's support for forceful action against apartheid. While not defending apartheid, the SACC regretted the means proposed for combating racism, but significantly added: "Our social order in South Africa is already to a considerable extent based on violence. The conclusion reached by the WCC Consultation on Racism in London that force may be resorted to by Christians in order to dislodge entrenched injustice, has been reached in part, on account of the failure of the churches."[5] The SACC criticized the WCC with the complaint that the churches in South Africa had not been properly informed about pending actions. The SACC also expressed unease at the WCC Uppsala Report's urging "the use of means usually associated with the civil power in the struggle against racism."[6] Bill Burnett[7] presented the SACC's appeal to the WCC Central Committee, but to no avail, and so the decision to set up the PCR was made.

Support came from Beyers Naudé,[8] Director of the Christian Institute, who called for understanding in the WCC's decisions. Having drawn attention to the millions of black people in South Africa who were voiceless, he said, "the more violent the reaction on the part of the whites, the more convinced the non-whites became that their salvation from the slavery of apartheid would not come from the white pharaohs, but that they could only expect it from a Moses from their own ranks, who at some time would speak the liberating word and perform the liberating deed."[9] There was no doubt that an accumulation of wealth and power in the hands of white people over a period of four hundred years had resulted in racism on all

---

4. "Uppsala to Jakarta," No. 5 (1–6), 4223.15.1, WCC Archives, Geneva, Switzerland.

5. Mbali, *Churches and Racism*, 46–47.

6. Mbali, *Churches and Racism*, 47.

7. Bill Burnett (July 31, 1917–August 23, 1994) was the Archbishop of Cape Town from 1974 to 1981. He became the Anglican Bishop of Bloemfontein in 1967 and also served as the first General Secretary of the South African Council of Churches (SACC).

8. Christiaan Frederick Beyers Naudé (May 10, 1915–September 7, 2004) was a renowned cleric and theologian in South Africa. A fervent critic of apartheid, after the Sharpeville massacre he denounced the political teachings of the Dutch Reformed Church (DRC).

9. Beyers Naudé, *Pro Veritate* 5, October 15, 1970, quoted in Sjollema, "Combating Racism," 470–79.

continents. Even those former colonies that had gained national independence still suffered from the aftermath of colonialism.[10]

The Central Committee recognized that the churches had participated
in racial discrimination and were still involved in the perpetuation of institutional racism. Therefore, it called upon churches "to move beyond charity,
grants, and traditional programming to relevant and sacrificial action" and
"to become agents for the radical reconstruction of society."[11] The churches
were to take a "significant moral lead" in the transfer of resources from the
powerful to the powerless.[12] Adler explains that these were strong words—
not too strong for the task that lay ahead, but perhaps overly optimistic. The
outline of the five-year program was so general that it hardly went beyond
traditional activities: terms of inquiry, consultations, assistance to member
churches, collection and circulation of analyses, examination of means for
political action, economic sanctions, etc. However, Adler notes that it was
significant that the Central Committee decided to make the Progamme to
Combat Racism a coordinated effort by the whole WCC under the direct
responsibility of Eugene Carson Blake.[13]

According to Pauline Webb, when the WCC launched its PCR, South
Africa became a major focus of its concern. Many of the WCC's member
churches, whose own countries had strong alliances with the South African
government, failed to recognize how deeply they themselves were impli-
cated in the injustices being perpetuated there. Therefore, the long struggle
began not only in solidarity with those in South Africa who were working
for the liberation of the oppressed, but also with the antagonism of many
others outside South Africa who did not accept the ramifications of that
oppression.[14] The report of the Commission on the PCR, "From Uppsala
to Jakarta," concluded that "any discussion about policies and programmes
in support of the racially oppressed must start with the assumption that the
liberation of oppressed people is an act that can only be validly undertaken
by the oppressed."[15] Thus, the question for the churches was how they could
positively support the liberation struggle. On the basis of this assumption,

10. "Uppsala to Jakarta," No. 5 (1–6), 4223.15.1, WCC Archives, Geneva,
Switzerland.

11. Adler, *Small Beginning*, 7.

12. Ibid.

13. Ibid.

14. Webb, *Long Struggle*, x.

15. "Uppsala to Jakarta," No. 5 (1–6), 4223.15.1, WCC Archives, Geneva,
Switzerland.

the PCR's main task was to isolate the root causes of oppression in order to discover ways of effectively combating racism.[16]

The PCR came into operation in January of 1970, developing a series of programs, policy actions, and guidelines to fulfill the Canterbury mandate. This mandate stipulated the major emphasis for the PCR:

a. White racism in its many organized ways was by far the most dangerous form of racial conflict.

b. It was institutional racism as reflected in the social, economic, and political power structures which must be challenged.

c. Combating racism must entail a redistribution of social, economic, political and cultural power from the powerful to the powerless.

d. No single strategy to combat racism was universally appropriate.

e. The need to analyze and correct the church's complicity in benefiting from the continuing white racism. This was an absolute priority if the churches wanted to make any contribution to the isolation of society's problems.[17]

A Special Fund was created at the 1969 WCC Control Committee meeting at Canterbury as part of the PCR. The Special Fund financed by the WCC supported various groups and organizations supporting victims of racial injustice throughout the world, laying special emphasis on the struggle for liberation in Southern Africa. The Special Fund was only one part of the PCR operations, but it soon became the focal point. The basic underlying concept of the Special Fund was the redistribution of power. Canterbury had decided that "there can be no justice in our world without a transfer of economic resources to undergird the redistribution of political power and to make cultural self-determination meaningful."[18] A fund of at least five hundred thousand dollars was required, of which two hundred thousand was to be taken from WCC reserves, with member churches expected to contribute the balance.[19] Considerable controversy surrounded these proposals. The original plans had passed by a narrow 11–7 vote in a sub-committee of the Central Committee. It required a reminder that "Onward Christian Soldiers" indeed reflected the view of many attendees for "combat" to be accepted as part of the PCR's title.[20] Proceeds from the

16. Ibid.

17. "Uppsala to Jakarta," No. 5 (1–6), 4223.15.1, WCC Archives, Geneva, Switzerland.

18. Adler, *Small Beginning*, 15.

19. Vincent, *Race Race*, 47.

20. Welch, "Mobilizing Morality," 880.

Special Fund were to be used to support organizations that "combat racism, rather than welfare organizations that alleviate the effects of racism."[21] The Special Fund was designed from the very beginning to do the following:

- Manifest solidarity with the racially oppressed in all parts of the world.

- Express the WCC's commitments to racial, economic, and political justice.

- Awaken people's consciousness about the struggle for racial justice.

- Raise the level of awareness and strengthen the organizational capability of the racially oppressed.[22]

The grants from the fund were to be used for humanitarian purposes and to strengthen the organizational capabilities of racially oppressed people, and they were to be given without direction as to the manner in which they were spent. South Africa was to have priority, and token grants were to be avoided. It was clear from the criteria that the WCC wanted to avoid paternalism and tokenism.[23] Adler questions that motive in view of the "smallness of the sums distributed" in amounts of two hundred thousand dollars to nineteen organizations, and whether in fact this constituted any "redistribution of power," but concludes that the symbolic act was important to show ecumenical solidarity.[24] Principal sources of support came from churches and ecumenical groups in the Netherlands, Germany, Sweden, Norway, Canada, and to a lesser degree, the US.[25] Regardless of the size of the grants, this was a clear departure from the past, when churches were often reluctant to be partisan in the "political" and controversial struggle for justice. Zolile Mbali raises this point, asking, "how could the church, through the Special Fund of the WCC, help the people involved without being identified as taking sides?"[26] Churches had generally taken a neutral position in situations of unequal power relationships, without realizing that in their neutrality, they were supporting the oppressive status quo. As Mbali notes, it became clear that for the churches to remain neutral would be interpreted as condoning the evil of racism.[27] Such a stance was no longer acceptable, and the WCC urged churches to be on the side of the racially oppressed.

21. Ibid., 882.

22. Ibid.

23. Barkat, "Personal Reflections, 1980–1990," 1994, 4223.17.1/1, WCC Archives, Geneva, Switzerland.

24. Adler, *Small Beginning*, 15.

25. Sjollema, *Isolating Apartheid*, 129.

26. Mbali, *Churches and Racism*, 21.

27. Ibid.

Anwar Barkat indicated that the WCC had never totally endorsed the political positions and methodologies of any given liberation movement, nor had it passed moral judgment on those driven by desperation to use violence against "the violence of racism."[28] The WCC found support to end all forms of racism, not to seek a victory for any ideological or political position. Nevertheless, it was precisely on this point that the WCC had been criticized—for being Marxist-oriented, supporting violence, or supporting organizations committed to the use of violence to achieve their goals. This was significant in light of the legacy of Martin Luther King Jr., and it was because of these allegations that the WCC requested a study on violent and nonviolent methods of social change. This would not compromise the Special Fund, for which the WCC continued to request support from member churches "as a minimum indication of their commitment to the objectives of Programme to Combat Racism."[29]

South Africa's Prime Minister Johann B. Vorster[30] manipulated contact between the WCC and SACC. The latter asked for a consultation with the WCC in 1971. Eugene Carson Blake agreed and requested visas for a delegation of WCC representatives. Vorster, however, laid impossible conditions: First, the delegation had to remain at Jan Smuts Airport in Johannesburg, and it could not travel into the country; second, the WCC grants to "terrorist" organizations to buy arms could be the only subject of discussion; third, the WCC delegation would have to be much smaller. Blake replied that the WCC could not agree to these terms and the consultation was called off.[31] The churches faced not only Vorster's anger over the WCC grants, but internal opposition as well, for they were interpreted as legitimizing organizations seeking the demise of the South African government. Churches that remained members of the WCC were seen as being against South Africa and in favor of violence and revolution. So-called "Patriotic Members" demanded withdrawal from the WCC. In this atmosphere, the annual synods convened. The Presbyterian Church gave a fearless reply: "(the Church's) only Lord and master is Jesus Christ, and it may not serve two masters. Its task is not necessarily to support the politics of the government in power,

---

28. Barkat, "Personal Reflections, 1980–1990," 1994, 4223.17.1/1, WCC Archives, Geneva, Switzerland.

29. Ibid.

30. Balthazar Johannes Vorster (December 13, 1915–September 10, 1983) was Prime Minister of South Africa from 1966 to 1978. Although he was a loyal supporter of apartheid, he was more pragmatic in his relationship with adjoining states.

31. Sjollema, "Eloquent Action," 16.

but to be faithful to the Gospel of its Lord and to seek justice for the afflicted and liberty for those who are oppressed."[32]

The other churches met as well, and the end result was a series of steps:

1. All decided to retain their membership in the WCC.

2. All criticized the WCC for its implicit support of violence in making grants to the liberation movements.

3. All strongly criticized racism in South Africa.

4. All desired further consultation with the WCC.

5. Most decided not to send funds to the WCC as a sign of protest.[33]

The WCC underestimated the controversy that arose when the Executive Committee met in Arnoldshain, Germany, in September of 1970 to approve grants from the Special Fund. The decision generated widespread controversy. "Never in its history has any action of the ecumenical movement received so much attention from the churches and the world," wrote one commentator.[34] Prime Minister Vorster, speaking for the white racist regime in South Africa, blasted the WCC for "subsidizing murder in the name of God."[35] This outrageous charge received extensive coverage, especially from conservative papers in West Germany and Great Britain. Responding to the furor, the Central Committee of the WCC met in Addis Ababa, Ethiopia, in January of 1971 to put forward a new resolution:

> The churches must always stand for the liberation of the oppressed and of victims of violent measures which deny basic human rights. [The Central Committee] calls attention to the fact that violence is in many cases inherent in the maintenance of the status quo. Nevertheless, the WCC does not and cannot identify itself completely with any political movement, nor does it pass judgment on those victims of racism who are driven to violence as the only way left to redress grievance and to open the way for a new and more just order.[36]

The PCR staff prepared a paper that gave some background details on the PCR's Special Fund to enable the Central Committee to determine its future. The report stated that the Special Fund moved the WCC beyond charity to involve itself, even if only symbolically, in the redistribution of

32. Mbali, *Churches and Racism*, 47–48.

33. Ibid., 48.

34. Welch, "Mobilizing Morality," 883.

35. Quoted in ibid., 884.

36. Mbali, *Churches and Racism*, 21.

power. Also, the Special Fund acted to influence several groups, organizations, and governments to make grants to liberation movements. Because the struggle against racial oppression had intensified and the need for humanitarian programs had increased, the financial and moral support of the WCC could not be withdrawn. If the Special Fund was to end, it would create the impression that the WCC no longer stood by the Canterbury decision to directly support the racially oppressed. It was noted that the grants had started the educational process among Christians about the churches' role in a world of racial oppression. This process was unprecedented and had to be continued. Furthermore, the grants had helped to start a process of growing confidence of oppressed people vis-à-vis the churches' commitment to justice. It was observed that pledges and plans for future support for the Special Fund were encouraging.[37]

The WCC Central Committee met in Utrecht in the Netherlands in August of 1972. It decided unanimously to extend the Special Fund to at least one million dollars and called upon member churches, groups, and individuals to support it as an indication of their commitment to the objectives of the PCR.[38] They urged the government of the United Kingdom to exercise its continuing responsibility until full political rights for all the peoples of Rhodesia were achieved. The WCC Finance Committee was instructed to sell existing holdings and to make no further investments in South Africa, Namibia, Zimbabwe, Angola, Mozambique, and Guinea-Bissau, urging all member churches, Christian agencies, and individual Christians outside Southern Africa to use their influence to press corporations to withdraw investments from and cease trading with these countries.[39]

In South Africa, John Rees, General Secretary of the South African Council of Churches, announced that the Special Grants had unleashed an avalanche of anger from the white establishment both in the church and in politics. Rees advised that it might be hard to understand why there was such a strong reaction, especially since the DRC had already withdrawn from the WCC following the Cottesloe Consultation in 1960 under pressure from the Verwoerd government. Other churches were known to be taking an enlightened view on the race question in general and on apartheid in particular. However, in South Africa, according to human rights lawyer and theologian Barney Pityana, the WCC was not regarded as a credible world

37. Adler, *Small Beginning*, 17–18.

38. Ibid.

39. "WCC's Statements and Actions on Racism, 1948–1979," 4223.16.3, WCC Archives, Geneva, Switzerland.

Christian organization.[40] In fact, the WCC had also come to understand that the church in South Africa did not represent the aspirations of the oppressed majority in the country. But a radical shift was underway from the institutional church to the church of the oppressed in those matters where the church could not or would not act.[41] As matters stood, the response of the South African churches and other organizations had been orchestrated by Prime Minister Vorster, who told the white minority parliament: "If they do not decide to dissociate themselves from this organization I would be neglecting my duty if I did not take action against them, if I allowed more money to be collected in South Africa for transmission to that organization, if I allowed churches which . . . remain members to send representatives to conferences of that body . . . if I failed to take action against clergymen who allow pamphlets . . . to be distributed in their churches."[42]

Since meeting in Addis Ababa in January of 1971, the Central Committee had been considering reactions to the first allocations decided upon at Arnoldshain. It concluded that the debate about violence and nonviolence was a major issue, especially since critics of the PCR were accusing the WCC of condoning violence because the grants financed groups engaged in armed struggle. Therefore, they decided to set up a two-year study project to examine this issue under the Church and Society Working Committee.[43]

Chinese Communist leader Mao Zedong is renowned for his oft-quoted statement, "power grows out of the barrel of a gun."[44] Martin Luther King Jr. would certainly not have agreed with the armed insurrection by MK in South Africa, for as he saw it: "There is more power in socially organized masses on the march than there is guns in the hands of a few desperate men. Our enemies would prefer to deal with a small armed group rather than with a huge, unarmed but resolute mass of people."[45] King went on to explain how the mass movement of the downtrodden could bring about change because "the determined movement of people incessantly demanding their rights always disintegrates the old order."[46]

The churches were strongly urged to be more imaginative in using nonviolent action, which was not intended as an excuse for not taking a political stance or challenging the existing system. There was a warning against

40. Pityana, "Tumultuous Response," 88–89.
41. Ibid., 89.
42. Ibid., 90.
43. Mbali, *Churches and Racism*, 22.
44. Wirmark, "International Solidarity," 4–15.
45. Ibid.
46. Ibid.

any tendency to sit in judgment on those who were driven to revolutionary violence. The Church and Society Working Committee's study explained that the greatest problem—often hidden by concern about violence—was Christian apathy and indifference to translating the commitment to Jesus Christ into action for social justice.[47] As Anglican bishop Kenneth Sansbury[48] wrote, the WCC report, "Violence, Nonviolence, and the Struggle for Social Justice," was convinced that "far too little attention has been given by the church and by resistance movements to the methods and techniques of nonviolence in the struggle for a just society."[49] The looming question was, under what circumstances might Christians participate in a violent conflict? The historic definition for a "just war" was laid down with seven conditions by the renowned Christian theologian Saint Thomas Aquinas in the Middle Ages:

a. The cause fought must be just.

b. The purpose of the warring power must remain just while the war goes on.

c. The war must be the last resort when peaceful methods have failed.

d. The means employed must be just.

e. The results for humanity must be expected to be better than if the war had not been fought.

f. The victory of the righteous cause must be assured.

g. The concluding peace must be just.

Sansbury concluded that in the case of South Africa, most if not all of these conditions had been met. The majority of colored people were oppressed and discriminated against "by an alien minority regime" and therefore the cause was "certainly just."[50] David M. Gill's "Violence and Non-violence: Resuming the Debate" refers to the WCC Central Committee statement in August of 1973, which explained that for those who accept violent resistance as a Christian option in extreme circumstances, the traditional restraints on the use of force might be restated as follows: "Not only must the cause be just and all other possibilities exhausted, but also there must be reasonable expectation that violent resistance will attain

47. Adler, *Small Beginning*, 32–33.

48. Cyril Kenneth Sansbury (January 21, 1905–August 25, 1993) was an Anglican bishop who served with distinction overseas. In 1956, he became General Secretary of the British Council of Churches (BCC), and he retired in 1973.

49. Sansbury, *Combating Racism*, 37.

50. Ibid., 43–45.

the ends desired, the method must be just, and there must be a positive understanding of the order which will be established after the violence succeeds."[51]

The difficulty of achieving a just order was monumental. An illustration of the intransigence of the South African apartheid regime was exposed in a paper titled "Détente of Delusion" at the annual meeting of the Commission on the PCR in early 1973. South Africa had been quietly penetrating the subcontinent and its investment then stood at two billion dollars. If that pattern of dependency was to continue, it was necessary to maintain good relations with neighboring African states. Internally, however, the apartheid regime had not changed. Reference was made to a recent speech by Prime Minister Volster, in which he promised publicly that blacks would never have a voice in "white South Africa."[52]

As Adler explains, that the Church and Society Working Committee's study did not provide an "alternative" program to the PCR, which may have been expected by some. The study recognized the complexity of the issue of violence, covert and overt, oppressive and liberating, and the use of nonviolence in politically motivated acts. The issue of unjust power structures and Christian engagement in the struggle for justice took center stage. The widely held view that the PCR was limited to supporting organizations engaged in a violent struggle was corrected. The Church and Society Working Committee emphasized that the PCR supported the humanitarian programs of those organizations because they were striving for economic, political, and racial justice. In fact, they were not excluded from support because they had used violence. Furthermore, this program had used nonviolent action more imaginatively than many others in discouraging white migration, supporting Portuguese deserters, and calling for a withdrawal of corporations from Southern Africa along with a cessation of trade. James Lawson, who worked closely with Martin Luther King Jr., did not hesitate to fully support the PCR when speaking before the Central Committee in Geneva. Adler raises an important point when she asks, "Is violence really the issue for those who oppose the Programme to Combat Racism?" Her response raises awkward questions for the morality of capitalist investment abroad, for "the peculiar turn taken by the debate on the violence/nonviolence statement makes one wonder whether it is not in fact a deep unconscious fear that the economic and political system of the West is at stake."[53]

51. Gill, "Violence and Non-Violence," 25–28.
52. "Ecumenical Diary," 164.
53. Adler, *Small Beginning*, 33.

In the first six years of the Special Fund, more than 1.5 million US dollars were received and disbursed to organizations supporting victims of racial injustice. These organizations agreed to use the grants according to the criteria approved by the WCC Executive Committee. The mission of the organizations were not to be inconsistent with the general purpose of the WCC and its units, and the grants were given for humanitarian activities (e.g., social, health, and educational purposes, legal aid, etc.). Grants from the Special Fund were intended to support organizations combating racism rather than welfare organizations alleviating the effects of racism, which were normally eligible for support from other units of the WCC. The focus of the grants was on raising awareness and on strengthening the organizational capacity of racially oppressed people. In addition, recognition was needed to support organizations that aligned themselves with the victims of racial injustice in pursuit of the same objective. The grants were intended as an expression of commitment by the PCR in the cause of economic, social, and political justice these organizations promoted. Baldwin Sjollema explains that while the WCC statements included significant reservations on the right to violent resistance, even as a last resort, the WCC was careful not to lay ground rules to oppose unending violence. The PCR quickly became identified with South Africa and was seen by some as a kind of church anti-apartheid movement.[54] The WCC took into account those places where the struggle was most intense and where grants might make substantial contributions to the process of liberation, particularly where racial groups were in imminent danger of being physically or culturally exterminated. In considering applications from countries of white and affluent majorities, attention was given to areas where political involvement precluded help from elsewhere. Grants were to be made with due regard to where they would have the maximum effect—token grants would not be made unless there was a possibility of stimulating a substantial response from other organizations.[55]

The WCC had supported the liberation movements in Southern Africa through humanitarian activities in accordance with the criteria set by the Executive Committee. Two organizations from former Rhodesia, the Zimbabwe African National Union (ZANU) and the Zimbabwe African People's Union (ZAPU), had received grants since 1970. However, when the WCC awarded grants to forty organizations in 1977, including a combined application from ZANU and ZAPU called the Patriotic Front, the

54. Sjollema, "Eloquent Action," 15.

55. "Programme to Combat Racism," 4223.17.1, WCC Archives, Geneva, Switzerland.

WCC came under intense criticism.[56] The political and military situations in Rhodesia (now Zimbabwe) were particularly sensitive in the late 1970s. Abel Muzorewa,[57] an African Methodist bishop, headed the government, but violence continued through guerrilla warfare. Tensions rose when a British missionary family was murdered, supposedly by guerrillas, early in 1978. On August 10, of the same year, the PCR granted eighty-five thousand dollars to the Zimbabwean Patriotic Front, a loose alliance of the two chief nationalist parties, ZAPU and ZANU. A civilian aircraft was shot down a few days later, allegedly by ZAPU forces. The WCC was again accused of supporting terrorism. A staff report at the time read: "In no single year since the Programme to Combat Racism started ten years ago, in 1970 have there been so many letters of protest, cables, statements, enquiries of all sorts, telephone calls, visits by groups, individual and church delegations . . . as a result of this action. These protests coincided with and were no doubt influenced by strong and well-orchestrated international campaigns against the World Council of Churches, and the Programme to Combat Racism in particular."[58]

In a background document dated August 11, 1978, concerning the WCC's Special Fund to Combat Racism's grant of eighty-five thousand dollars to the humanitarian programs of the Patriotic Front of Zimbabwe, WCC officers sought to clarify their decision in view of severe criticism from church and political circles. The criteria for the grants made it clear that the money must not be used for purposes "in conflict with the general purposes of the WCC and its units."[59] The WCC made it clear that it did not endorse violence "any more than a padre endorses the bullets of the soldier he serves." The WCC's own commitment to nonviolent change was clear. But that did not mean that it must desert those in need of humanitarian support when their struggle turned violent. In giving the grant, the WCC in no way aligned itself with all the policies and pronouncements of the Patriotic Front. The WCC's policy was clearly defined in 1971: "It believes that the churches must always stand for the liberation of the oppressed, and of victims of violent measures which deny basic human rights."[60] Furthermore,

---

56. Barkat, "Personal Reflections, 1980–1990," 1994, 4223.17.1/1, WCC Archives, Geneva, Switzerland.

57. Bishop Abel Muzorewa (April 14, 1925–April 8, 2010) was a Methodist bishop who served as Prime Minister of Zimbabwe-Rhodesia for a short period up to the Lancaster House Agreement in 1979. Robert Mugabe assumed power in March 1989 after an allegedly rigged election.

58. Welch, "Mobilizing Morality," 890.

59. "Special Fund Grants," 380–82.

60. Ibid.

the WCC drew attention to the fact that violence was in many cases inherent in the maintenance of the status quo. Nevertheless, the WCC refused to identify itself completely with any political movement, nor would it pass judgment on those victims of racism who were driven to violence as the only option to redress grievance and bring about a just social order.[61]

In his address to the Central Committee in Jamaica in January of 1979, WCC General Secretary Philip A. Potter raised the issue of the armed struggle against racist regimes in which innocent people, including missionaries, were killed. He pointed out that several churches and groups raised the question of supporting violence, "which cannot be the action of the church."[62] As Potter argued, "it seems to be easier to tolerate the violent institutions and practices of the racist regimes, which claim to be upholding Christian civilization, and which are maintained by external economic investments and military support, than to understand the violent struggle of the oppressed who have been deprived of every nonviolent means of travailing for their liberation, and have been forced as a last resort to take up arms." Potter went further in asking the compelling question, "How are we to evaluate the relationship between violence of oppression and violence of liberation?" The WCC had no guarantee that the money would be spent in the manner stipulated—only the good faith they had from the 120 other groups that the PCR had supported in educational and humanitarian work since 1970. The WCC affirmed that "the Programme to Combat Racism grants are specifically made as an expression of commitment to the groups in question and their causes."[63] The WCC thus awarded grants as part of their statement of trust. The WCC officers faced the question of whether a grant to the Patriotic Front's humanitarian work would free other funds for military purposes. In response, the WCC found that this and other Southern African liberation movements going back to 1970 had given no reason to believe the money was used for anything other than the purposes for which it was requested.[64]

The WCC had originally envisioned a brief, concentrated, special effort, optimistically dubbed by staff as a program to *end* racism. Supporters believed they could change institutionalized white racism in Southern Africa within five years. They did not and could not, for the staying power of racist structures was greater than anticipated. WCC-funded studies found that the campaign for change would have to continue, despite the controversies that

61. Ibid.
62. Potter, "Churches and the World Council," 133–45.
63. "Special Fund Grants," 380–82.
64. Ibid.

had come from many quarters. Important lessons had been learned in the early years of the PCR, as mobilizing morality had turned out to be complex and challenging. Summing up the PCR's accomplishments in 1974 as part of the evaluation process, Adler concludes that churches lived within very limited horizons, and the PCR proved a shock treatment for many. Most churches had adapted to their environment and were part of the social and political climate of their countries, where few were ready to criticize elected officials. According to Adler, theology played a limited and even ambiguous role in conflict situations.[65] Also, the PRC raised questions about the WCC's character. Welch agreed with Adler, but added that the "crusading sense" in the early years from 1968 to 1970 was unduly optimistic.[66] Although some former colonies in Africa such as Guinea-Bissau and Mozambique gained independence, strong resistance remained in Namibia, Rhodesia, and South Africa, where minority governments continued to hold power by military might.[67]

Adler identified some unfinished tasks in the WCC's campaign. The PCR had not really been a world program insofar as particular situations of racial oppression had been neglected while others had been analyzed without subsequent action. The churches of Latin America, Asia, and Africa had been on the fringe of the PCR, and the global pattern of white racism had not been studied in its entirety. Adler noted that the racially oppressed had not been granted sufficient agency in determining the direction of the PCR. Finally, the WCC and its member churches had only begun to move beyond charity. If it really wished to combat racism until it was eliminated, it had to go deeper.[68]

The Special Fund had played a controversial role in the WCC's response to racism. Another set of moral issues arose in connection with economic ties. Economic sanctions had been discussed long before the WCC took up the idea, having been a subject of debate in South Africa since the late 1950s. From the start, it was understood that sanctions would affect black people already suffering under oppression. As Luthuli observed in 1959, "the economic boycott of South Africa will entail undoubted hardship for Africans. We do not doubt that. But if it is a method which shortens the day of bloodshed, the suffering to us will be a price we are willing to pay."[69]

65. Adler, *Small Beginning*, 61–62.

66. Welch, "Mobilizing Morality," 891.

67. Ibid.

68. Adler, *Small Beginning*, 61–62.

69. Quoted in Mbali, *Churches and Racism*, 145.

Professor Steenkamp of the University of South Africa said in 1971 that "foreign money is flowing in to South Africa, and it is instrumental in the maintenance of apartheid."[70] In 1976, as South Africa's vulnerability became more obvious, Reed Kramer of Africa News wrote in the December 11 issue of *The Nation* that "with falling gold prices and heightened black resistance, Pretoria is under tremendous pressure. It is hard to imagine where it would be right now without borrowed funds."[71] Public opinion was divided on whether sanctions would produce the desired effect. As reported in *Africa Today*, "other scholars have frequently pointed out that even if sanctions do have a significant economic impact on the target country, there is no presumption that this will necessarily lead to desirable political changes."[72] Instead they might induce proponents to "rally around the flag" rather than promote reform.[73] An alternative viewpoint from William H. Kaempfer and Anton D. Lowenberg maintained "that even sanctions that have weak economic impacts on the target nevertheless serve to signal foreign support or disapproval to influence interest groups in the target country, thereby helping to foster political change."[74] Harry M. De Lange observed that "the political stability of South African governments is considered sufficient by Western business, and that, conversely, their stability is strengthened by the arrival of Western enterprise."[75] Apartheid South Africa depended on the supply of capital from abroad; therefore such investments supported this racist regime. Any withdrawal of investments would be seen by the WCC as a nonviolent method of bringing about change. Should the churches lobby governments and private corporations to take moral responsibility by withdrawing investments in South Africa? Such direct pressure might raise further criticism about the "politicization" of the WCC.

At Uppsala in 1968 and at Notting Hill, racism was linked with economic and political exploitation, and member churches were encouraged to "withdraw investments from institutions that perpetuate racism."[76] Deliberations over reparations were also very confrontational, and the Central Committee in 1969 stated that the issue of reparations "cannot be avoided," but that simple reparation fell short, "for it seeks simply to apportion guilt

---

70. Kirby and the WCC, *Bank Loans to South Africa*, 7.

71. Kramer, "Hock to U.S. Banks," 624–26.

72. Lowenberg, "Economic Sanctions on South Africa," 63.

73. Kirby and the WCC, *Bank Loans to South Africa*, 7.

74. Kaempfer and Lowenberg, "International Economic Sanctions," 786–93.

75. De Lange, "Foreign Investments," 383–93.

76. Quoted in Welch, "Mobilizing Morality," 892–93.

for the past."[77] Accordingly, it was important to "move beyond charity, grants, and traditional programming to relevant and sacrificial action . . . There can be no justice in our world without a transfer of economic resources to undergird the redistribution of political power and to make cultural self-determination meaningful."[78]

Some businessmen contended that further investment and growth would help ameliorate the harshness of apartheid. De Lange dismissed this supposition outright, observing that over a ten- to fifteen-year period South Africa had experienced a massive economic expansion that had coincided with the imposition of even tighter discriminatory legislation. As De Lange explains, "to think that economic activity (resulting in growth, higher incomes, the acquisition of more skills) is a means of undermining apartheid is to indulge in illusions."[79] Zolile Mbali describes how foreign investment was sought for big 1970s projects like the Richard's Bay Port Complex located in the Kwazulu homeland of Natal and plant projects for the South African Coal, Oil, and Gas Corporation (SASOL) and the Electricity Supply Commission.[80] These projects benefited the white economy, and some such as SASOL were strategic, for the fastest growing sections of the South African economy were the military and ancillary industries required to back up the militarization of South Africa. In general, the black population did not gain from such investment.

By the early 1970s, many in the WCC and its member churches believed that financial disengagement, both as an alternative to armed struggle and as a meaningful response to the pressure for reparations, was the answer. The application of effective economic pressure could accomplish nonviolent change in the white minority regimes of Southern Africa, especially South Africa, through a peaceful campaign of disinvestment and isolation.[81] Sjollema argues that the entanglement of the church with business was part of South Africa's problem: "The collaboration between the apartheid system and external business interests in an unholy alliance. Churches which at this stage still remain opposed to policies of disengagement are effectively becoming partners in this unholy alliance, especially when they themselves are investors in companies which derive large profits from the oppression of the black people in South Africa."[82]

77. Ibid.
78. Ibid.
79. De Lange, "Foreign Investments," 383–93.
80. Mbali, *Churches and Racism*, 139.
81. Welch, "Mobilizing Morality," 893.
82. Sjollema, *Isolating Apartheid*, 101.

Rev. Andrew Young, King's former senior aide, was appointed as one of the first Commissioners of the PCR. He adopted a robust approach, and at the second meeting of the Commission held in Geneva in March of 1971, he denounced the historic role of Christianity: "We've had our chance to be missionaries among the masses, and look what a mess we made of that. Lets look at ourselves now, and save our own souls."[83] Young also castigated the multinational companies, saying, "it is the corporations that are the enemy as they cut across national boundaries—more important than nations." He said that any success achieved with these multinationals would have re-percussions elsewhere, arguing, "if there is a breakthrough here it will be a blow for racism everywhere. When you attack South Africa, you attack US corporations' involvement and US racism at the same time."[84]

The WCC proceeded by good example and checked its own policies. Having obtained a list of 650 corporations in the Netherlands, Switzerland, United Kingdom, and USA with significant investments in six minority-ruled African states, the WCC initiated the following action:

1. The WCC decided to sell all its holdings in these companies (some 1.5 million dollars of the WCC's total portfolio of 3.25 million dollars),

2. To deposit no funds in banks maintaining direct operations in these countries, and

3. To urge "all member churches, Christian agencies, and individual Christians outside Southern Africa to use all their influence, includ-ing stockholder action and disinvestments, to press corporations to withdraw investment from and cease trading with these countries."[85]

The aim of the resolution was to put pressure on multinational cor-porations investing and trading in Southern Africa. It was recognized that such multinationals were giving economic, political, and moral support to apartheid and colonialism. The WCC would take a symbolic action by disinvesting at once, whereas member churches were asked to use their influence to make the multinationals themselves withdraw and cease trad-ing. Adler notes that the Central Committee debate was controversial as to whether a symbolic act would produce this desired effect.[86] At Utrecht, the discussion centered on either forcing complete withdrawal by multination-als or attempting policy reform. The Evangelical Church in Germany (EKD) suggested that it was necessary to calm things down and avoid economic

---

83. Welch, "Mobilizing Morality," 898–99.

84. Ibid.

85. Ibid., 893; Adler, *Small Beginning*, 26.

86. Adler, *Small Beginning*, 25–26.

pressure from outside. If improved conditions for black workers could be obtained from the multinationals, it may have been possible to conform with South African laws. In the end, a radical resolution for withdrawal was passed, but the EKD proposal was included in a footnote to demonstrate "multiple strategies."[87]

The WCC Central Committee meeting in 1973 was the first occasion since the PCR was launched for meetings with representatives of South African churches. There was no unanimity on the grants or the disinvestment policy, but the meeting did allow time to sort out some misunderstandings. The South African representatives were able to satisfy themselves that the WCC was trying to respond to the needs of the oppressed, and important initiatives were discussed and documented. The WCC Central Committee recommended a statement on violence, nonviolence, and the struggle for social justice to member churches. Three observations were made with direct relevance to South Africa:

1. There are some forms of violence in which Christians may not participate and which the church must condemn . . . the conquest of one people by another or the deliberate oppression of one class or race by another, which offend divine justice.

2. Too little attention has been given by the church and by resistance movements to the methods and techniques of nonviolence.

3. We regret some facile assumptions about nonviolence which have been current in the recent debate. Nonviolent action is highly political. It may be extremely controversial.[88]

The 1973 statement was carefully crafted and noncommittal in relation to what action was acceptable against unbearable violence.

The British Council of Churches (BCC) published "Investments in Southern Africa" in April of 1973, a document which set out four lines of argument for people and institutions interested in the disinvestment debate. The first was that economic growth would in all probability lead to social and political change, which would weaken racial discrimination and help end the oppressive system. Investments were therefore to be encouraged. The second was that the most useful and encouraging action for the churches, institutions, and individuals was to retain investments, and possibly buy more in order to increase pressure and improve working conditions in companies based in Southern Africa. Churches, institutions, and individuals could take a third approach by selling existing holdings and making

87. Sjollema, "Eloquent Action," 20.
88. Ibid., 23.

no further investments in companies trading or investing in South Africa. Finally, companies and banks in Britain could be pressured to withdraw capital investments from Southern Africa and to cease trading with those countries.[89]

In the summer of 1973, the WCC sought to assess the involvement of banks with which the organization held accounts in white-ruled Africa. The named banks were Bankers Trust Company, New York; Midland Bank Ltd., London; Schroder, Munchmeyer, Hengst, and Co., Frankfurt; Odier, Bungener, Courvoisier, and Cie, Paris; Algemene Bank Nederland, Amsterdam; Skandiniska Enskilda Banken, Stockholm; Hentsch and Cie, Geneva; Lombard, Odier, and Cie, Geneva; Morgan Guaranty Trust Co., New York; and Union de Banques Suisses, Zurich. A letter sent to the banks by the WCC's Director of Finance asserted that "you are aware of our deep concern about the situation in Southern Africa, where white minority regimes oppress the black majorities, withhold from them democratic and basic human rights, and impose conditions of social injustice."[90] It went on to request answers to the following questions regarding the extent of their bank's activities in South Africa, Namibia (South-West Africa), Zimbabwe, Angola, Mozambique, and Guinea-Bissau:

a. Do you have branches in any of the six countries named?

b. Do you have correspondents or banking representation in any of the countries named?

c. Do you hold any deposits from the governments or public corporations of the named countries?

d. Do you have any loans outstanding to any of the governments or public corporations of the named countries?

e. Do you hold any bonds of any of the governments or public corporations of the named countries?

f. Does your bank act as the agent for the marketing of gold production originating in any of the named countries?

g. Do you hold deposits from companies registered or based in any of the named countries?

89. British Council of Churches Department of International Affairs, *Investment in Southern Africa*, Conference of British Missionary Societies, London, April 1973. Quoted in Mbali, *Churches and Racism*, 137–38.

90. Quoted in Kirby and the WCC, *Bank Loans to South Africa*, 16–17.

Of the ten banks contacted, nine replied to the WCC letter, the exception being the Algemene Bank Nederland.[91]

The next important action taken by the WCC was its "Resolution on Bank Loans" made at West Berlin in 1974, which instructed the Finance Department to communicate with the European American Banking Corporation (EABC).[92] Mr. Frank Norton, the WCC Director of Finance, sent letters to the EABC and four of its owners in 1975 requesting that they terminate loans to the South African government. The named banks were Deutsche Bank, West Germany; Amsterdam-Rotterdam Bank N.V., the Netherlands; Société Générale de Banque S.A., Belgium; and the Creditanstalt-Bankverein, Austria. The EABC was reported to have provided over 210 million dollars to the South African government and its agencies since 1970.

Following the WCC Central Committee meeting in West Berlin, where its Finance Committee sought to "solicit assurances" from various banks, including the Midland Bank in the UK, "that they will stop granting loans to the South African government and its agencies," action was initiated in Britain, and it is worth recalling that it was by far the largest single investor in the South African economy. In 1976, the total European Economic Community investment in South Africa was 7,660 million pounds, of which 63 percent came from the UK, representing 36 percent of all foreign investment.[93] The Methodist Church started a dialogue with the leadership of the Midland Bank, and the Church Commissioners of the Church of England also entered the fray. Further pressure on this issue came from an action group called "End Loans to South Africa" (ELTSA), in which Pauline Webb, former Vice President of the WCC, played a prominent part. She convened a discussion among the WCC's British member churches, along with WCC President Dr. Ernest Payne and Charles Henry Gordon Lennox, Chairman of the WCC Finance Committee. They asked the British Council of Churches (BCC) to make a joint approach with the WCC to the Midland Bank. No immediate public action was taken by the bank.[94]

It is important to assess what the PCR was hoping to achieve in lobbying the banks. In the first instance, the debate between the churches and

---

91. Kirby and the WCC, *Bank Loans to South Africa*, 16–17.

92. The European American Banking Corporation (EABC) is one of the top banking organizations in the US. It was jointly owned by six of Europe's largest banks: the Deutsche Bank, West Germany; Société Générale, France; Midland Bank, Britain; Amsterdam-Rotterdam Bank N.V., the Netherlands; Société Générale de Banque S.A., Belgium; and the Creditanstalt-Bankverein, Austria.

93. Mbali, *Churches and Racism*, 148–49.

94. Sansbury, *Combating Racism*, 51.

the banks aired the issue of public accountability, a subject that neither the banks nor the churches had confronted. Previously, the churches had left Christians involved in business alone where social and political ethics were concerned. The issues were now openly debated with renewed responsibility in the hope of working for justice. Corporate ethics and public accountability were now opened for discussion at all church and business levels. This triggered an additional need for education in the churches and the development of systematic strategies for Christian agencies and individuals to combat institutional racism and injustice. Finally, in dealing with the banks and multinational companies, the churches had learned an important lesson to maximize the effect of policy decisions: In order to take on the titans of trade unions, political parties, and lobby groups, churches must act in concert with one another and with outside organizations.[95]

Sjollema emphasizes that in this correspondence with the banks in 1975 and 1976, the response of Amsterdam-Rotterdam Bank (AMRO) was of considerable political and ethical importance.[96] AMRO stated in its reply to the WCC that it "always refrained from using the apparatus of the bank (either in a positive or negative sense) for political ends."[97] AMRO said that bank officials would have to be guided by the question, "are the transactions for which the cooperation is being asked legally permissible?" They added that if it was legally possible to continue the "rendering of services" despite the "social or political situation in a certain country," then "the management of the bank has no call to boycott the country in question." Demonstrating their commercial orientation, AMRO concluded, "we consider it to be out of the question that conscience could make a definite decision on how to act in the actual practice of these extremely complicated issues." WCC representatives showed concern with two issues in their reply: the state of South Africa and the attributes of AMRO as a bank, and the raison d'être of the WCC: "WCC believes that South Africa is a special case . . . It is a special case because it has declared itself to be one . . . what makes South Africa unique is the fact that its constitution denies any possibility of the emergence of a society in which human beings are treated on their human values and not on their skin color."[98]

The WCC went on to say that such a policy is "basically anti-Christian." This was not imposed on South Africa; they freely chose it for themselves. The WCC said by embarking on such a policy, South Africa had isolated

---

95. Sjollema, *Isolating Apartheid*, 65.

96. Ibid., 61.

97. Quoted in ibid.

98. Quoted in ibid.

itself and that this was the reality they had to deal with: "To talk of the withholding of loans from the South African government as 'isolating' that country is therefore to ignore the fact that over 80 percent of the country's people are already isolated from all the processes of decision-making in the country."[99] The WCC referred to the "State of South Africa Yearbook 1971," in which the South African government lauded the fact that increased foreign investment reflected "the confidence in South Africa's economic stability and growth."[100] This, in fact, coincided with the increased brutality of apartheid over the last two decades. The WCC alleged that the "argument that disinvestment would delay the end of apartheid, apart from being categorically denied by the South African government, has never been tried in practice. The WCC claimed that South Africa was a bitterly isolated and polarized country "and that this would continue for as long as others, even 'right-thinking people,' were enthusiastic in supporting the continuance of apartheid. If one needed a reality check, the recent Soweto,[101] (1976) uprising indicated the road ahead.[102]

The Central Committee of the WCC reiterated the Acting General Secretary's statement about the Soweto massacre of June 16, and called "upon the South African regime urgently to end violence against the oppressed majority, to recognize immediately their full human rights."[103] Pleas were made to release all political prisoners and to end apartheid. The WCC urged all its member churches, and particularly churches in South Africa, to do everything in their control to hinder the repressive violence of the regime and to show their empathy with the oppressed by their actions. Furthermore, the WCC urged member churches in countries that maintained military and economic links with South Africa to lobby their governments to end this collaboration and to increase their efforts to discourage white emigration to South Africa by encouraging the press and other agencies to refuse to advertise or hire white labor for South Africa.[104]

The WCC had to observe divine love, which was "oriented to the poor, the marginalized, and the oppressed," which had practical implications for the WCC such that "the church should reflect the same partisanship in the

99. Ibid., 62.

100. Quoted in ibid.

101. The Soweto uprising was led by protesting high school students in South Africa that began on June 16, 1976. Up to 20,000 students participated in the protests, and security forces killed at least 176 students and possibly many more.

102. Sjollema, "Isolating Apartheid," 62.

103. "Ecumenical Chronicle," 460–63.

104. Ibid.

way it lives, the way it acts, how it uses its resources."[105] The WCC perceived
that the only permissible use of Christian capital was primarily to free the
poor and the oppressed, but this very process in itself would liberate the
rich: "So capital is for WCC a means, while for AMRO, it appears to be
an end in itself." The WCC then proceeded to take a swipe at capitalism
and how profits might be dispensed, insisting that "it can never be right for
Christians to allow the capital of which they are trustees to be used solely
as an end in itself, for the accumulation of more capital."[106] In criticizing
AMRO and capitalism's failures, the WCC called for a "new international
economic order" wherein capital did not exist for the benefit of the few, but
for the common good: "If the poor are to become less poor, the rich must
become less rich, and we should deny the gospel if we failed to say so." The
WCC took AMRO to task over the restrictions of free market forces in South
Africa, saying, "it seems strange to us that you can involve yourselves in a
country where there is no free market, in which buyers of goods or services
can obtain the highest degree of satisfaction of their needs wherever they
can."[107] The WCC stated that because capital was a form of power, it was
often used for political ends. South Africa used loans for the perpetuation
of apartheid, which was an immoral political end. WCC therefore accused
AMRO, "we do not think you can claim to have faced squarely the implications of your current policy unless you acknowledge your own interest in
the status quo in South Africa, and the degree to which your interest would
be threatened by the precipitate disappearance of the existing South African
government."[108]

Finally, the WCC told AMRO that they had no choice in their dealings
with South Africa but to accept how apartheid was practiced. Their acquiescence to apartheid only sustained the system. Having acknowledged that
WCC action had commenced in 1972 against the bank, AMRO eventually
answered the letters in September of 1976: "We should like to point out that
we have recently stated that our bank, and the affiliates it controls, have not
granted any credits to South Africa since the Spring of 1973, other than in
connection with the economic relations between the Netherlands and that
country."[109] Furthermore, AMRO continued, "without fundamental changes
in the situation in South Africa, we do not envisage that this policy, followed

105. Quoted in Sjollema, *Isolating Apartheid*, 62–63.
106. Ibid.
107. Ibid.
108. Ibid.
109. Ibid., 64.

since 1973, will be modified."[110] As Sjollema observes, the bank had changed its policy, which was most interesting. The WCC had mustered its forces to launch a concentrated moral and ethical assault on a capitalist fortress, which resulted in the bank's enlightened retreat from supporting a rotten apartheid regime. The other banks did not engage in the same ethical debate as AMRO, but the WCC arguments were applicable to all the others. The multinational companies fought back against WCC policy, quoting statements from Chief Mangosuthu Gatsha Buthelezi[111] and other Bantustan leaders suggesting that black workers were against disinvestment because it could result in wholesale job losses. In a somewhat exaggerated claim, these leaders argued that WCC policies sought "pauperization" of black people to precipitate a revolution.[112] Other member churches in the United Kingdom, West Germany, and Switzerland put forward similar arguments. However, the WCC, along with an increasing number of member churches, saw the policy as a last-ditch effort for change by nonviolent means. Like the Special Fund, disinvestment was highly controversial, but for the WCC it meant "a further move on the part of the WCC as a whole towards its involvement in the struggle for racial justice. In many ways, the decision on a withdrawal of investment is of much more fundamental importance than the preceding one on the grants, because it questions fundamentally the social, economic, and political structures of both the West and Southern Africa."[113]

This left the churches in a dilemma, for such statements called the whole basis of the capitalist systems in their own countries into question. The result, according to the PCR's Director, was "lots of flak" for linking church policies with political involvement, which "set in motion hot debate in local congregations, which went down to local levels. That was exactly what the PCR was supposed to do, to make churches at local and national and regional level aware of their own responsibilities."[114] In West Germany, this "political" outlook would prove sensitive, for the Evangelical Church was heavily reliant on state tax exemptions. There were repercussions in Switzerland as well, where church and state relationships were under extreme pressure from banks and Swiss multinational corporations. Under criticism, the banks robustly defended their loans and investments in

110. Ibid., 57–64.

111. Mangosuthu Gatsha Buthelezi (August 27, 1928) has been President of the Inkatha Freedom Party since its foundation in 1975. He became Minister of Home Affairs in South Africa in 1994.

112. Sjollema, "Eloquent Action," 20.

113. "WCC Background Documents for the 1973 Central Committee Meeting," quoted in ibid., 21.

114. Welch, "Mobilizing Morality," 896.

Southern Africa. First, they argued that their loan policy was in line with both the national and foreign policies of their respective countries, which maintained economic ties with South Africa. Second, they asserted that economic disengagement would backfire: "Instead of capitulation [by the South African government, a boycott] will sooner lead to an aggravation of the present situation in which the reactionary forces will consolidate their position of authority."[115] Third, the banks observed that political neutrality was the best policy, arguing that if "we were to allow ourselves to be influenced in our business dealings by political views of this kind—whether favorable or unfavorable to a particular government—our international business would rapidly become impossible. In our view, therefore, our right and proper course is to observe a strict political neutrality in all our dealings."[116]

The WCC had decided that private ethics and corporate ethics should be brought into agreement. Apartheid could only be toppled if the economic foundation bolstering white racism could be eroded. The WCC attempted to persuade the EABC and its associated banks to end economic support to South Africa by emphasizing the immorality of apartheid and its dependency on their coffers for survival. The EABC failed to give in, and the Executive Committee of the WCC decided in November of 1975 to withdraw all of its funds from member banks of the EABC. Member churches of the WCC were encouraged to begin their own campaigns of consultation, shareholder action, and closure of accounts if required.[117]

According to a 1977 WCC publication, "the initiative in raising the issue of bank loans to the South African government and its agencies came originally from local church and secular groups, and it is they who are maintaining the momentum of the debate and the campaign now."[118] However, the approval given by the WCC Central Committee in its 1974 Berlin meeting, coupled with the advocacy and network-building coordinated by PCR in Geneva, made the effort international.[119] The Central Committee of the WCC perceived a deterioration in efforts to abolish apartheid when they pronounced in 1979 that "the Western nations have substantially increased their economic involvement in Southern Africa as a whole, and in South Africa in particular."[120] The Central Committee noted with disappointment

115. Ibid., 895–96.
116. Ibid.
117. Ibid., 896–97.
118. Ibid.
119. Welch, "Mobilizing Morality," 863–910; Adler, *Small Beginning*, 26.
120. "Statement of the Central Committee," 194–98.

that there were more foreign-controlled firms in South Africa than there had been two years earlier. Some overseas firms had reduced their South African involvement, but sales to South Africa by British, West German, Japanese, and French firms had increased substantially.

The WCC's next major policy decision was the "Resolution on Comprehensive Sanctions against South Africa" issued in Geneva in 1980. The Central Committee called upon the WCC and its member churches "to press governments and international organizations to enforce comprehensive sanctions against South Africa, including a withdrawal of investments, an end to bank loans, arms embargo and oil sanctions, and in general for the isolation of the state of South Africa."[121] This went further than previous resolutions by essentially designating South Africa as a pariah state.

Zolile Mbali explains that the campaign for withdrawing bank assistance to South Africa began with rather vague directions from the WCC, which became more pointed as research revealed the degree to which banks were involved in lending there. In 1979, the Centre Against Apartheid at the UN produced a comprehensive document listing all the major loans made to South Africa so as to make ethical choices possible. British banks and finance houses provided more money for South Africa than any other country. In the three-year period from 1979 to 1982, British banks had provided 1068 million dollars in loans, while Switzerland had come in second with loans totaling 998 million dollars, with Germany and the US trailing close behind.[122] As Mbali comments, "high financiers in the West appear to be insulated from the moral arguments by the persistent Western traditions of amoral economics and money-making—of 'following the market movements' with no initiatives or judgments involved."[123] Although the WCC's campaign for the withdrawal of financial backing in South Africa began in the 1970s, it was another decade before it became a serious political consideration there.

The difficult periods after the Sharpeville massacre in 1960 and the Soweto killings in 1976 did cause the banks and multinationals to reflect on their futures in South Africa. It is hard to distinguish whether it was the insecurity brought about by apartheid and its consequent violence or "nervous Nellie" financiers with pangs of conscience that contributed to increasing fear for their money. The instability of South African society became more apparent as Western investors began to feel the heat.[124] South African

121. Sjollema, *Isolating Apartheid*, 59–60.
122. Mbali, *Churches and Racism*, 155.
123. Ibid.
124. Ibid., 154–55.

religious leaders were proactive in giving encouragement to the growing resistance at home, but they also continuously called on the international community to pressure Pretoria. The National Council of Churches of Christ (NCC) in the US and the United States Catholic Conference (USS-CC) convened a consultation in New York, where Bishop Desmond Tutu[125] pleaded with international partners, "the West has a critical role to play to ensure the survival of all in our subcontinent, and you shouldn't abdicate your moral responsibility . . . You in the West have undergirded apartheid, injustice, and oppression by your investments, by your use of your veto in South Africa's favor at the United Nations. You must decide where you want to be."[126] Bishop Tutu, as General Secretary of the South African Council of Churches (SACC), pleaded in 1981 with the international community "for the sake of the children of all South Africans, black and white, for God's sake, for the sake of world peace," to be proactive in compelling change in South Africa using "political pressure, and above all, economic pressure."[127]

In his 1980 article, "The Black Church and the Struggle in South Africa," theologian Allan Boesak[128] made the case that the oppression of black South Africans over the past three hundred years was going to be difficult and costly to overcome. Reconciliation was essential, but in order to bring it about "the Church must initiate and support programs of civil disobedience on a massive scale, and challenge white Christians especially on this issue."[129] Boesak went on to urge people not to obey unjust laws, "because non-cooperation with evil is as much a moral obligation as is co-operation with good," and so it was imperative to "obey God rather than man in South Africa." He concluded that there was no point in conducting new studies on the investment problem, "but direct and forceful action will show these companies how serious the church really is about the plight of our people."[130]

125. Bishop Desmond Tutu (October 7, 1931) is Anglican bishop who headed the Truth and Reconciliation Commission after the demise of apartheid. In 1986, he became Archbishop of Cape Town and went on to become a tireless worker for democracy, freedom, and human rights worldwide. He received the Nobel Peace Prize in 1984, as well as numerous other honors over the years.

126. Quoted in Katzin, "Economic Strategies," 59.

127. Ibid., 60.

128. Allan Aubrey Boesak (February 23, 1945) is a political activist and a cleric of the Dutch Reformed Church. He vehemently opposed apartheid as patron of the United Democratic Front (UDF) from 1983 to 1991.

129. Boesak, "Struggle in South Africa," 16–24.

130. Ibid.

In 1981, the WCC solidified its stance on banking investments in South Africa. They adopted a set of five criteria to serve as objective guidelines for WCC relations with such banks. These actions were in line with the policy first articulated at the 1968 WCC's Assembly at Uppsala. Each criterion could be evaluated independently, but together they could be used to gauge the depth of banks' involvement to help the WCC bring about change by assessing:

1. Did the bank maintain facilities in South Africa?

2. Did the bank regularly appear as a 'manager' of loans and/or bond issues in South Africa?

3. Did the bank continue substantive lending since the troubles in Soweto in 1976?

4. Did the bank loans have direct or indirect military purposes?

5. Did the bank loans benefit the nuclear industry?

The WCC agreed that relationships with banks could be continued if they openly implemented a no loans policy to the South African government. The Executive Committee decided in August of 1981 that the following six banks met the WCC criteria:

- Algemene Bank Nederland
- Skandinaviska Enskilda Banken
- Bankers Trust Company
- Banque Scandinave en Suisse
- Union Bank of Finland Ltd.
- Lloyds Bank Ltd.

It was decided that WCC relations with the following banks were to end:

- Union Bank of Switzerland
- Dresdner Bank
- Swiss Bank Corporation

WCC relations with these banks were to be provisionally retained pending further discussion:

- American Express Bank (Switzerland)
- Banque Worms
- Schroder, Munchmeyer, Hengst, and Co.

- Banque International pour l'Afrique Occidentale

- Morgan Guaranty Trust Co. of New York

That the WCC would consider opening or extending accounts to the banks below, which served as alternative institutions to those listed above:

- International Genossenschaftsbank

- Algemene Bank Nederland

- Lloyds Bank Ltd.[131]

Wesley Kenworthy, WCC Assistant General Secretary for Finance and Administration, explained that the WCC's actions were not in any way a criticism of the "entirely satisfactory" services rendered by these banks over the years. The WCC's sole objective was to foster "nonviolent change towards a genuine multi-racial society in South Africa."[132] Some further clarification may be needed about these lists. The banks designated as acceptable were judged to be so on the basis that they either made no loans to the South African government and its agencies or would not extend any in the future. The banks deemed unacceptable were heavily involved in financing South Africa in various ways, while other banks were only "moderately involved" in that their relationship with South Africa was shallow and so did not warrant the closure of WCC accounts.[133] It is important to note that the argument with the banks was not about banking per se, but rather about the morality of dealing with a racist regime. The WCC had argued "that corporate ethics are no different from private ethics in that just as each of us had to give account of those actions (and inactions) for which we are alone responsible, so we are obliged, when we act with others, to account for what we do together."[134]

The WCC analyzed the results of this ongoing debate with the banks and came to four conclusions:

1. The first result was a clarification of the role of the Algemene Bank Nederland, and the realization that it was very closely identified with the judgment and conduct of the other Dutch merchant banks.

2. The second result was seen as potentially more far-reaching. It was the debate's success in making public accountability more open, a point that neither the banks nor the churches had previously faced. Corporate ethics were now widely discussed.

131. Sjollema, *Isolating Apartheid*, 65–67. See also "Ecumenical Diary," 82–83.

132. "Ecumenical Diary," 82–83.

133. Sjollema, *Isolating Apartheid*, 65–67. See also "Ecumenical Diary," 82–83.

134. Kirby and the WCC, *Bank Loans to South Africa*, 43.

3. The third result highlighted that with bank loans and other issues, no single strategy would work, for multiple strategies were much more effective.

4. The fourth result was the development of a strategy to combat racism on an institutional basis rather than at the level of the individual. Speculation had not previously taken place on the motives for lending to South Africa, or whether prejudice by bank directors prevailed.[135]

One could say that Zolile Mbali was prescient when he wrote in 1987 that "South Africa is vulnerable to the refusal of financial loans, as the events of 1985–86 show. Governments, in particular the United States government, exercise control over the International Monetary Fund, but private banks are more open to direct public pressures. In the short term the 1970s have shown that financial managers are not swayed by moral argument alone, as these raised by the Programme to Combat Racism. However, there are signs that a growing number of corporate bodies can be persuaded to consider ethical criteria."[136]

The collapse of apartheid in 1989 came about as the result of economic forces. By the mid-1980s, South Africa had become heavily dependent on short-term international loans that had to be rolled over frequently. It was the reaction by Western banks in 1985 that broke the intransigence of the South African government. When Chase Manhattan Bank called in its loans, Swiss and German institutions quickly followed. When F. W. de Klerk replaced Botha as head of the National Party, peace initiatives swiftly followed through the ANC. With the ANC unbanned, constitutional negotiations could begin, and history was made when Nelson Mandela was freed on February 11, 1990.[137] Nelson Mandela rejoiced, "let us join hands and march together into the future . . . We have reached the end of the era."[138] Perhaps Martin Luther King Jr. looked down and smiled, as he had fought long and hard to spotlight South African's apartheid hell on the international stage.

---

135. Ibid., 46–47.

136. Mbali, *Churches and Racism*, 205.

137. Welch, "Mobilizing Morality," 902–903.

138. Mandela, Nelson, "Presidential Inauguration Speech," address at Union Buildings Amphitheatre, Pretoria, South Africa, May 10, 1994, quoted in Potter, "Task Ahead," 116.

9

Remembering a Drum Major

Final Reflections on Aspects of King's Freedom and Social Justice Crusades

MARTIN LUTHER KING JR. was a "drum major for justice,"[1] a towering figure in the twentieth century who captured the imagination of countless millions of Christians and people of other faiths throughout the world. He was a courageous leader who challenged both political and ecclesiastical authority by taking controversial stands against racism at home and overseas. King opposed the Vietnam War as early as 1965, when few clergymen were prepared to criticize US foreign policy in Southeast Asia. His stance with the WCC on that war has long since been vindicated, though the tragic events have left a scar on the American psyche that will be difficult to heal. Ten years after the war, *Time*'s cover story on April 15, 1985, captured the national feeling: "A Bloody Rite of Passage, Viet Nam Cost America Its Innocence and

1. Paraphrasing a 1952 homily, "Drum-Major Instincts," by Methodist preacher J. Wallace Hamilton, King explained to his congregation that the desire for personal greatness should be achieved through service and love, saying, "there is deep down within all of us an instinct. It's a kind of drum major instinct—a desire to be out front, a desire to lead the parade, a desire to be first . . . Yes, if you want to say that I was a drum major, say that I was a drum major for justice. Say that I was a drum major for peace. I was a drum major for righteousness. And all of the other shallow things will not matter" ("The Drum Major Instinct," address at Ebenezer Baptist Church, Atlanta, GA, February 4, 1968, Box 14, King Center Library and Archives, Atlanta, GA).

Still Haunts Its Conscience."[2] King and the representatives of the WCC had seen the futility of the conflict and mourned the massive loss of life in an unnecessary theater of war. Indeed, historian Robert McMahon argues that despite the deaths of over fifty-eight thousand Americans and between two and three million Vietnamese, Cambodians, and Laotians, the expenditure of billions of dollars, and the most extensive bombing campaign in world history, Americans had failed in their principal objective, just as figures like King and Blake had predicted. American intervention could not preserve the independent South Vietnamese government that so much US blood, money, and prestige had been tied to, nor could they prevent the emergence of Communist regimes in any of the three countries that once constituted French Indochina.[3]

The US was too traumatized to become embroiled in another Vietnam War scenario for a quarter century, but the attacks on the Twin Towers in New York on September 11, 2001, awoke the sleeping giant. King's legacy of conflict resolution through nonviolence, embraced by many in the WCC, may have seemed irrelevant in face of the nearly three thousand people killed in that devastating terrorist act. The term, "the Lost Decade," has been used to describe the disastrous invasions of Iraq and Afghanistan in pursuit of nonexistent weapons of mass destruction, amongst other nebulous objectives.[4] Some lessons in restricting combat losses have been learned from Vietnam, but the casualty rate amongst the armed forces is nevertheless alarming: "While we know how many US soldiers have died in the wars (over 6,600), what is startling is what we don't know about the levels of injury and illness in those who have returned from the wars. New disability claims continue to pour into the VA, with over 750,000 disability claims already approved. Many deaths and injuries among US contractors have not been identified."[5]

It has also been confirmed that 137,000 civilians have died in the conflict in Afghanistan and Iraq, while nearly eight million people have been displaced.[6] The cost of the wars has been staggering, leading a report by Brown University to estimate a cost of 4.4 trillion dollars, and along with the

2. Morrow, "Bloody Rite of Passage," 20. See also McMahon, "Contested Memory," 159–84.

3. Ibid.

4. See Rogers, "9/11 and the Lost Decade," http://www.opendemocracy.net/paul-rogers/911-and-lost-decade.

5. Watson Institute for International Studies, Brown University, "Over 330.000 Killed by Violence, $4 Trillion Spent and Obligated," Costs of War Project, http://costsofwar.org/.

6. Ibid.

counterinsurgency efforts in Pakistan, overall civilian and soldier casualties of 225,000.[7] As the US should have learned from Vietnam, the so-called "War on Terror" requires a nonmilitary solution, as King and the WCC would have advised. Shortly before his death, Martin Luther King Jr. had prepared some notes for a speech titled "Ten Commandments on Vietnam," which was delivered shortly after his death by Mrs. Coretta Scott King. These could be easily adapted to cover the wars in Iraq, Afghanistan, and perhaps even Syria, were King alive to observe:

1.] 1. Thou shalt not believe in a military victory.

2. Thou shalt not believe in a political victory.

3. Thou shalt not believe that the Vietnamese people love us.

4. Thou shalt not believe that the Saigon government has the support of the people.

5. Thou shalt not believe that the majority of the South Vietnamese look upon the Viet Cong as terrorists.

6. Thou shalt not believe the figures of killed enemies or killed Americans.

7. Thou shalt not believe that the generals know best.

8. Thou shalt not believe that the enemies' victory means communism.

9. Thou shalt not believe that the world supports the United States.

10. 10.Thou shalt not kill.[8]

Following from the 1968 Martin Luther King Jr. Resolution on Nonviolence, which was passed at the WCC Uppsala Assembly in 1968, the WCC continued to emphasize the importance of nonviolent approaches to its ongoing witness for peace:

> *1975 Fifth Assembly, Nairobi*
> The Nairobi Assembly adopted a guideline on "The need to exercise a ministry of peace and reconciliation to explore further the significance of nonviolent action for social change and the struggle against militarism."

> *1979 Central Committee, Jamaica*
> The Central Committee in 1979 encouraged "further exploration and continuing implementation of the report on violence and nonviolence, and the struggle for Social Justice, paying

---

7. Ibid.

8. Krieger, "Legacy of Peace," Nuclear Age Peace Foundation, April 4, 2008, https://www.wagingpeace.org/articles/2008/04/04_krieger_king_legacy.php.

serious attention to the rights of conscientious objectors, and the need to promote peaceful resolution of conflicts."

1983 Sixth Assembly, Vancouver
The churches were called to "emphasize their willingness to live without the protection of armaments." In a statement on Peace and Justice, it affirmed that "Christians should give witness to their willingness to participate in any conflict involving weapons of mass destruction or indiscriminate effect." And it instructed the WCC to "engage the churches in a conciliar process of mutual commitment (covenant) to justice, peace and the integrity of all creation (JP IC)."

1990 World Convocation on JPIC, Seoul
Participants in the JPIC Convocation endorsed an appeal "to reject the spirit, logic and practice of deterrence based on weapons of mass destruction," and called for the development "of a culture of active nonviolence which is life-producing, and is not a withdrawal from situations of violence and oppression, but is a way to work for justice and liberation."

1992 Central Committee, Geneva.
Following a debate on the conflict in the former Yugoslavia, the Central Committee agreed "that active nonviolent action be affirmed as a clear emphasis in programmes and projects related to conflict resolution."[9]

Stanley Mogoba, a Methodist bishop who was imprisoned for his opposition to apartheid, informed delegates to the WCC Central Committee meeting in Johannesburg in January of 1994 that the WCC's PCR had been an important force in the demise of apartheid. Bishop Mogoba then called for a new program—this time to combat violence. The Central Committee responded to this call by establishing a program to overcome violence "with the purpose of challenging and transforming the global culture of violence in the direction of a culture of just peace."[10] The resulting "Ecumenical Decade to Overcome Violence" ran from 2001 to 2010. In a press release dated January 30, 2001, His Holiness Aram I, Catholicos of Cilicia and Moderator of the WCC's Central Committee, said, "people of different nations, cultures, and backgrounds should engage in 'creative dialogue' to

9. "Ecumenical Decade, 2001–2010," Final Report on the WCC Decade for Overcoming Violence, 16.

10. "Ecumenical Decade, 2001–2010," Final Report on the WCC Decade for Overcoming Violence, 12–13.

seek nonviolent solutions to problems. That should be the intention of the 'Decade to Overcome Violence.'"[11]

January 12, 2004, saw the NCC and WCC launch a year-long effort to overcome violence in the US with a worship service commemorating the life and ministry of Martin Luther King Jr. The service was held in the Chapel of the Interchurch Center in New York City, and it marked the opening of a year dedicated to strengthening churches and movements working for peace in the US. The American focus was coordinated by the US Decade to Overcome Violence (DOV) Committee under the auspices of the US Office of the WCC and the NCC. During the opening remarks of the service, King was called to mind by the Very Reverend Leonid Kishkovsky, Archpriest of the Orthodox Church in America and Moderator of the US Conference of the WCC: "We are gathered as peacemakers from various regions of the world to launch this year-long focus in the United States by lifting up the legacy of Martin Luther King Jr., whose work and ministry has inspired peacemakers around the globe."[12] In summing up the DOV, Hansulrich Gerber, a Swiss Mennonite minister, wrote, "the Decade has not been an unmitigated success, but it has had some real successes, and it has set in motion a process of prioritizing peace in the ecumenical movement that cannot be stopped."[13]

Martin Luther King Jr. and the WCC actively supported the elimination of apartheid in South Africa, and that country's fortune since the introduction of democratic elections in 1994 under Nelson Mandela has been mixed. King was aware of the pernicious effect of white supremacy, but he warned, "I am convinced that 'black supremacy' is as dangerous as 'white supremacy.' It only serves to substitute one tyranny for another."[14] In a tragedy reminiscent of the Sharpeville massacre in 1960, the South African police opened fire on miners striking at the Lonmin platinum mine in Marikana, South Africa, on August 16, 2012, killing thirty-four people and injuring at least seventy-eight others. *The Guardian* described the event in dramatic detail: "In scenes that evoked memories of some of the country's

11. WCC Office of Communication, "Creative Dialogue Key to Decade to Overcome Violence, Moderator Says," news release, January 30, 2001, http://www.wcc-coe.org/wcc/news/press/01/cc-releases/04pre.html.

12. National Council of Churches, "NCC, WCC Launch Year-Long Effort to Overcome Violence in the U.S. at January 12 Service Honoring the Rev. Dr. Martin Luther King, Jr.," news release, January 13, 2004, http://www.ncccusa.org/news/04dovlaunchservice.html.

13. "Ecumenical Decade, 2001–2010," Final Report on the WCC Decade for Overcoming Violence, 131.

14. King, "Man Who Was a Fool," 4–6.

darkest days, national television showed pictures of police in helmets and body armor shooting at workers on Thursday amid shouting, panic, and clouds of dust at Lonmin's Marikana platinum mine. After three minutes of gunfire, bodies littered the ground in pools of blood."[15] At the time of writing, the government-appointed Commission of Inquiry into the massacre headed by Ian Farlam, a retired Supreme Court of Appeal judge, has yet to make its report. Unfortunately, King's pronouncement on the changing of the guard of racial supremacy seems all too relevant here.

There have, however, been some good news stories in South Africa. British journalist R. W. Johnson has reported that by 2006 the proportion of households using electricity had risen to 81.4 percent and that 71.3 percent of households enjoyed running water.[16] Increased use of mobile phones has meant that far more people are able to communicate. Basic housing units, "little matchbox-like RDP houses," sprang up all over the veld, and over one million had been built by 2006.[17] Free basic education is available and 90 percent of school-age children are in school. Unfortunately, the increased budget on education has not been spent wisely, and standards continue to fall. Johnson describes the scramble for power in South Africa in observing that Nelson Mandela "was clearly too old to be more than an interim leader, and he has little appetite for power," cynically reflecting that "just ahead lay a division of the spoils on a scale never seen before in Africa. Everything hinged on who won the struggle to succeed Mandela."[18] Thabo Mbeki emerged from this struggle, but his stewardship of South Africa will be remembered for its incompetence, particularly in the fight against AIDS. Mbeki's refusal to accept any connection between HIV and AIDS led Douglas Foster to lament in 2012 that "one in eight South Africans [is] living with HIV, and two million people [are] dead from AIDS already."[19]

In 2009, *World Focus* reported that South Africa was still coming to terms with the fallout of apartheid. Although legalized racism was gone, the legacy remained. Inequality continues, and many of the poverty-stricken are black, with few prospects for socioeconomic improvement. Black South Africans may hold positions in government, but white South Africans control the two most important things: the money and the minds of a people

15. Smith and Macalister, "South African Police Shoot," *The Guardian*, August 16, 2012.

16. Johnson, *South Africa's Brave New World*, 583.

17. Ibid., 584.

18. Ibid., 21.

19. Foster, *After Mandela*, 89. See also Johnson, *South Africa's Brave New World*, 182–85.

who have been taught to think of themselves as an inferior race.[20] On the other hand, a new phenomenon has been noted by the *Christian Science Monitor*, which has reported that "more white South Africans struggle in post-apartheid economy."[21] White South Africans are increasingly living below the poverty line as the job market adjusts to a post-apartheid era, which lacks the government support once afforded to whites. Although unfortunate, King and WCC leaders like Blake understood the possibility of such a scenario.

Recent statistics from the Bureau for Market Research in South Africa reveals that 650,000 whites aged sixteen and above are out of work, with a projected increase of 15 percent a year.[22] The increasing poverty among whites can be seen in the sixteen mostly white families who live in an assortment of canvas and wooden shacks beside the Grand West Casino frequented by the city's wealthier inhabitants. Resident Russel du Toit, a father of five, says, "it's apartheid in reverse," adding, "we can't get jobs or houses because they're given to black people and we're bottom of the list. We don't have electricity and we have [water] taps in the street and those toilets," pointing to temporary latrines.[23] Certainly King would have been dismayed by this turn of events, for he sought equality for all regardless of color, knowing that the poor white population in the US exceeded that of the African American poor.

In "Poverty and Inequality after Apartheid," Jeremy Seekings writes,

> Democratic South Africa was born amidst high hopes for the reduction of income poverty and inequality from their high levels under apartheid. The reality has been disappointing; despite steady economic growth, income poverty rose in the late 1990s before a muted decline in the early 2000s . . . It is also clear that economic growth alone will not reduce poverty or inequality; pro-poor social policies are important, but not as important as a pro-poor economic growth path.[24]

20. Seemungal and McGinn, "Poverty Preserves Racial Lines," *World Focus*, February 23, 2009.

21. Evans, "More White South Africans Struggle," *Christian Science Monitor*, October 14, 2010.

22. Quoted in ibid.

23. Ibid.

24. Seekings, Jeremy, "Poverty and Inequality after Apartheid," Centre for Social Science Research Working Paper No. 200, University of Cape Town, September 2007, http://www.cssr.uct.ac.za/sites/cssr.uct.ac.za/files/pubs/WP200.pdf.

With the departure of Thabo Mbeki in September of 2005, President Jacob Zuma pulled off a remarkable political comeback in May of 2009, but Douglas Foster remains skeptical: "He has done his level best in the past three years to knit his party together, but in this he had largely failed. His ambition now was to be seen as the heroic figure who managed to ease the country into its post-Mandela, post-Mbeki, and even post-Zuma reality."[25]

Among the more visible gains from King's legacy in the US was the election of Barack Obama as president. This can be seen as a fulfillment in part of the goals the civil rights movement of the 1950s and 1960s sought. Rev. Bernice Powell Jackson wrote to President Barack Obama on behalf of the members of the board and the US Conference for the WCC on January 20, 2009, greeting his inauguration as the forty-fourth President of the United States, "especially because you have been part of the fellowship of the World Council of Churches."[26] Jackson and her colleagues acknowledged that President Obama faced enormous and formidable challenges, but in order to overcome worldwide poverty and arrive at a peaceful coexistence for all, proffered a vision by the prophet Micah as a source of great hope: "Nation shall not lift up sword against nation, neither shall they learn war anymore; but they shall all sit under their own vines and under their own fig trees, and no one shall make them afraid; for the mouth of the Lord of hosts has spoken" (Mic 4:3–4). The letter went on to express the same hopes and aspirations that Martin Luther King Jr. had expounded in years past to bring about a "beloved community." King's lasting legacy finds expression in the conclusion, "we close with a pastoral prayer by Martin Luther King, Jr., whose words in 1956 are most fitting as we step into this new day:

> O God, our Heavenly Father, we thank thee for this golden privilege to worship thee, the only true God of the universe. We come to thee today, grateful that thou hast kept us through the long night of the past and ushered us into the challenge of the present and the bright hope of the future. We are mindful, O God, that man [*sic*] cannot save himself, for man is not the measure of things and humanity is not God. Bound by our chains of sins and finiteness, we know we need a Savior. We thank thee, O God, for the spiritual nature of man. We are in nature but we live above nature. Help us never to let anybody or any condition pull us so low as to cause us to hate. Give us strength to love our enemies and to do good to those who despitefully use us

25. Foster, *After Mandela*, 542.

26. WCC US Conference to President Barack Obama, January 20, 2009, http://www.oikoumene.org/en/resources/documents/other-ecumenical-bodies/wcc-us-conference-letter-to-president-obama.

and persecute us. We thank thee for thy Church, founded upon thy Word, that challenges us to do more than sing and pray, but go out and work as though the very answer to our prayers depended on us and not upon thee. Then, finally, help us to realize that man was created to shine like stars and live on through all eternity. Keep us, we pray, in perfect peace, help us to walk together, pray together, sing together, and live together until that day when all God's children, Black, White, Red, Brown, Yellow, will rejoice in one common band of humanity in the kingdom of our Lord and of our God, we pray. Amen.[27]

In his "Presidential Proclamation" on January 14, 2011, President Obama declared:

Dr. King guided us towards a mountaintop on which all Americans— regardless of skin color—could live together in mutual respect and brotherhood. His bold leadership and prophetic eloquence united people of all backgrounds in a noble quest for freedom and basic civil rights . . . Their courage and dedication have carried us even closer to the promised land Dr. King envisioned, but we must recognize their achievements as milestones on the long path to true opportunity and equal rights.[28]

That promise of fulfillment remains after President Obama's first term, which enjoyed some notable successes and suffered some defeats due to failure to agree on a bipartisan approach on several key issues. Nevertheless, in his second inaugural address on January 21, 2013, President Obama again invoked King's name in proclaiming the common struggle in which all men share:

We, the people, declare today that the most evident of truth— that all of us are created equal—is the star that guides us still; just as it guided our forebears through Seneca Falls, and Selma, and Stonewall; just as it guided all those men and women, sung and unsung, who left footprints along this great Mall to hear a preacher say that we cannot walk alone; to hear a King proclaim that our individual freedom is inextricably bound to the freedom of every soul on Earth.[29]

27. WCC US Conference to President Barack Obama, January 20, 2009, http://www.oikoumene.org/en/resources/documents/other-ecumenical-bodies/wcc-us-conference-letter-to-president-obama.

28. Obama, Barack, "Presidential Proclamation—Martin Luther King, Jr., Federal Holiday," January 14, 2011, http://www.whitehouse.gov/the-press-office/2011/01/14/presidential-proclamation-martin-luther-king-jr-federal-holiday.

29. Obama, Barack, "President Obama's Second Inaugural Address, January 2013,"

In a reminder that the problem of racism in the US is still raw, George Zimmerman's acquittal by a Florida jury in July 2013 in the shooting of Trayvon Martin, a young African-American, highlighted the dangers of complacency once more. As President Barack Obama said, the slain seventeen-year-old "could have been me thirty-five years ago," and that the case conjured up a hard history of racial injustice "that doesn't go away."[30] Indeed, the penal system in the US suffers from some disturbing statistics. The Washington, DC–based Sentencing Project says a black male born in 2001 has a 32 percent change of imprisonment at some point in his life, whereas a white male has a 6 percent chance. On any given day, one in every ten black males in their thirties are in prison or jail, reports the group. African-Americans represent 38 percent of all US prisoners, but just 13 percent of the general population.[31] Michelle Alexander, a law professor and civil rights activist, in her book *The New Jim Crow: Mass Incarceration in the Age of Colorblindness*, "found that the racial caste system had not been eliminated but merely redesigned by the criminal-justice system and law enforcement. The targeting of black men in the war on drugs has created a substitute for the racist Jim Crow laws of the 1960s and turned millions of black Americans into second-class citizens."[32] It is no exaggeration to say that Dr. King's call for a "beloved community" is as relevant today as it ever was.

---

address at the White House, Washington, DC, January 21, 2013, http://www.white-house.gov/the-press-office/2013/01/21/inaugural-address-president-barack-obama.

30. Obama, Barack, "Remarks by the President on Trayvon Martin," address at the James S. Brady Press Briefing Room, Washington, DC, July 19, 2013, http://www.white-house.gov/the-press-office/2013/07/19/remarks-president-trayvon-martin.

31. Quoted in Carswell, Simon. "Can Florida Stick to Its Guns?" *Irish Times*, July 20, 2013, 3, http://www.irishtimes.com/news/world/us/can-florida-stick-to-its-guns-1.1469157?page=3.

32. Ibid.

Bibliography

Adler, Elizabeth. *A Small Beginning: An Assessment of the First Five Years of the Programme to Combat Racism.* Geneva: World Council of Churches, 1974.

"American in Geneva." *Time* 87, February 18, 1966, http://content.time.com/time/magazine/article/0,9171,899037,00.html.

Anderson, Lowrie J. "Roundup: Foreign Tributes to Dr. King." *Christian Century* 85, May 8, 1968, 629–30.

Ansbro, John J. *Martin Luther King: The Making of a Mind.* Maryknoll, NY: Orbis, 1982.

Baldwin, Lewis V. "Martin Luther King, Jr., the Black Church and the Black Messianic Vision." In vol. 2 of *Martin Luther King Jr.: Civil Rights Leader, Theologian, Orator,* edited by David J. Garrow, 1–16. Martin Luther King, Jr. and the Civil Rights Movement. Brooklyn, NY: Carlson, 1989.

———. "Martin Luther King Jr., a 'Coalition of Conscience,' and Freedom in South Africa." In *Freedom's Distant Shores: American Protestants and Post-Colonial Alliances with Africa,* edited by R. Drew Smith, 53–82. Waco, TX: Baylor University Press, 2006.

———. "The Minister as Preacher, Pastor, and Prophet: The Thinking of Martin Luther King, Jr." In vol. 1 of *Martin Luther King, Jr., Civil Rights Leader, Theologian, Orator,* edited by David J. Garrow, 39–57. Martin Luther King, Jr. and the Civil Rights Movement. Brooklyn, NY: Carlson, 1989.

———. *Toward the Beloved Community: Martin Luther King Jr. and South Africa.* Cleveland: Pilgrim, 1995.

———. *The Voice of Conscience: The Church in the Mind of Martin Luther King, Jr.* Oxford: Oxford University Press, 2010.

Barnett, Bernice McNair. "A Structural Analysis of the Civil Rights Movement and the Leadership Roles of Martin Luther King, Jr." PhD diss., University of Georgia, 1989.

Bennett, Lerone, Jr. *What Manner of Man: A Biography of Martin Luther King, Jr.* Chicago: Johnson, 2000.

Benson, Mary. *Chief Albert Lutuli of South Africa.* London: Oxford University Press, 1963.

Beschloss, Michael R., editor. *Reaching for Glory: Lyndon Johnson's Secret White House Tapes, 1964–1965.* Vol. 2 of Johnson White House Tapes. New York: Simon & Schuster, 2001.

Blake, Eugene Carson. *The Church in the Next Decade.* New York: Macmillan, 1966.

———. "The Church in the Next Decade," *Christianity and Crisis* 26, February 21, 1966, 15–18.

———. "The Moral Responsibility of the Church in a Secular Society." Rauschenbusch Lectures. New York: New York State Council of Churches, 1960.

Boesak, Allan. "The Black Church and the Struggle in South Africa." *Ecumenical Review* 32 (1980) 16–24.

Borstelmann, Thomas. *The Cold War and the Color Line: American Race Relations in the Global Arena.* Cambridge: Harvard University Press, 2001.

Brackenridge, R. Douglas. *Eugene Carson Blake: Prophet with Portfolio.* New York: Seabury, 1978.

Branch, Taylor. *At Canaan's Edge: America in the King Years, 1965–1968.* New York: Simon & Schuster, 2006.

Burns, Stewart. *To the Mountaintop: Martin Luther King Jr.'s Sacred Mission to Save America: 1955–1968.* New York: HarperCollins, 2004.

Carson, Clayborne. "Martin Luther King, Jr., and the African-American Social Gospel." In *African-American Christianity: Essays in History,* edited by Paul E. Johnson, 159–77. Berkeley: University of California Press, 1994.

"The Churches' Influence on Secular Society." *Time* 89, April 21, 1967.

Cone, James H. "Martin Luther King, Jr., Black Theology—Black Church." In vol. 1 of *Martin Luther King, Jr.: Civil Rights Leader, Theologian, Orator,* edited by David J. Garrow, 203–15. Martin Luther King, Jr. and the Civil Rights Movement. Brooklyn, NY: Carlson, 1989.

Cook, Robert. *Sweet Land of Liberty? The African-American Struggle for Civil Rights in the Twentieth Century.* New York: Longman, 1998.

Cort, John. *Christian Socialism: An Informal History.* Maryknoll, NY: Orbis, 1988.

Couper, Scott Everett. "Emasculating Agency: An Unambiguous Assessment of Albert Luthuli's Stance on Violence." *South African Historical Journal* 64 (2012) 564–86.

———. "'An Embarrassment to the Congresses?' The Silencing of Chief Albert Luthuli and the Production of ANC History." *Journal of Southern African Studies* 35 (2009) 331–48.

———. "Irony upon Irony upon Irony: The Mythologizing of Nationalist History in South Africa." *South African Historical Journal* 63 (2011) 339–46.

———. "My People Let Go." *International Congregational Journal* 5 (2005) 101–23.

Crow, Paul A., Jr. "Eugene Carson Blake: Apostle of Christian Unity." *Ecumenical Review* 28 (1986) 228–36.

Cuddy, Edward. "Vietnam: Mr. Johnson's War or Mr. Eisenhower's?" *The Review of Politics* 65 (2003) 351–74.

Dallek, Robert. *Flawed Giant: Lyndon Johnson and His Times, 1961–1973.* New York: Oxford University Press, 1998.

Darby, Henry E., and Margaret N. Rowley. "King on Vietnam and Beyond." In vol. 1 of *Martin Luther King, Jr.: Civil Rights Leader, Theologian, Orator,* edited by David J. Garrow, 249–56. Martin Luther King, Jr. and the Civil Rights Movement. Brooklyn, NY: Carlson, 1989.

De Gruchy, John W. *The Church Struggle in South Africa.* 2nd ed. London: Collins, 1986.

De Lange, Harry M. "Foreign Investments in Southern Africa: The Beginning of a Dialogue." *Ecumenical Review* 29 (1977) 383–93.

Dombrowski, James A. *The Early Days of Christian Socialism in America.* New York: Octagon, 1977.

Du Boulay, Shirley. *Tutu: Voice of the Voiceless.* London: Hodder & Stoughton, 1988.

Dulles, John Foster. "Religion: American Malvern." *Time* 39, March 16, 1947, 43–48.

Dyson, Michael Eric. *I May Not Get There With You: The True Martin Luther King, Jr.* New York: Simon & Schuster, 2001.

"Ecumenical Chronicle." *Ecumenical Review* 28 (1976) 460–63.

"Ecumenical Diary." *Ecumenical Review* 27 (1975) 159–70.

Eskidjian, Salpy, and Sarah Estabrooks, editors. *Overcoming Violence: WCC Statements and Actions 1994–2000.* Geneva: World Council of Churches, 2000.

Evans, G. Russell. *Apathy, Apostasy, and Apostles: A Study of the History and Activities of the National Council of Churches of Christ in the USA with Sidelights on Its Ally, the World Council of Churches.* New York: Vantage, 1973.

Evans, Ian. "More White South Africans Struggle in Post-Apartheid Economy." *Christian Science Monitor,* October 14, 2010, http://www.csmonitor.com/World/Africa/2010/1014/More-white-South-Africans-struggle-in-post-apartheid-economy.

Fager, Charles. *Uncertain Resurrection: The Poor People's Washington Campaign.* Grand Rapids: Eerdmans, 1969.

Fairclough, Adam. *Better Day Coming: Blacks and Equality, 1890–2000.* London: Penguin, 2001.

———. *Martin Luther King, Jr.* Athens: University of Georgia Press, 1995.

———. "Martin Luther King, Jr. and the War in Vietnam." In vol. 2 of *Martin Luther King Jr.: Civil Rights Leader, Theologian, Orator,* edited by David J. Garrow, 311–32. Martin Luther King, Jr. and the Civil Rights Movement. Brooklyn, NY: Carlson, 1989.

———. *To Redeem the Soul of America: The Southern Christian Leadership Conference and Martin Luther King, Jr.* Athens: University of Georgia Press, 1987.

Findlay, James F. "Religion and Politics in the Sixties: The Churches and the Civil Rights Act of 1964." *The Journal of American History* 77 (1990) 66–92.

Foster, Douglas. *After Mandela: The Struggle for Freedom in Post-Apartheid South Africa.* New York: Liveright, 2012.

Frazier, E. Franklin, and C. Eric Lincoln. *The Negro Church in America/The Black Church Since Frazier.* New York: Schocken, 1974.

Friedland, Michael B. *Lift Up Your Voice Like a Trumpet: White Clergy and the Civil Rights and Antiwar Movements, 1954–1973.* Chapel Hill: University of North Carolina Press, 1998.

Gaines, David P. *The World Council of Churches: A Study of Its Background and History.* Peterborough, NH: R. R. Smith, 1966.

Gall, Susan Bevan, and Timothy L. Gall, editors. "U Thant's Stand on the Vietnam War." In *United Nations,* 51–52. Vol. 1, Worldmark Encyclopedia of the Nations. 8th ed. New York: Gale Research, 1995.

Garber, Paul R. "King Was a Black Theologian." In vol. 2 of *Martin Luther King Jr.: Civil Rights Leader, Theologian, Orator,* edited by David J. Garrow, 395–412. Martin Luther King, Jr. and the Civil Rights Movement. Brooklyn, NY: Carlson, 1989.

Garrow, David J. *Bearing the Cross: Martin Luther King, Jr. and the Southern Christian Leadership Conference.* New York: Quill, 1999.

———. *The FBI and Martin Luther King, Jr.: From "Solo" to Memphis.* Harmondsworth, Middlesex, UK: Penguin, 1983.

————. *We Shall Overcome: The Civil Rights Movement in the United States in the 1950s and 1960s.* 3 vols. Brooklyn, NY: Carlson, 1989.

Gill, David M. "Violence and Non-Violence: Resuming the Debate." *Ecumenical Review* 32 (1980) 25–28.

Haley, Alex. "Playboy Interview: Martin Luther King." *Playboy* 22, January 1965, 65–68, 70–74, 76–78.

Hall, Mitchell K. *Because of Their Faith: CALCAV and Religious Opposition to the Vietnam War.* New York: Columbia University Press, 1990.

Hall, Simon. *Peace and Freedom: The Civil Rights and Antiwar Movements in the 1960s.* Philadelphia: University of Pennsylvania Press, 2005.

Harbutt, Fraser J. *The Cold War Era.* Malden, MA: Blackwell, 2002.

Harding, Vincent. *Martin Luther King, the Inconvenient Hero.* Maryknoll, NY: Orbis, 2003.

Heschel, Abraham Joshua. "Conversation with Martin Luther King." *Conservative Judaism* 22 (1968) 1–19.

Holt, Thomas C., and Elsa Barkley Brown, editors. *Major Problems in African-American History: Documents and Essays*, 316–17. Vol. 2. Boston: Houghton Mifflin, 2000.

Honey, Michael K. *Going Down Jericho Road: The Memphis Strike, Martin Luther King's Last Campaign.* New York: Norton, 2008.

Houck, David W., and David E. Dixon, editors. *Rhetoric, Religion and the Civil Rights Movement, 1954–1965.* Waco, TX: Baylor University Press, 2006.

Jackson, A. B. "Funny Things Do Happen." *Sunday News and Tribune* (Jefferson City, MO), October 29, 1967.

Jackson, Thomas F. "Recasting the Dream: Martin Luther King, Jr., African American Political Thought, and the Third Reconstruction, 1955–1968." PhD diss., Stanford University, 1994.

Jackson, Thomas F. *From Civil Rights to Human Rights: Martin Luther King, Jr. and the Struggle for Economic Justice.* Philadelphia: University of Pennsylvania Press, 2007.

Johnson, R. W. *South Africa's Brave New World: The Beloved Country Since the End of Apartheid.* London: Allen Lane, 2009.

Kaempfer, William H., and Anton Lowenberg. "The Theory of International Economic Sanctions: A Public Choice Approach." *American Economic Review* 78 (1988) 786–93.

Karis, Thomas, and Gwendolen Margaret Carter, editors. *From Protest to Challenge: A Documentary History of African Politics in South Africa, 1822–1964.* Vol. 4 of *Political Profiles, 1882–1964.* Hoover Institution Publications 161. Stanford, CA: Hoover Institution on War, Revolution, and Peace, 1977.

Katzin, Donna. "Economic Strategies: An Evolving Prophetic Partnership between South African and US Churches." In *A Long Struggle: The Involvement of the World Council of Churches in South Africa*, edited by Pauline M. Webb, 58–68. Geneva: World Council of Churches, 1994.

King, Coretta Scott. *My Life with Martin Luther King, Jr.* New York: Holt, Rinehart, & Winston, 1969.

King, Martin Luther, Jr. *Chaos or Community?* London: Hodder & Stoughton, 1968.

————. *The Autobiography of Martin Luther King, Jr.* Edited by Clayborne Carson. New York: Warner, 1998.

————. "The Church and the Race Crisis." *Christian Century* 75, October 8, 1958, 1140–41.

―――. *"In a Single Garment of Destiny": A Global Vision of Justice.* Edited by Lewis V. Baldwin. Boston: Beacon, 2012.

―――. *A Knock at Midnight: Inspiration from the Great Sermons of Reverend Martin Luther King, Jr.* Edited by Clayborne Carson and Peter Holloran. New York: Warner, 1998.

―――. "Letter from Birmingham Jail." *Christian Century*, June 12, 1963, 767–73.

―――. "The Man Who Was a Fool." *The Pulpit* 32 (1961) 4–6.

―――. "My Dream—Peace: 'God's Man's Business.'" *Chicago Defender*, January 1–7, 1966.

―――. "People in Action: The Role of the Church." *New York Amsterdam News*, September 15, 1962.

―――. "People in Action: Segregation in the Church." *New York Amsterdam News*, February 2, 1963.

―――. "Pilgrimage to Nonviolence." *Christian Century* 77, April 13, 1960, 439–41.

―――. "A Profound Moral Issue." *New York Amsterdam News*, July 20, 1963.

―――. "The Social Organization of Nonviolence." *Liberation* 4, October 1959, 5–6.

―――. *Strength to Love.* New York: HarperCollins, 1977.

―――. *Stride Toward Freedom: The Montgomery Story.* New York: Harper & Row, 1964.

―――. "A Time to Break Silence." In *A Testament of Hope: The Essential Writings and Speeches of Martin Luther King, Jr.*, edited by James M. Washington, 231–44. San Francisco: HarperCollins, 1991.

―――. *The Trumpet of Conscience.* New York: Harper & Row, 1967.

―――. "Who Is Their God?" *Nation* 195, October 13, 1962, 209–13.

―――. *Why We Can't Wait.* New York: Signet, 1964.

Kirby, Alexander, and the World Council of Churches Programme to Combat Racism. *The World Council of Churches and Bank Loans to Apartheid.* Geneva: World Council of Churches, 1977.

Kirk, John A. *Martin Luther King, Jr.* Profiles in Power. Harlow, UK: Pearson Longman, 2005.

Kotz, Nick. *Judgment Days: Lyndon Baines Johnson, Martin Luther King Jr., and the Laws That Changed America.* Boston: Houghton Mifflin, 2006.

Kramer, Reed. "In Hock to U.S. Banks." *The Nation*, December 11, 1976, 624–26.

Krieger, David. "Martin Luther King's Legacy of Peace." Nuclear Age Peace Foundation, April 4, 2008, https://www.wagingpeace.org/articles/2008/04/04_krieger_king_legacy.php.

Lentz, Richard. "Resurrecting the Prophet: Dr. Martin Luther King, Jr., and the News Magazines." PhD diss., University of Iowa, 1983.

―――. *Symbols, the News Magazines, and Martin Luther King.* Baton Rouge: Louisiana State University Press, 1990.

Lewis, David L. *King: A Biography.* Urbana: University of Illinois Press, 1978.

Lincoln, C. Eric. "The Black Church and a Decade of Change." Part II, *Tuesday at Home* (1976) 7.

Ling, Peter J. *Martin Luther King, Jr.* New York: Routledge, 2002.

Logevall, Fredrik. *Choosing War: The Lost Chance for Peace and the Escalation of War in Vietnam.* Berkeley: University of California Press, 1999.

Lokos, Lionel. *House Divided: The Life and Legacy of Martin Luther King.* New Rochelle, NY: Arlington House, 1968.

Lowenberg, Anton D. "Measuring the Effectiveness of Economic Sanctions on South Africa." *Africa Today* 37 (1990) 63.

Luthuli, Albert. "Africa and Freedom: The Recognition and Preservation of the Rights of Man." *Vital Speeches of the Day* 28, February 15, 1962, 267–71.

———. *Let My People Go*. London: Collins, 1962.

———. "Man of the People: Chief A. J. Lutuli." Johannesburg: Afrika Publications, 1961.

———. "Nobel Lecture: Africa and Freedom." In *Nobel Lectures, Peace 1951–1970*, vol. 3, edited by Frederick W. Haberman, Amsterdam, Netherlands: Elsevier, 1972.

Mandela, Nelson. *Conversations with Myself*. London: Macmillan, 2010.

———. *The Long Walk to Freedom: The Autobiography of Nelson Mandela*. Boston: Little, Brown, 1994.

"March on Gwynn Oak Park." *Time* 82, July 12, 1963, 1–25.

May, Ernest, et al., editors. *The Presidential Recordings: Lyndon B. Johnson*. Vol. 4–6 of *Presidential Recordings*. New York: Norton, 2005.

Mbali, Zolile. *The Churches and Racism: A Black South African Perspective*. London: SCM, 1987.

McGraw, James, "An Interview with Andrew J. Young," *Christianity and Crisis* 27, January 22, 1968, 324–30.

McKnight, Gerald D. *The Last Crusade: Martin Luther King, Jr., the FBI, and the Poor People's Campaign*. Boulder, CO: Westview, 1998.

McMahon, Robert J. "Contested Memory: The Vietnam War and American Society, 1975–2001." *Diplomatic History* 26 (2002) 159–84.

———. *Major Problems in the History of the Vietnam War: Documents and Essays*. Lexington, MA: D.C. Heath, 1995.

Meer, Ismail. *A Fortunate Man*. Cape Town: Zebra, 2002.

Mehnert, Anza. "Memory and Heritage: How Memory Functions and How It Can Be Used in Heritage; Chief Albert Luthuli as a Case Study." *Quarterly Bulletin of the National Library of South Africa* 65 (2011) 85–91.

Miller, Keith D. *Voice of Deliverance: The Language of Martin Luther King, Jr., and Its Sources*. Athens: University of Georgia Press, 1998.

Morrow, Lance. "A Bloody Rite of Passage: Viet Nam Cost America Its Innocence and Still Haunts Its Conscience." *Time* 125, April 15, 1985, 20–21.

Moses, Greg. *Revolution of Conscience: Martin Luther King, Jr., and the Philosophy of Nonviolence*. New York: Guilford, 1997.

Mufamadi, Thembeka Doris. "The World Council of Churches and Its Programme to Combat Racism: The Evolution and Development of Their Fight against Apartheid, 1969–1994." PhD diss., University of South Africa, 2011.

Oates, Stephen B. *Let the Trumpet Sound: A Life of Martin Luther King Jr*. Edinburgh: Payback, 1998.

O'Reilly, Kenneth. *Racial Matters: The FBI's Secret File on Black America, 1960–1972*. New York: Free, 1989.

"Overcoming Violence: The Ecumenical Decade, 2001–2010," Final Report on the WCC Decade for Overcoming Violence, International Ecumenical Peace Convocation, Kingston, Jamaica, 2011. Geneva: WCC, 2011. http://www.overcomingviolence.org/fileadmin/dov/files/OvercomingViolence.pdf.

Peters, William. "Our Weapon Is Love." *Redbook*, August 1956.

Pillay, Gerald. *Albert Luthuli*. Vol. 1 of *Voices of Liberation*. Pretoria, South Africa: Human Sciences Research Council, 1993.

Pityana, Barney. "Tumultuous Response: The Voices of South African Churches." In *A Long Struggle: The Involvement of the World Council of Churches in South Africa*, edited by Pauline Webb, 84–101. Geneva: World Council of Churches, 1994.

Potter, Philip. "The Churches and the World Council After Thirty Years." *Ecumenical Review* 31 (1979) 133–45.

———. "The Task Ahead." In *A Long Struggle: The Involvement of the World Council of Churches in South Africa*, edited by Pauline Webb, 116–26. Geneva: World Council of Churches, 1994.

Quinley, Harold E. "The Protestant Clergy and the War in Vietnam." *Public Opinion Quarterly* 34 (1970) 43–52.

Rogers, Paul. "9/11 and the Lost Decade." *OpenDemocracy*, September 8, 2011, http://www.opendemocracy.net/paul-rogers/911-and-lost-decade.

Saint Laurent, Philip. "The Negro in World History." *Tuesday Magazine* 3, July 3, 1968, 16–33.

Sansbury, Cyril Kenneth. *Combating Racism: The British Council of Churches and the WCC Programme to Combat Racism*. London: British Council of Churches, 1975.

Seemungal, Martin, and Sean McGinn. "Poverty Preserves Racial Lines in Post-Apartheid Africa." *World Focus*, February 23, 2009. http://worldfocus.org/blog/2009/02/23/poverty-preserves-racial-lines-in-post-apartheid-south-africa/4161/.

Sithole, Jabulani, and Sibongiseni Mkhize, "Truth or Lies? Selective Memories, Imagings, and Representations of Chief Albert John Luthuli in Recent Political Discourses." *History and Theory* (2000) 69–85.

Sjollema, Baldwin. "Combating Racism: A Chapter in Ecumenical History." *Ecumenical Review* 56 (2004) 470–79.

———. "Eloquent Action." In *A Long Struggle: The Involvement of the World Council of Churches in South Africa*, edited by Pauline Webb, 12–44. Geneva: World Council of Churches, 1994.

———. "The Initial Challenge." In *A Long Struggle: The Involvement of the World Council of Churches in South Africa*, edited by Pauline Webb, 1–11. Geneva: World Council of Churches, 1994.

———. *Isolating Apartheid: Western Collaboration with South Africa: Policy Decisions by the WCC and Church Responses*. Geneva: World Council of Churches, 1982.

Slovo, John. *Slovo: The Unfinished Biography of ANC Leader Joe Slovo*. London: Ravan, 1995.

Smith, David, and Terry Macalister. "South African Police Shoot Dead Striking Miners." *The Guardian*, August 16, 2012, http://www.theguardian.com/world/2012/aug/16/south-african-police-shoot-striking-miners.

Smith, R. Drew, editor. *Freedom's Distant Shores: American Protestants and Post-Colonial Alliances with Africa*. Waco, TX: Baylor University Press, 2006.

"South Africa: Prize and Prejudice." *Time* 78, November 3, 1961.

"Special Fund Grants to the Patriotic Front," *Ecumenical Review* 30 (1978) 380–82.

"Statement of the Central Committee: Public Issues." *Ecumenical Review* 31 (1979) 194–98.

Suttner, Raymond. "'The Road to Freedom Is Via the Cross': 'Just Means' in Chief Luthuli's Life." *South Africa Historical Journal* 62 (2010) 693–715.

Tawney, Richard Henry. *Religion and the Rise of Capitalism: A Historical Study.* Holland Memorial Lectures, 1922. London: John Murray, 1960.

Thomas, M. M. and Paul Abrecht. *World Conference on Church and Society, Geneva, July 12–26, 1966: Christians in the Technical and Social Revolutions of Our Time: The Official Report with a Description of the Conference.* Geneva: World Council of Churches, 1967.

Vermaat, J. A. Emerson. *The World Council of Churches and Politics, 1975–1986.* Focus on Issues 6. New York: Freedom House, 1989.

Vincent, John, *The Race Race.* London: SCM, 1970.

Von Eschen, Penny M. "Challenging Cold War Habits: African American Race and Foreign Policy." *Diplomatic History* 20 (1996) 627–38.

Wadlow, René. "Martin Luther King, Jr.: Nonviolence with People We Do Not Know." *Newropeans Magazine*, January 20, 2008, http://www.newropeans-magazine.org/content/view/7531/881.

Webb, Pauline, editor. *A Long Struggle: The Involvement of the World Council of Churches in South Africa.* Geneva: World Council of Churches, 1994.

Welch, Claude Emerson. "Mobilizing Morality: The World Council of Churches and Its Programme to Combat Racism, 1969–1994." *Human Rights Quarterly* 23 (2001) 863–910.

Williams, Buntu, and Mandla Ngwenya. "The Legacy of a Legend." DVD, 52 min. Amman, Jordan: Amandla Communications, 2004.

Williams, Robert F. "Can Negroes Afford to be Pacifists?" *Liberation* 4, September 1959, 4–7.

Wilmore, Gayraud Stephen, Jr. "The Case for a New Black Church Style." *Church in Metropolis* 18 (1968) 18–22.

Wilson, Emile LeRoy. "An Analysis and Interpretation of the Life, Writings, and Philosophy of Martin Luther King, Jr." PhD diss., University of Oxford, 1981.

Wirmark, Bo. "Violence, Non-Violence and International Solidarity." *Ecumenical Review* 32 (1980) 4–15.

Woods, Jeff. *Black Struggle, Red Scare: Segregation and Anti-Communism in the South, 1948–1968.* Baton Rouge: Louisiana State University Press, 2004.

Woodson, Dorothy C. "Albert Luthuli and the African National Congress: A Bio-Bibliography." *History in Africa* 13 (1986) 345–62.

Zepp, Ira G. *The Social Vision of Martin Luther King, Jr.* Brooklyn, NY: Carlson, 1989.

Index

www.ingramcontent.com/pod-product-compliance
Lightning Source LLC
Chambersburg PA
CBHW071100280326
41928CB00050B/2572